Richard Saul Wurman

Published under license from Los Angeles Olympic Organizing Committee

ACCESSPRESS Ltd. is the publisher of the **Official Los Angeles Guidebook LA**ACCESS

OLYMPIC SITES (VENUES)

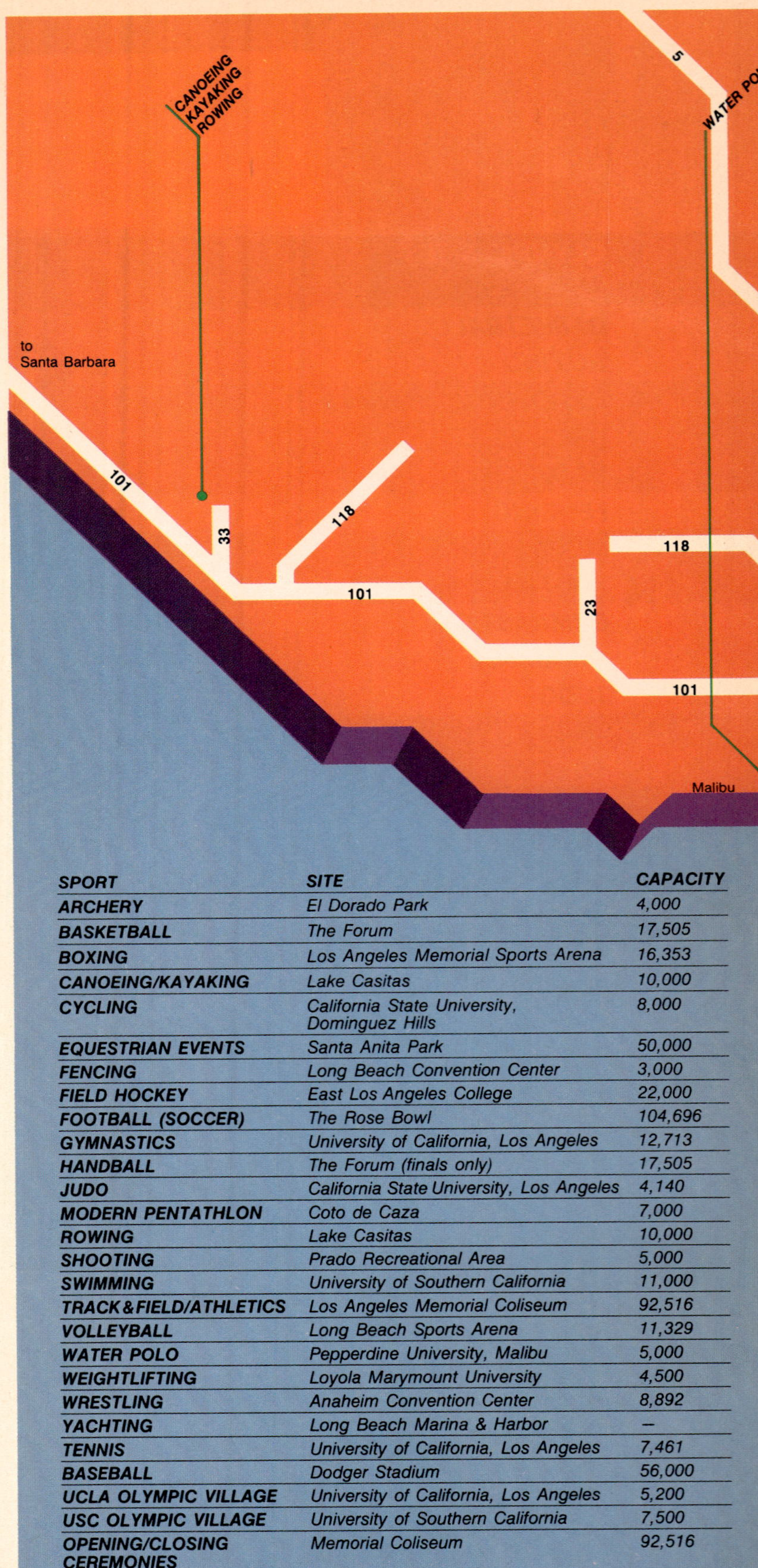

SPORT	SITE	CAPACITY
ARCHERY	El Dorado Park	4,000
BASKETBALL	The Forum	17,505
BOXING	Los Angeles Memorial Sports Arena	16,353
CANOEING/KAYAKING	Lake Casitas	10,000
CYCLING	California State University, Dominguez Hills	8,000
EQUESTRIAN EVENTS	Santa Anita Park	50,000
FENCING	Long Beach Convention Center	3,000
FIELD HOCKEY	East Los Angeles College	22,000
FOOTBALL (SOCCER)	The Rose Bowl	104,696
GYMNASTICS	University of California, Los Angeles	12,713
HANDBALL	The Forum (finals only)	17,505
JUDO	California State University, Los Angeles	4,140
MODERN PENTATHLON	Coto de Caza	7,000
ROWING	Lake Casitas	10,000
SHOOTING	Prado Recreational Area	5,000
SWIMMING	University of Southern California	11,000
TRACK & FIELD/ATHLETICS	Los Angeles Memorial Coliseum	92,516
VOLLEYBALL	Long Beach Sports Arena	11,329
WATER POLO	Pepperdine University, Malibu	5,000
WEIGHTLIFTING	Loyola Marymount University	4,500
WRESTLING	Anaheim Convention Center	8,892
YACHTING	Long Beach Marina & Harbor	–
TENNIS	University of California, Los Angeles	7,461
BASEBALL	Dodger Stadium	56,000
UCLA OLYMPIC VILLAGE	University of California, Los Angeles	5,200
USC OLYMPIC VILLAGE	University of Southern California	7,500
OPENING/CLOSING CEREMONIES	Memorial Coliseum	92,516

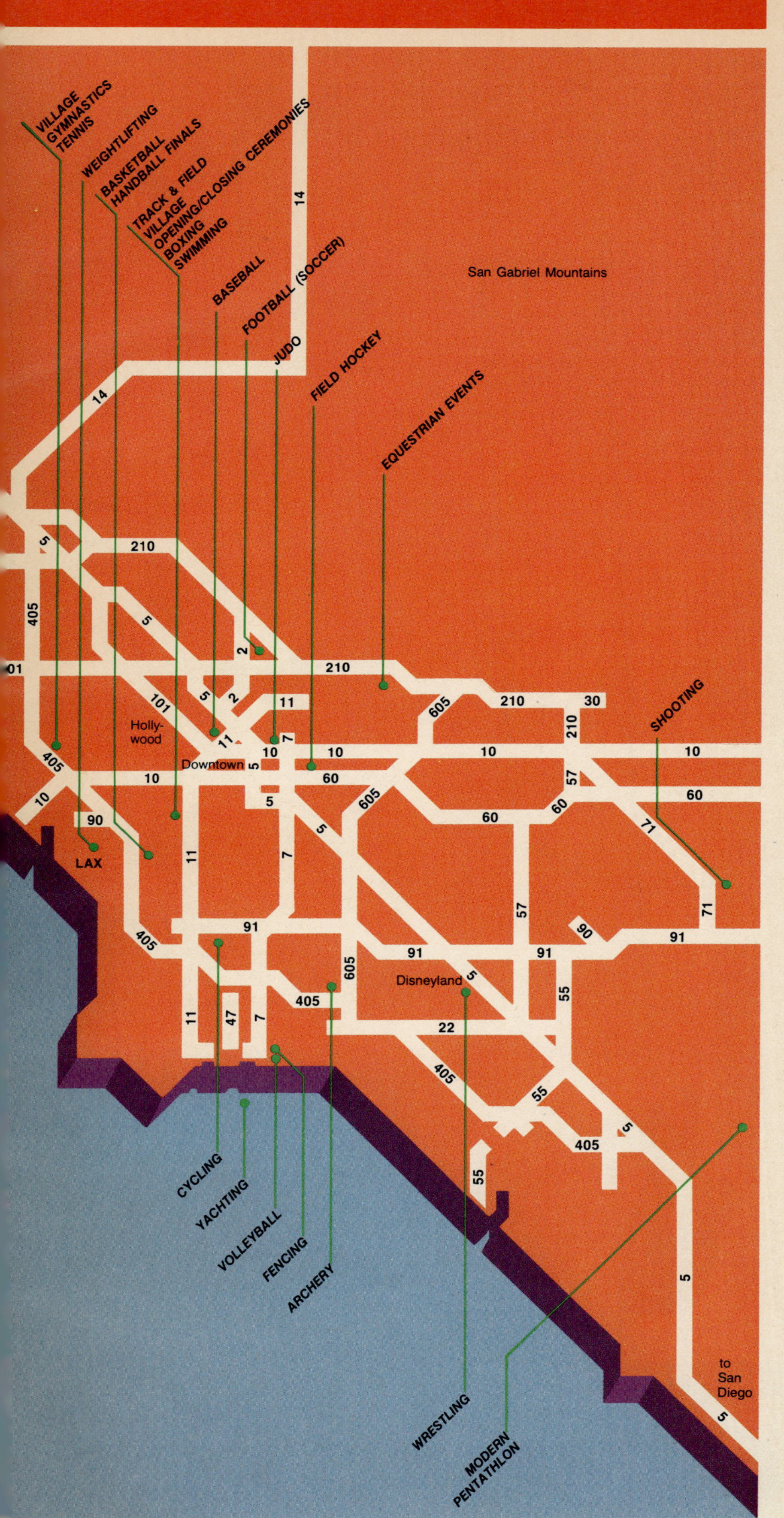
VILLAGE
GYMNASTICS
TENNIS
WEIGHTLIFTING
BASKETBALL
HANDBALL FINALS
TRACK & FIELD
VILLAGE
OPENING/CLOSING CEREMONIES
BOXING
SWIMMING
BASEBALL
FOOTBALL (SOCCER)
JUDO
FIELD HOCKEY
EQUESTRIAN EVENTS
San Gabriel Mountains
SHOOTING
Hollywood
Downtown
LAX
Disneyland
CYCLING
YACHTING
VOLLEYBALL
FENCING
ARCHERY
WRESTLING
MODERN PENTATHLON
to San Diego

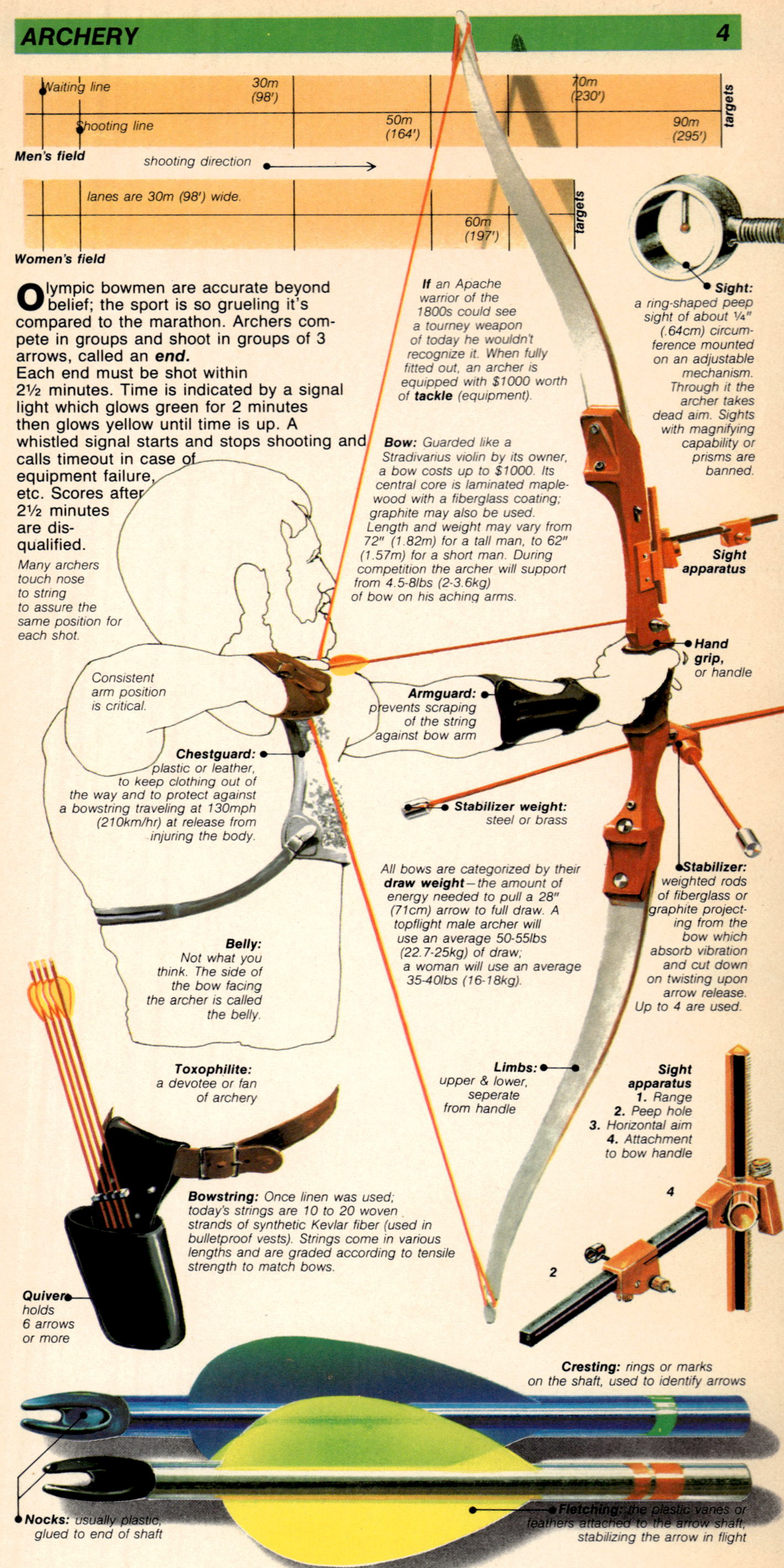
Waiting line
30m
(98')
70m
(230')
Shooting line
50m
(164')
90m
(295')
targets
Men's field
shooting direction
lanes are 30m (98') wide.
60m
(197')
targets
Women's field
Olympic bowmen are accurate beyond belief; the sport is so grueling it's compared to the marathon. Archers compete in groups and shoot in groups of 3 arrows, called an **end.**
Each end must be shot within 2½ minutes. Time is indicated by a signal light which glows green for 2 minutes then glows yellow until time is up. A whistled signal starts and stops shooting and calls timeout in case of equipment failure, etc. Scores after 2½ minutes are disqualified.
Many archers touch nose to string to assure the same position for each shot.
If an Apache warrior of the 1800s could see a tourney weapon of today he wouldn't recognize it. When fully fitted out, an archer is equipped with $1000 worth of **tackle** (equipment).
Sight: a ring-shaped peep sight of about ¼" (.64cm) circumference mounted on an adjustable mechanism. Through it the archer takes dead aim. Sights with magnifying capability or prisms are banned.
Bow: Guarded like a Stradivarius violin by its owner, a bow costs up to $1000. Its central core is laminated maplewood with a fiberglass coating; graphite may also be used. Length and weight may vary from 72" (1.82m) for a tall man, to 62" (1.57m) for a short man. During competition the archer will support from 4.5-8lbs (2-3.6kg) of bow on his aching arms.
Sight apparatus
Hand grip, or handle
Consistent arm position is critical.
Armguard: prevents scraping of the string against bow arm
Chestguard: plastic or leather, to keep clothing out of the way and to protect against a bowstring traveling at 130mph (210km/hr) at release from injuring the body.
Stabilizer weight: steel or brass
All bows are categorized by their **draw weight**—the amount of energy needed to pull a 28" (71cm) arrow to full draw. A topflight male archer will use an average 50-55lbs (22.7-25kg) of draw; a woman will use an average 35-40lbs (16-18kg).
Stabilizer: weighted rods of fiberglass or graphite projecting from the bow which absorb vibration and cut down on twisting upon arrow release. Up to 4 are used.
Belly: Not what you think. The side of the bow facing the archer is called the belly.
Toxophilite: a devotee or fan of archery
Limbs: upper & lower, seperate from handle
Sight apparatus
1. Range
2. Peep hole
3. Horizontal aim
4. Attachment to bow handle
4
2
Bowstring: Once linen was used; today's strings are 10 to 20 woven strands of synthetic Kevlar fiber (used in bulletproof vests). Strings come in various lengths and are graded according to tensile strength to match bows.
Quiver holds 6 arrows or more
Cresting: rings or marks on the shaft, used to identify arrows
Nocks: usually plastic, glued to end of shaft
Fletching: the plastic vanes or feathers attached to the arrow shaft, stabilizing the arrow in flight

Shooting glove or **finger tab:** The 3 fingers which cock the string would become sore or bloodied without these protectors.

El Dorado Park will host the '84 archery competition.

Hollywood
Santa Barbara
El Dorado Park
Long Beach
Distance from Coliseum 23mi (37km)

At 90m, the whole target looks about the size of a silver dollar to the archer, informs head coach **John Williams** of the 1984 USA Archery team. The gold, or bullseye, is just a pinpoint at long range.

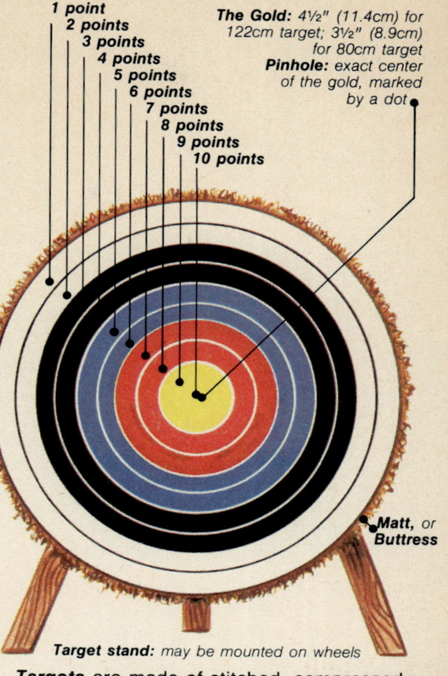

Target stand: may be mounted on wheels

After an end, competitors walk to the target and one calls out all scores, with the other 2 teammates verifying. Disputes are settled by officials of the sport's international governing body, the ***Federation International de Tir a l'Arc***.

Shooting continues for 2½ hours, or until 36 arrows have been shot. The next afternoon another 36 bolts are fired. Five hours are spent on the range each day for 4 days, at which time each entrant will have shot a ***double FITA*** round of 288 arrows at varying distances during a total 20 hours.

The action: Bowmen, concentrating fiercely, go through 7 distinct, rhythmic motions: ***a)*** taking their stance, ***b)*** gripping their bow, ***c)*** nocking their arrow, ***d)*** drawing the bow, ***e)*** anchoring the string under their chin or jawbone, ***f)*** making the final adjustment of aim through their bowsight, ***g)*** loosening their 3-finger grip to release the arrow. The final act of releasing is vital. Fingers must part smoothly and simultaneously or a bad shot results. The bow hand must be absoluteley steady. Upon firing and on the follow-through, bowmen remain in *status quo.* "We call it *lashing the body to the bow,*" says '76 Olympic Champion **Darrell Pace** of the USA.

*One of the earliest archery tournaments was the **Ancient Scorton Arrow,** dating to England in 1673. Archery was included in the Olympic Games from **1900** to **1920**, but was dropped until **1972.** Now it's a permanent fixture.*

Scoring: 1. An arrow landing on the dividing line between 2 color zones earns the higher value. **2.** A deflected arrow scores where it lands. **3.** An arrow which rebounds from the matt or passes through it will only be scored if its mark can be determined by the judges. **4.** An arrow embedded in another arrow scores the same as the first arrow. **5.** An arrow is considered not shot if the archer can touch it with his bow without moving his feet from behind the starting line.

Targets are made of stitched, compressed straw rope called a ***matt*** or ***buttress*** and have a thick paper ***face*** on which 5 concentric color zones narrow to a gold bullseye. The face is slanted 15° away from the archer. Targets come in 2 sizes: 4′ (1.22m) and 2′7″ (80cm). Men shoot at the larger target from distances of 229.7′ (70m) and 295.3′ (90m); women shoot from 197′ (60m) and 229.7′ (70m). The smaller target is shot at from 98.4′ (30m) and 164′ (50m) by both men and women.

What to watch for: ***1)*** Size and beginning score are not always indicative of the eventual winner: **Darrell Pace,** USA, the '76 gold winner, weighs only 130lbs (59kg); **Luann Ryon,** USA, who was in 7th place on the first day of the '76 Games, finally won, setting a new world record.

2) The most important clue to a likely victor is ***steadiness:*** the bowperson who allows no variation to creep into his style has the superior ***muscle memory*** and will steadily earn points while others wax and wane.

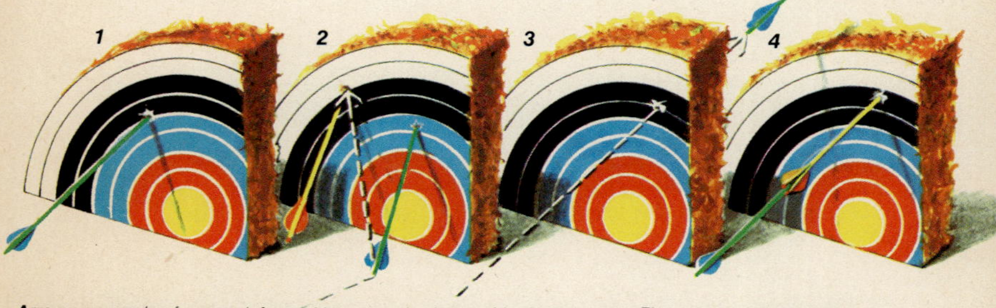

***Arrows** are made of **a.** wood, **b.**graphite, or **c.** aluminum tubing.*

*The point is called the **Pile.***

***Shaft:** section of arrow between the pile and the nock. Lengths between 24" (61cm) and 32" (81.3cm).*

*Shot from a 50lb (22.7kg) bow, arrows travel at an average **speed** of between 185′-198′ (56.4-60m) per second, or between 126-135mph (202-217km/hr).*

Current world records
***Men:** 1341 (**Darrell Pace,** USA, 1979)*
***Women:** 1324 (**Natalia Boutouzova,** USSR, 1982)*

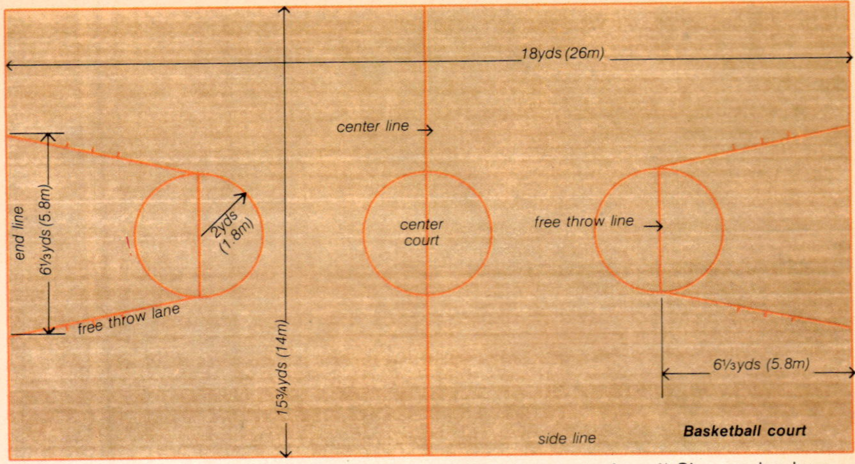

Basketball court

Basketball, one of the few sports the USA has contributed to the Olympic roster, was invented by **Dr. James Naismith** in 1891 at Springfield (Massachusetts) College, then known as the School for Christian Workers. The game was added to the Olympic men's team sports schedule in 1936, and women's basketball competition was added 40 years later.

Procedure: Basketball is played by 2 teams of 5 players each. The purpose of each team is to throw the ball into its own basket and to prevent the other team from scoring. The ball may be thrown, batted, rolled or dribbled in any direction, subject to the restrictions laid down in the playing rules, but may not be carried or deliberately kicked.

Offensive strategies: *1)* Slow pacing by a superior team, allowing a timed, controlled game; *2)* fast-paced games relying on the fast-break play, for teams with speed and height; *3)* a combination, where the team controls a slow-paced game until opportunities for a fast-break present themselves.

The Rules: *Basketball rules, were, initially, a simple text of 13 typewritten statements which Naismith tacked on the bulletin board adjacent to the inside of the gymnasium door.*

At 7'3" (2.21m), Russian ***Yan Kruminsh*** *was the tallest Olympic athlete. He played center on the USSR basketball team*

Officials: There are only 2—a single **referee** and a single **umpire**—but they have absolute power on the court. Neither official can set aside a ruling of the other official.

Scoring: Teams score 2pts by putting the ball through the basket and score 1pt for each made free throw. TV viewers shouldn't expect to see many games over 100pts; championship games of the last 3 Olympics have had an average winning score of 77.1pts; the losers averaged 67.0pts.

Offense: When a team gets possession of the ball, it dribbles or passes the ball among teammates in order to position a player for a good shot. **Dribbling** is bouncing the ball off the floor with one hand. If a player puts both hands on the ball, he must shoot or pass, but may not continue to dribble. Teammates of the ball handler try to position themselves to take a pass from the man with the ball and score.

Olympic jumper **Charles Dumas** *(USA) became the first man to break the 7' (2.15m) highjump barrier and took the gold at Melbourne in 1956. After failing to place 4 years later, Dumas retired to play professional basketball. Other USA Olympic highjumpers who turned pro included* **Walter *Buddy* Davis** *(1952) and* **John Rambo** *(1964).*

Defense Strategies: Defending team members must try to block scoring moves by the offense and also must try to steal the ball without touching *(**fouling**)* an opponent Various team defenses are used. The 2 most common are: man-to-man, with each player matched to an opponent; zone, with each player assigned an area of the court to defend.

Basketballs *are between 30-31" (75-78cm) in circumference and weigh about 1⅓lbs (600-650g). High-topped* ***shoes*** *help prevent ankle injuries, the most common injury basketball players suffer.*

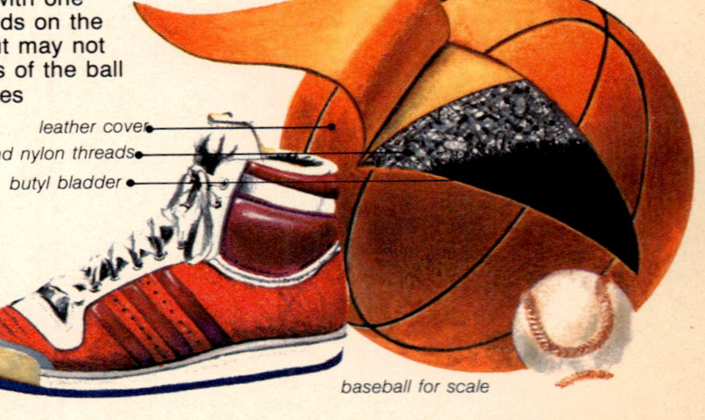

baseball for scale

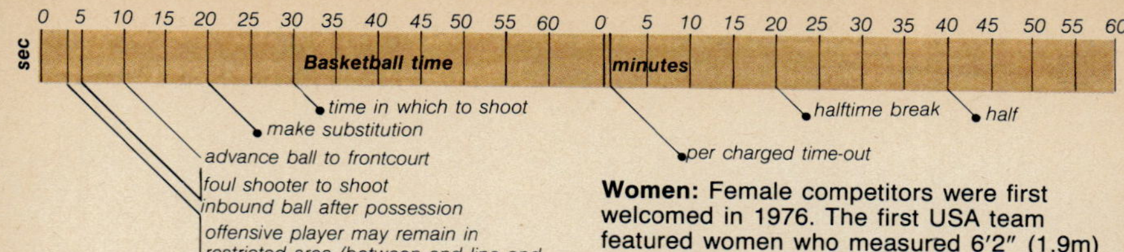

Duration: *Games comprise 2 20min halves with a 10-15min break period in between.*

Time Limitations: Much of the fast-paced action of basketball is based on the special limitation: 30 seconds are allowed for a team to ***shoot*** after gaining control of the ball. The ball must be ***advanced*** from the backcourt to the frontcourt—toward the offense's goal—within 10sec.

Basket

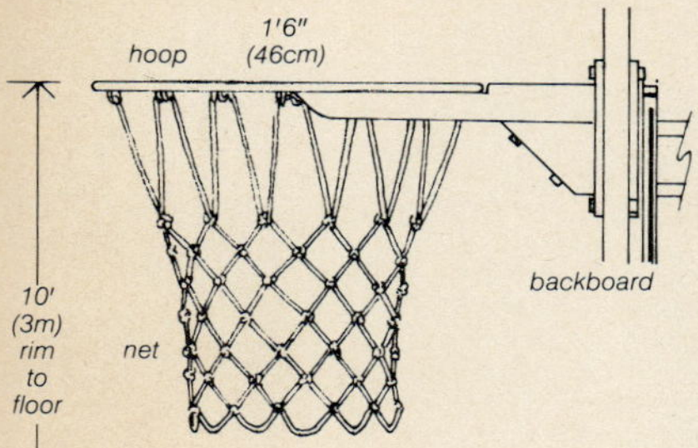

hoop

1'6" (46cm)

backboard

10' (3m) rim to floor

net

Bill Russell, *9-time USA National Basketball Association most valuable player, was a team member of the 1956 Olympic gold-medal squad. That same year he was ranked as the world's 11th best highjumper, leaping 6'9¼" (2.06m), ¼" over his own height.*

Women: Female competitors were first welcomed in 1976. The first USA team featured women who measured 6'2" (1.9m) and 6'5" (2m) tall. One Russian player, **Luli Semanova,** towered 7'2" (2.18m). Semanova scored 43pts and 40 rebounds in the first 3 contests, and the USSR easily won the title over the 2nd-place USA, 112-77. The Soviets triumphed again in 1980. The USA boycotted the 1980 Games, hence did not compete.

From the outset, men's basketball has been a Yankee sport. In 1936, when teams met on muddy outdoor fields, the USA won. In 1948, when indoor courts were finally provided, the USA won. In fact, American teams took the first 7 basketball titles.

The average winning margin through 1968 was 26.2 points, and Olympic basketball proved one of the least thrilling of Olympic competitions. American teams were loaded with the cream of the collegiate crop. Then 2 developments changed the ho-hum forecast of Olympic basketball:

First, **Russia,** studying coaching books by **Adolph Rupp** of Kentucky and **Red Auerbach** of the Boston Celtics, made basketball a priority. By 1960, its state-supported teams were the finest in Europe, featuring 6-footers galore.

Second, **USA collegians** rejected Olympic berths to turn pro. **Lew Alcindor** (Kareem-Abdul Jabbar), **Bill Walton, Julius *Dr. J* Erving, Jim Chones** and **Bob McAdoo** all skipped Olympic gold for the big money of the pros.

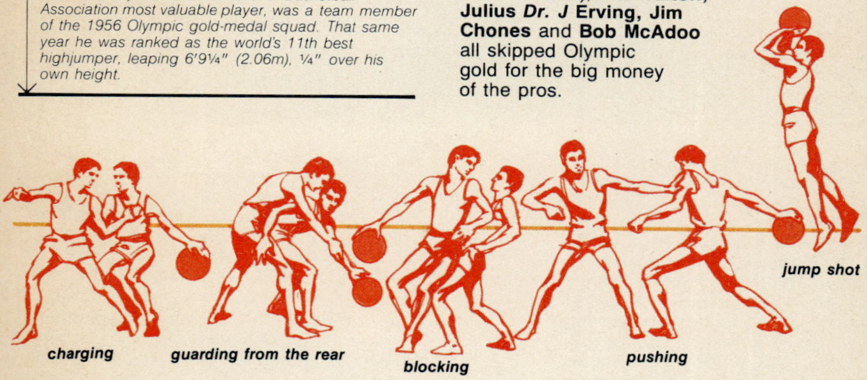

charging ***guarding from the rear*** ***blocking*** ***pushing*** ***jump shot***

When a ball goes ***out-of-bounds,*** it must be in-bounded within 5sec.

Teams have 20sec to make a ***substitution.***

Fouls: After a team has committed 8 fouls in a half, it is penalized by awarding the opponent 2 free throws. When fouled in the act of shooting and the basket is made, the shooter is awarded 1 free throw attempt. If the basket is not made, however, the fouled player is awarded 3 shots to make 2pts. An intentional foul carries a 2-shot penalty. Technical fouls are a 1-shot penalty on the bench and 2 shots on the player.

Classifying: Olympic teams are classified in **pools,** named A, B and sometimes C. A round robin is played in each pool. A team win counts as 2 points, and a loss is one point. If 2 teams finish with the same number of points, the team which won the pool game between the 2 tied teams wins the superior medal. Following is the result of the last Olympic Games in which all FIBA-member nations competed:

Men: The USSR led Group A with 10pts to Canada's 9; the USA led Group B with 10pts to Yugoslavia's 9. Yugoslavia eliminated the USSR, the USA eliminated Canada. In the final, the USA beat Yugoslavia.

With those 2 changes, the tide turned. Led by the giant **Aleksandr Below,** the USSR beat the USA in the 1972 finals at Munich, ending the longest winning streak in any Olympic sport (63 straight victories for the USA). While competition added sparkle to the game, it also added controversy: In 1972, with the score 51-50, officials kept re-setting the time clock in the final 10sec and the USSR finally won. The USA team, protesting the time re-setting as being favorable to the USSR, refused to accept its 2nd-place silver medals, which to this day sit in the vaults of a Munich bank.

Four years after the Munich controversy, the USA, coached by **Dean Smith** of North Carolina regained the crown. Russia was ousted in the semi-finals by fast-improving Yugoslavia and the USA beat the Yugoslavians for the gold, 95-74.

1980's boycott brought up a surprise runner-up: Italy. In the final, Yugoslavia again defeated the USSR.

What to watch for: Memorize the jersey number of the best offensive player and the best defensive player; focus your attention on them.

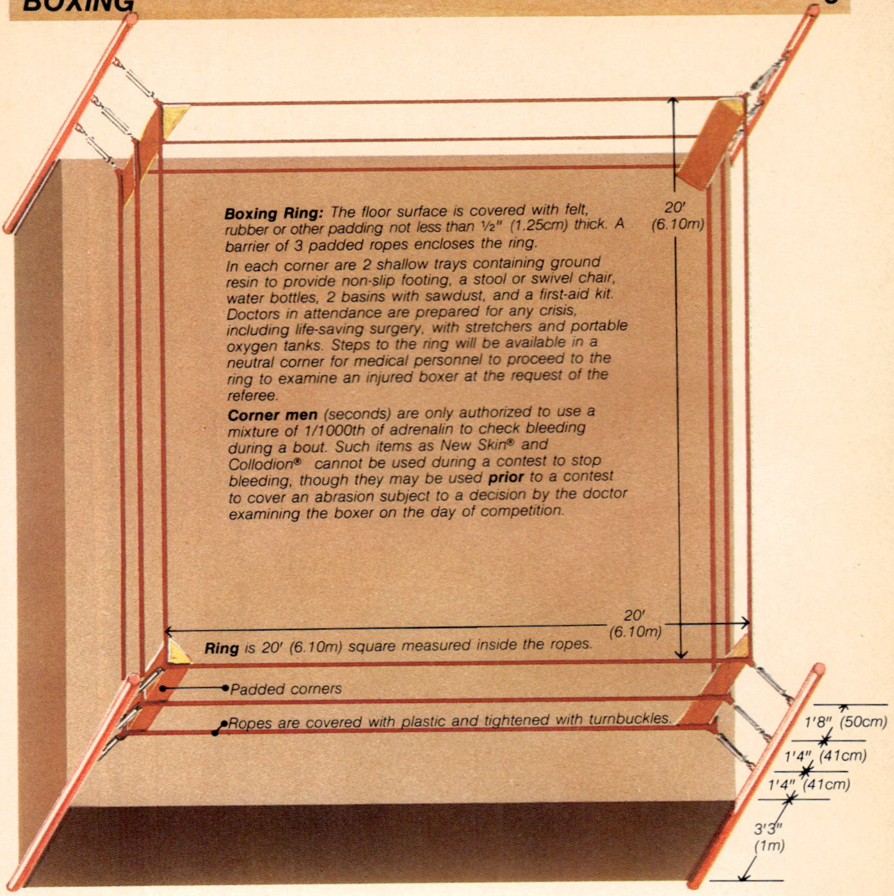

Boxing Ring: *The floor surface is covered with felt, rubber or other padding not less than ½" (1.25cm) thick. A barrier of 3 padded ropes encloses the ring.*
In each corner are 2 shallow trays containing ground resin to provide non-slip footing, a stool or swivel chair, water bottles, 2 basins with sawdust, and a first-aid kit. Doctors in attendance are prepared for any crisis, including life-saving surgery, with stretchers and portable oxygen tanks. Steps to the ring will be available in a neutral corner for medical personnel to proceed to the ring to examine an injured boxer at the request of the referee.
Corner men *(seconds) are only authorized to use a mixture of 1/1000th of adrenalin to check bleeding during a bout. Such items as New Skin® and Collodion® cannot be used during a contest to stop bleeding, though they may be used* **prior** *to a contest to cover an abrasion subject to a decision by the doctor examining the boxer on the day of competition.*
20' (6.10m)
20' (6.10m)
Ring *is 20' (6.10m) square measured inside the ropes.*
Padded corners
Ropes are covered with plastic and tightened with turnbuckles.
1'8" (50cm)
1'4" (41cm)
1'4" (41cm)
3'3" (1m)

1980 Games Champions:
106lb (48kg) **– Shamil Sabirov** (USSR)
112lb (51kg) **– Petar Lessov** (BUL)
119lb (54kg) **– Juan Hernandez** (CUB)
125lb (57kg) **– Rudi Fink** (GDR)
132lb (60kg) **– Angel Herrera** (CUB)
139lb (63.5kg) **– Patrizio Oliva** (ITA)
147lb (67kg) **– Andres Aldama** (CUB)
156lb (71kg) **– Armando Martinez** (CUB)
165lb (75kg) **– Jose Gomez** (CUB)
178lb (81kg) **– Slobodan Kacar** (YUG)
201lb (91kg) **– Teofilo Stevenson** (CUB)

The Los Angeles Olympic boxing meet will be the largest in Games history. More than 80 nations affiliated with the **Association Internationale de Boxe Amateur** (AIBA), the international governing body, will box 34 times per day (16 morning bouts, 18 afternoon) for 11 days. There's nothing like the Olympics for action involving the world's finest non-professional ringmen.

Before the boxing program ends at Los Angeles, approximately ***450 bouts*** will be staged in 12 weight divisions. A new bracket has been added to the 1984 tournament: ***Superheavyweights,*** or fighters weighing more than 20lbs (91kg).

Contestants: Ranging from diminutive 106lb (48kg) **light flys** to superheavyweights, boxers must be at least 17 years old. One fighter per nation per weight division is allowed. Contestants must be cleanly shaved, with no goatees or beards.

Boxers are medically examined each day they compete, preventing abnormal weight gains between competitions.

Competition for gold, silver and bronze medals is torrid among the preeminent boxing countries: Cuba, USSR, Yugoslavia, USA, Bulgaria, Poland, German Democratic Republic (East Germany), Federal Republic of Germany (West Germany) and Italy.

Knockouts and **Referee Stops Contest** (RSC) are not as frequent as in professional boxing and competitors are trained in the skill of delivering more effective legal blows and in the art of self-defense. Many have gone on to become professional World Champions utilizing and exploiting the skills learned as amateur boxers.

The decisions of referees and judges have caused many controversies in many previous Olympic Games. They come from many lands and have varying ideas on who won a fight. At the 1976 Games, 3 officials were fired or suspended for poor judgement. In 1964, no less than 14 refs and judges were removed from the Games after violent protests by fans.

Weight divisions:

Light Flyweight 106lbs (48kg)
Flyweight 112lbs (51kg)
Bantamweight 119lbs (54kg)
Featherweight 125lbs (57kg)

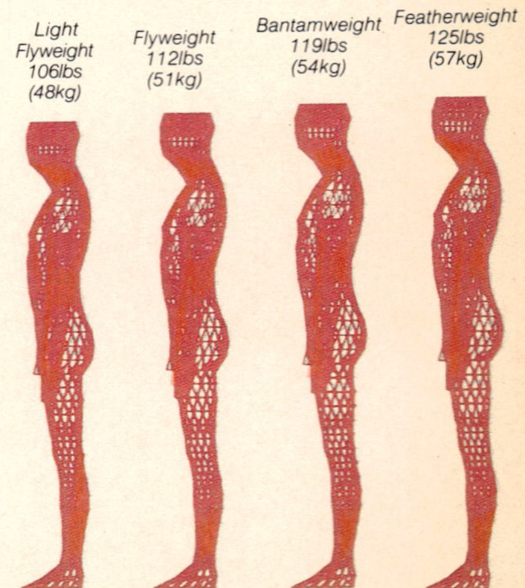

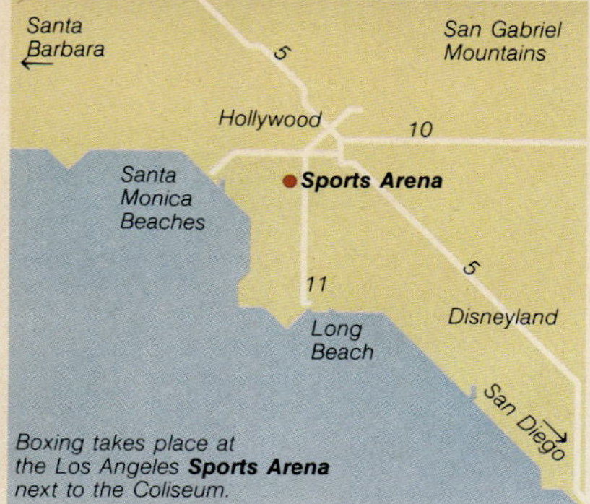

Boxing takes place at the Los Angeles ***Sports Arena*** *next to the Coliseum.*

Olympic style boxing is considerably different from professional boxing. The rules and regulations of amateur boxing are consistent for international competition all over the world. The major differences are:

1) **The *20pt must* system:** The winner of a round must receive 20pts with the loser receiving a lesser number as described below. This judging method determines the scoring of points leading to victory or defeat. Twenty points are awarded the winner of each round. A proportionate number of points—less than 20—are given the man losing the round. Often the per-round points are very close—for instance, a winner may score 20pts while the loser earns 19pts. If a round is judged to be even, each contestant is awarded 20pts. But an Olympic even round is a rarity. Judges almost always give 1 man the edge in their scoring.

2) **Tie bouts:** Under international rules, judges use 3 elements to determine the winner of a bout where equal points have been awarded both boxers. Credit is given, in order of value:

For ***aggressiveness,*** wherein a boxer is pressing forward and delivering scoring blows outnumbering his opponent;

For a ***strong defense*** which enables a boxer to block, parry, etc., to avoid receiving blows;

For ***clean boxing,*** which includes use of clever boxing and the complete elimination of fouls and unfair tactics.

Mandatory 8-count: When a boxer is knocked down, the referee begins to count at 1sec intervals from 1-10. A mandatory count of 8 must be given before the referee gives the command to continue the bout with the command, ***box!*** If a boxer who has received an 8 count falls to the floor again, or is considered incapable of defending himself and is in poor condition, the referee may continue the count to 10, thus resulting in the decision of a knockout. ***A man is considered down*** if he touches the floor with any part of his body other than his feet as a result of a blow or series of blows, or if he hangs helplessly on the ropes as a result of a blow or series of blows, or if he is outside or partly outside the ropes as a result of a blow or series of blows, or if, following a hard punch, he has not fallen and is not lying on the ropes, but is in a semi-conscious state and cannot, in the opinion of the referee, continue the bout. An Olympic referee, or any other referee in amateur boxing, has the prime responsibility for the safety of the boxers. This is a major difference between amateur and professional boxing, where the professional referees are influenced by crowds, boxers' reputations, etc.

End of round: *If a man is down at the end of a round, the bell terminating the 3min round is not sounded. The referee continues the count and, if the man doesn't rise before a 10-count is reached, he is considered out. As in all amateur boxing, "saved by the bell" is eliminated in the Olympics. The theory is that a fighter who is flattened shouldn't be saved by a gong, dragged to a corner for a few seconds rest, then forced to continue the punishment. The only exception to this rule is the last round of the final championship match of each weight division, when the continued-count provision does not apply.*

Other scoring factors: *The value of hits made during* ***infighting*** *is assessed by the judges at the end of each such rally. They are credited to the boxer according to the number of effective blows landed.*

Non-scoring blows *which have no point value whatever include: while infringing on the rules; struck with the side, heel or inside of the glove; struck with an open glove; those which land on the arms or connect without the power of body and shoulders behind them.*

Knockdowns *are not given the special consideration in amateur boxing that they are in professional boxing. Judges only award points to the boxer who has scored the knockdown by giving credit for an effective blow, such as a right hook or a left jab.*

Weighing scales *manned by 2 weighers must be of the* ***doctor's scales*** *or balance-beam type in 16lb (7.25kg) weights. Weigh-ins for all boxers are conducted prior to the first day of competition. Daily weigh-ins will be only for those boxers scheduled to compete that day. Weigh-ins are conducted in the nude.*

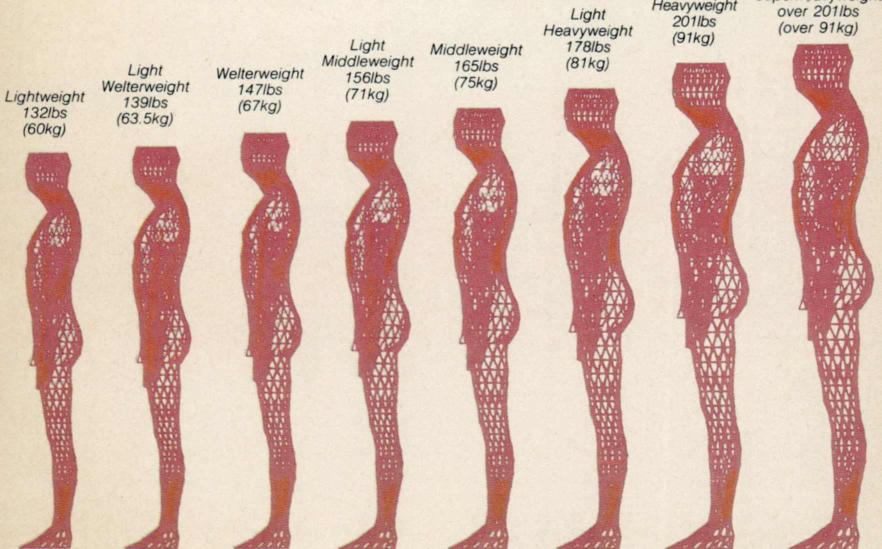

Computer Graphics by William Fetter

Bandages: *Soft surgical wraps not exceeding 8″ (20cm) in length and 2″ (5cm) in width are allowed, except for a type called Velpeau, which cannot exceed 6′6″ (1.98m) in length. Tape, rubber and adhesive plaster are strictly forbidden.*

Grease, *or any other slippery substance on the face, arms or body is prohibited.*

Most common boxing injuries: *cuts above the eye (causes bleeding so a boxer can't see), broken noses and displaced septums, and fractures of the lower bone of the first finger.*

Unconsciousness results from a nervous system overload caused by hard blows or a blow to the head causing a mild concussion.

Unlike bare-torsoed pro fighters, Olympic boxers wear a vest (sleeveless shirt) covering the chest and back. This is worn to reduce gloves becoming permeated with sweat, dirt, etc., and also provides means of proper identification of the boxer.

Custom-fit mouth-piece, *if knocked from the mouth, causes the bout to be stopped while the piece is washed and replaced.*

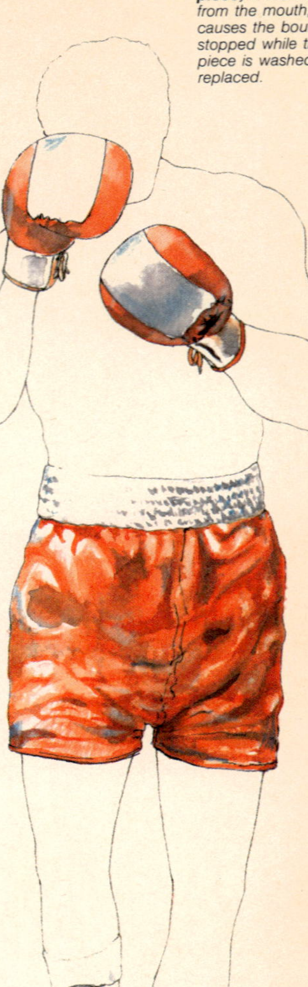

High-topped soft-soled ***ring shoes,*** *without cleats*

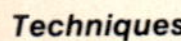

Techniques

right to head

right hook

uppercut

right to body

blocking a punch

slipping a punch

Techniques: *Often, a Games bout resembles a fencing match (from which modern boxing rules are, indeed, derived). The accent is on quick, sharp hitting and clever defense, unlike many pro-style slugfests. But the basic* ***blows*** *are standard:*

left jab *to the chin*
straight left *to body*
straight right *to the head*
left hooks *to head and body*
right hook *to head*
right cross *over opponent's blow*
left and right uppercuts
feints, counterpunches *and* ***combination jab-and-hook***

Footwork *reaches an apex in Olympic boxing where contestants' lateral movements make them moving targets for the opponent.*

Foul boxing: *Referees can give a warning for each major* ***harm foul.*** *The 3rd warning results in immediate disqualification. The warnings do not have to be for the same type of foul: for example, one for holding and hitting, illegal use of the head, and one for a low blow will result in automatic disqualification. The referee must give the 3rd warning and make it known to the boxers and the judges and jury, then disqualify the boxer.*

A long list of defined ***fouls*** *includes:*

hitting below the belt
butting *or hitting with head, shoulder or forearm*
holding, *tripping or kicking*
hitting to the back of the neck *or head*
kidney punches
striking with the open glove *or side of glove*
throttling *an opponent*
pivot blows
hitting while holding the ropes *or* ***making unfair use of the ropes***
hitting a man who's down *or in the act of rising*
locking of opponent's arm or head
pulling and hitting
offensive utterances
not stepping back *on the command of* ***break***
hitting on the break
falling down *to avoid a blow, or other passive defense*
lying on, wrestling and throwing *in the clinch*
assaulting a referee at any time

Harm fouls *may result in the offender being warned and 1pt deducted from his round score. In close matches, warnings may result in the decision being given to the offended boxer as a result of lost points by the offender.*

Procedure: Before the tournament begins, competitors draw numbers to determine their sequence of matches. Two ***seconds*** may mount the ring apron, but only one may enter the ring in the boxer's corner. No advice or encouragement may be given by a second during a bout. A second may throw in a sponge or towel on behalf of his man to signal ***we retire the boxer.***

Normally, a boxer would have to emerge as a winner in 5 to 6 bouts in his class to reach the finals for a shot at the gold medal.

The **winner** is determined by a ***knockout, referee stops contest (RSC)*** or based on the ***points of each boxer.*** The decision of the 5 AIBA-appointed judges may be overruled, in the case of a 3-2 decision, by the appointed technical jury if a minimum of 4 jury members are in favor of the decision for the other boxer.

Match duration is 3 rounds of 3min each, with a 1min interval between rounds.

Locking of opponent's arm or head

Hitting below the belt

Striking with open glove or side of glove (a slap)

Kneeing

Kidney punches

Elbowing

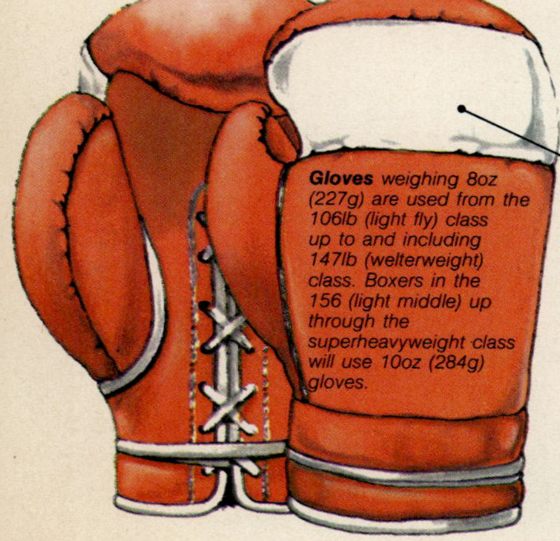

Gloves *weighing 8oz (227g) are used from the 106lb (light fly) class up to and including 147lb (welterweight) class. Boxers in the 156 (light middle) up through the superheavyweight class will use 10oz (284g) gloves.*

In the Olympics, there are 3 decision authorities: the ***referee,*** *the* ***5 judges*** *and the* ***5-man technical jury.***

Referee: *He has no scoring vote, but is empowered to stop any bout that is too one-sided, to enforce the rules and to disqualify rule-breakers. He cannot wear eyeglasses, but contact lenses are allowed. The referee wears a white shirt and white trousers and light colored shoes or boots without raised heels. To ensure neutrality, the referee must come from a nation* ***different*** *from those of the fighters he is supervising. To surmount the language problem, referees use* ***international sign language.***

To signal, referee: *taps palm of hand with his fingers of his other hand to warn fighter he is illegally hitting with an open glove or edge of glove (a* ***slap****)*

signals ***holding*** *by the gesture of holding*

taps forehead to signal ***butting*** *violation*

bends body forward to signal ***lying on opponent***

points below waist to show ***hitting below belt***

touches back of head, neck, kidney area to show ***blows to prohibited areas***

Referees use only 3 verbal commands: ***box, stop*** *and* ***break.***

Judges: *A panel of 5 surrounds the ring, keeps score on pads and awards points on the* ***20pt must system.*** *The total of their scores decides the winner (other than in a knockout).*

To assure neutrality, the judges from each bout must come from ***5 different continents:*** *Africa, Asia, Australia/Oceania, Europe, America. No judge can hail from the same country as either boxer.*

Technical jury: *This is the* ***Supreme Court*** *of Games boxing. A 3-5 man panel sits in judgement of the work of judges and referees. It can call any official on the carpet and recommend his dismissal to the Executive Committee of the AIBA, or overrule the actions or decisions of any referee or judge who acts in conflict with the articles and rules of the AIBA. This is one of the most coveted positions in the Olympic Games.*

What to watch for: Do what Olympic judges do in keeping track of the swift action—direct your gaze **not** on either boxer, but on a point midway between the pair. If you watch just one man (and following both is very difficult), you miss the overall ebb-and-flow. Games judges never concentrate on an individual, but direct their attention to the actions of both boxers.

Watch for boxers who jab often, then follow with a hook, cross or straight punch delivered with power.

Notice the condition of the boxers. Competitors are often required to box the length of the tournament and even though a boxer may win in his early competitions, the efforts put forth in winning the early bouts may result in a diminishing of strength and condition.

Keep score on a pad. Games judges award 1pt for 3 scoring blows delivered and keep running totals for each boxer. Fouls are clearly indicated by the referee, when he warns a boxer. If the judges agree, 1pt is awarded the offended boxer. If a judge disagrees with the warning, he marks an X in the scoring column and does not deduct points.

Marked gloves: In international amateur boxing, judges are aided in knowing when a scoring blow has been delivered by the requirement that the regular hitting surface of the glove is painted (normally it is white). This makes a blow more visible to the judges' eyes and lets them know when a scoring blow has been delivered in the scoring area. The scoring blow is defined as a blow struck with the knuckle part of the closed glove of either hand on any part of the front or sides of the head or the body above the belt. Any blow delivered with the fist not closed is not considered to be a scoring blow.

1980 Olympic Canoeing Champions
Men's 500m singles: S. Postrekhin, USSR
Men's 1000m singles: L. Lubanov, BUL

1980 Olympic Kayak Champions
Men's 500m singles: Vasily Parfenovich, USSR
Men's 1000m singles: Rudiger Helm, GDR
Women's 500m singles: Birgit Fischer, GDR

Canoes and canoe-like boats have been a common means of transportation since primitive man first took to the water, but perhaps the most universally noted version is the birch bark-covered boats of the North American Indian. In Alaska, Eskimos built their own version of the canoe, of whalebone and sealskin, called a **kayak.**

Weigh-in: *2 days before a race, the craft are weighed and must conform to strict standards. Weights are added if necessary to eliminate any advantage. One of the famous acts of high sportsmanship happened in kayaking in the Olympics. When a 1-man kayak belonging to the USA was discovered to be 1/8" too narrow and was disqualified, 7 rival countries offered to lend a legal kayak to the USA team—one similar to their lost boat. One of the offers was accepted, but the Yanks still didn't win the medal.*

After the 1700s, canoeing quickly evolved from a way to travel America's waterways into a popular water sport. In the 1924 Olympics, 4 national teams joined for the Games' first demonstration of canoeing and 12 years later it became an official competition. Shortly after WWII, the ***International Canoe Federation*** was formed to govern the sport.

Modern Olympic competition is divided into **kayak** and **Canadian canoe** contests. Calm, flatwater courses are wanted for these races. Lake Casitas, the 1984 site, will be the first natural lake used in the Games since 1960, when Italy's Lake Albano, in the crater of an extinct volcano, was the location.

Procedure: *Olympic sprint courses of 547yd (500m) and 1093yd (1000m) are marked by* ***bouys*** *and* ***flags*** *for their entire length. Red flags signify the start and finish lines.* ***Lanes*** *are 29'6" (9m) wide for each boat. Straying from lanes or coming closer than 16' (5m) to another boat is prohibited.*

Start: *An official* ***aligner*** *sees that boats are lined up evenly with bows on the starting line. When all entries are level and still, held by officials so that their sterns touch starting pontoons, a* ***ready*** *signal is given by the starter. After a 2sec pause, he fires the starting pistol.*

If an entrant's ***paddle breaks*** *within 49' (15m) of the start, there's a recall; the paddle is replaced and the race restarted. The 15m mark is designated by a flag.*

Finish: *1st boat to pass its bow between the red finishing flags is the winner.*

A variety of styles of knee pads are used by canoeists. They protect the knee, and along with an optional brace for the foot, afford the paddler maximum stability and power.

Canadian canoe*—an open boat (deck not enclosed) and propelled with a single-bladed, unfixed paddle. Canoeists operate from 1 or both knees.*

Technique: *Canoeists paddle from a high-kneeling position. The paddling motion is divided into 4 parts:* ***set-up,*** *shoulders and torso are positioned for correct strength and flexibility;* ***catch*** *and* ***power,*** *a quick thrust of the paddle into the water and application of body weight and muscle against the water's resistance to push the boat foward;* ***steering*** *and* ***exit,*** *making a J-hooked motion with the paddle to steer the boat and remove the paddle from the water simultaneously without deceleration of the boat;* ***mid-recovery,*** *a critical recovery of balance and set-up position without shifting weight in a way that slows the canoe.*

Kayak*—a boat with an enclosed deck with cockpit opening for the athlete's seat (2 openings for a 2-man team, 4 openings for the K-4). It is paddled from a sitting position with a double-bladed paddle.*

Technique: *double and quadruple paddlers use a similar cycle to the canoeist. It is divided into* ***set-up, immersion*** *of paddle,* ***power*** *and* ***exit.*** *A fluid, rhythmic stroke is the kayaker's goal.*

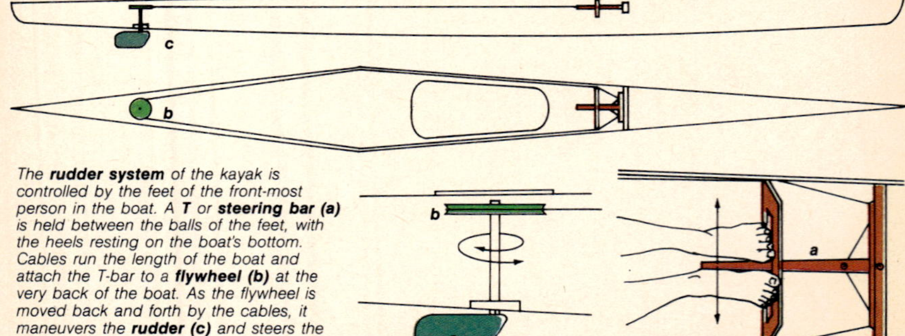

The ***rudder system*** *of the kayak is controlled by the feet of the front-most person in the boat. A* ***T*** *or* ***steering bar (a)*** *is held between the balls of the feet, with the heels resting on the boat's bottom. Cables run the length of the boat and attach the T-bar to a* ***flywheel (b)*** *at the very back of the boat. As the flywheel is moved back and forth by the cables, it maneuvers the* ***rudder (c)*** *and steers the boat.*

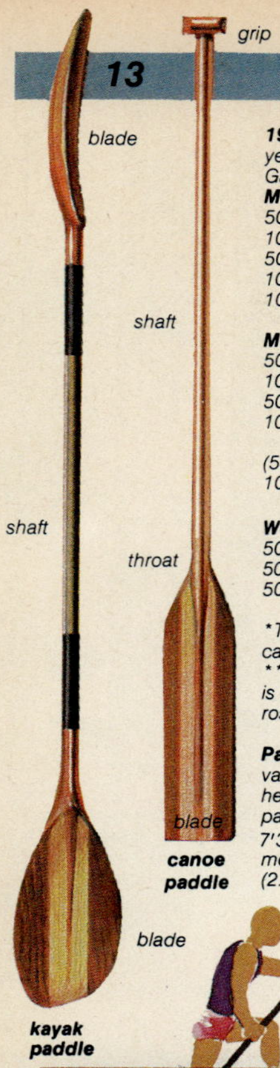

grip

blade

shaft

shaft

throat

blade

canoe paddle

blade

kayak paddle

1984 Olympic Events *(with year introduced to the Games)*

Men's Kayak
500m singles (K-1) (1976)
1000m singles (K-1) (1936)
500m pairs (K-2) (1976)
1000m pairs (K-2) (1936)
1000m fours (K-4) (1964)

Men's Canadian Canoe
500m singles (C-1) (1976)
1000m singles (C-1) (1936)
500m pairs (C-2) (1976)
1000m pairs (C-2) (1936)

(500m = 547yds; 1000m = 1,094yds)

Women's Kayak*
500m singles (K-1) (1948)
500m pairs (K-2) (1960)
*500m fours (K-4) (1984)***

**There are no women's canoeing events.*
***4-woman team kayaking is new to the Olympic roster.*

Paddles: *Canoe paddles vary in length with the height of the racer. Kayak paddles usually measure 7'3"-7'6" (2.21-2.9m) for men and 7'1"-7'4" (2.16-2.24m) for women.*

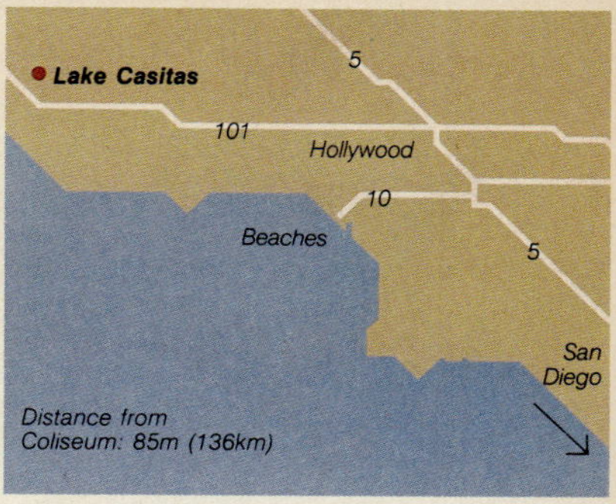

Lake Casitas
5
101
Hollywood
10
Beaches
5
San Diego

Distance from Coliseum: 85m (136km)

Strategy: *Unlike a footrace, where the racers can pace each segment of their race and save a burst of energy for the finish, canoe and kayak racers are often faced with trying to be the last ones to tire out. Only the East Germans have mastered the technique of pacing so that their* **splits** *(times for each portion of the race) hardly differ.*

Another facet of paddle race strategy takes advantage of the complex system of heats, repeat heats (repechages) and semifinals. Rather than place first in an early heat and be faced with the top-notch competition in the next heat, a team may purposely place 2nd or 3rd. In this way, it will be placed in a repechage against weaker teams, affording a greater chance for a win and potential progression to the finals.

steering & exit

mid-recovery

Boat dimensions:

C-1 *(canoe singles)—17' (5.18m) maximum length, 2'6" (75cm) beam, 35lbs (16kg) minimum weight*

C-2 *(canoe doubles) 21'4" (6.5m) maximum length 2'6" (76cm) beam, 44lbs (20kg) minimum weight*

Steering: *Canoes are maneuvered with a* **J stroke,** *a twisting of the paddle away from the canoe before it is pulled from the water. In the C-2, the stroke is used by the rear man only. Kayaks are guided with a foot-controlled rudder, which is always operated by the front-most person in the boat.*

1984 competition: *1 boat per nation per event may be entered in the Games. Thirty-five countries are expected to compete. To give all teams the advantage of quality equipment, the LAOOC will be purchasing top-quality Danish racing boats, and offering their use to all nations.*

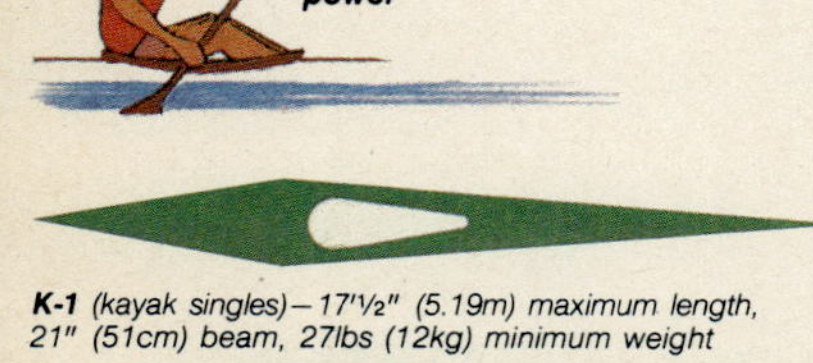

exit

Numberplates: *A big aid to TV viewers, kayaks must carry large black-and-yellow numbers on their afterdecks, canoes on their foredecks.*

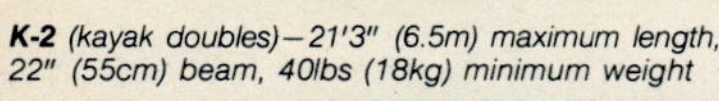

K-1 *(kayak singles)—17'½" (5.19m) maximum length, 21" (51cm) beam, 27lbs (12kg) minimum weight*

K-2 *(kayak doubles)—21'3" (6.5m) maximum length, 22" (55cm) beam, 40lbs (18kg) minimum weight*

Whitewater slalom (racing over a rapid river course) will not be held in 1984. It cost more than $4 million to construct an artificial slalom course for the 1972 Games and the event was dropped after that.

K-4 *(kayak fours)—36' (11m) maximum length, 23½" (60cm) beam, 66lbs (30kg) minimum weight*

What to watch for: Expect an explosive start and a heated early sprint. The race will then level off to a rhythmic pinwheel of paddles as racers catch their breath and try to maintain a front position. A combination of superb rhythm and an unyielding supply of power is needed for a win.

Construction: *The long, slim boats are made of laminated fiberglass or plywood. Most canoes are of wood, kayaks of fiberglass or wood. Paddles are often of maple, ash or spruce.*

Speed: *Velocity of close to 12mph (19.3km/hr) is attained in the short sprints at upward of 125 strokes per minute—a furious rate. Olympic times have been improved by phenomenal degrees. The 1976 Olympic winning time in 500m canoe men's singles was 1:59.23 and in 1980 it was 1:53.37. Kayak singles went from 1:45.41 to 1:43.43. Women cut their kayak doubles clocking from 1:51.15 to 1:43.88. A strong K-4 team builds up enough speed to pull a water-skiier!*

CYCLING

Track: *The 1984 Olympic track is of buffed concrete, rather than wood as used at the 1980 Moscow Games.*

Velodrome
e.
a.
b.
c.
Track Markings:
a. Pole line: Black line 7.8″ (20cm) wide around the track's inner edge.
b. Sprinter's line: Red line 35.4″ (90cm) up from the inner edge of the track.
c. Pacer or Relief line: Blue line halfway up the track above which riders travel during warmups.
d. 200m line: Black line 656.1′ from finish line, used for sprint timing.
e. Finish line: Black and painted in the center of a wide, white strip of 28.4″ (72cm) width.
Signal light system: Red and green flashing lights set on each side of the track tell the audience and racers who is leading at any point.
Banking at ends: 33°
33°
d.

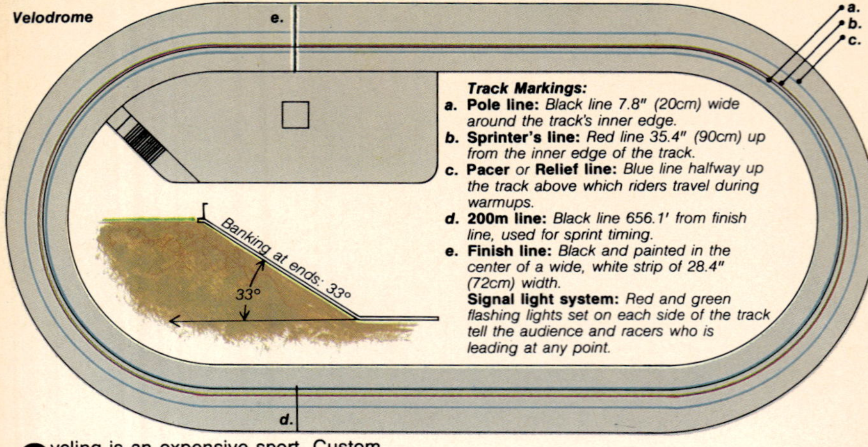

Cycling is an expensive sport. Custom made single and multispeed bikes cost up to $3000 apiece. Their special construction includes alloy tubing and silk-thread tires: the most strength at the least weight. National teams competing at Los Angeles will bring several of these cycles for each person entered, in case of breakdowns, crashes or other mishaps.

More than 500 cycle racers are anticipated at Los Angeles, easily replacing the 1972 Munich record of 360 competitors. The dominant nations in the 2 types of contests on the program—***road*** and ***track*** racing—have traditionally been France, Denmark, East Germany, West Germany, Holland, Poland, Italy and the USSR.

In 1976, ***Klaus-Peter Thaler*** *of West Germany made a wild dash for the finish line and got there first. But officials ruled he'd fouled the field by cutting across the path of others and Thaler was sent back to 9th place.*

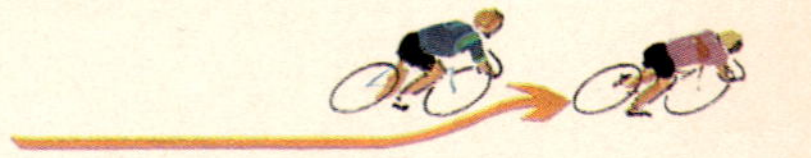

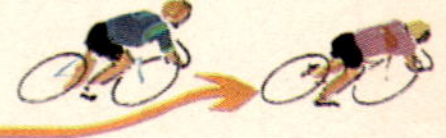

It is illegal ***to cross in front of*** *(cut off) another rider or to* ***push another cyclist*** *in time trials or individual races.*

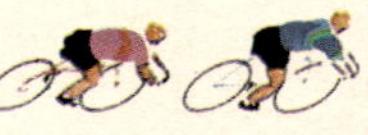

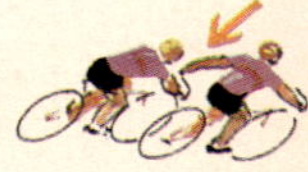

It's illegal ***to hold on to*** *an opponent's bike or to* ***push*** *a teammate's bike.*

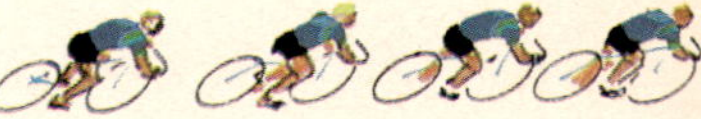

Drafting: *Riding close behind another cyclist in order to take advantage of lessened air resistance.*

Track bike

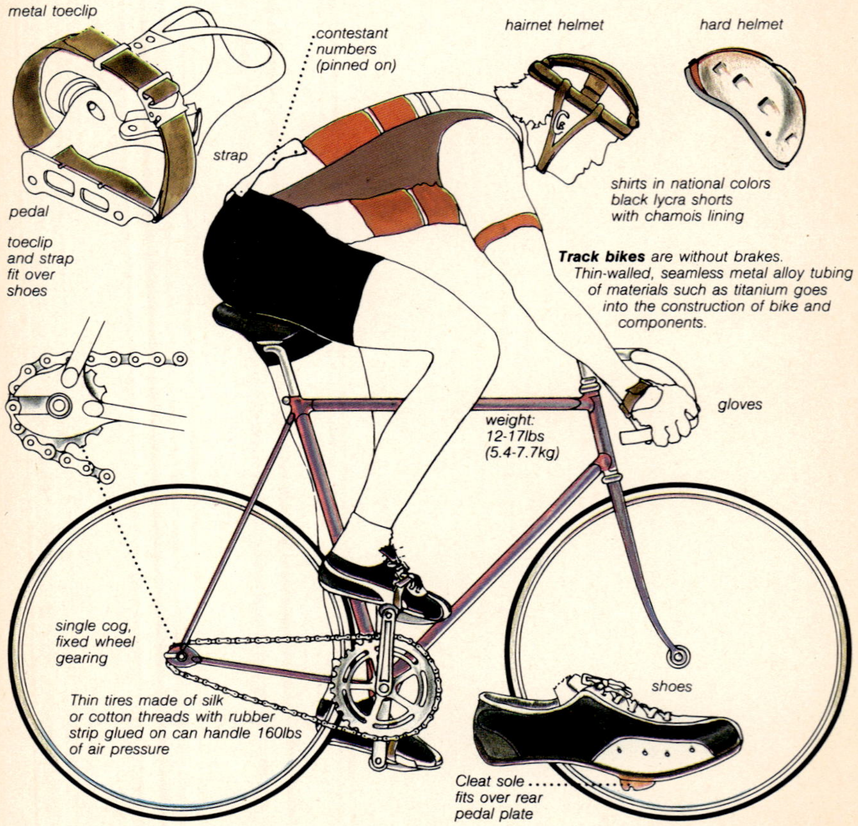

metal toeclip
strap
pedal
toeclip and strap fit over shoes
contestant numbers (pinned on)
hairnet helmet
hard helmet
shirts in national colors
black lycra shorts with chamois lining
Track bikes are without brakes. Thin-walled, seamless metal alloy tubing of materials such as titanium goes into the construction of bike and components.
gloves
weight: 12-17lbs (5.4-7.7kg)
single cog, fixed wheel gearing
Thin tires made of silk or cotton threads with rubber strip glued on can handle 160lbs of air pressure
shoes
Cleat sole fits over rear pedal plate

CYCLING

*In 1896 **Leon Flameng** of France and **G. Kolettis** of Greece had far outstripped their rivals in the 100km cycle race and were fighting it out for the gold medal. When Kolettis' bike broke down not far from the finish line, Flameng stopped pedaling and waited until the Greek could secure a new bike—then they continued the race. All of Athens cheered the fine sportsmanship of the French champ, who went on to beat Kolettis.*

(a)
(b)
(c)

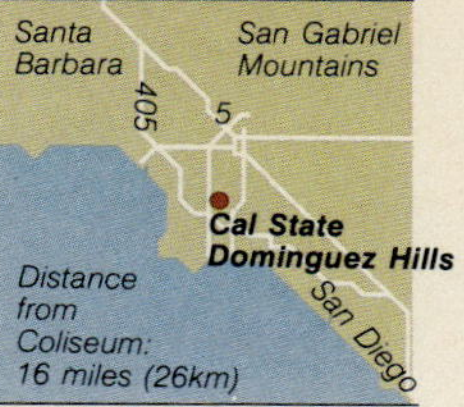

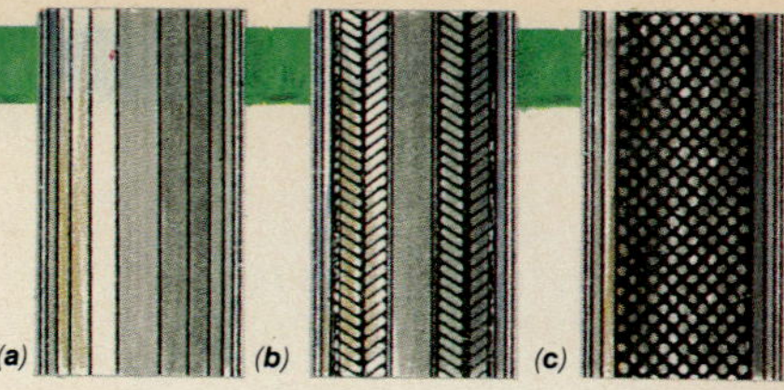

*Tread patterns range from **(a) grooves** for speed to **(b) herringbones** for cornering, to **(c) raised dot** designs for wet conditions.*

***Track racing will take place** in the $3 million open-air velodrome erected in 1982 at **California State University, Dominguez Hills.** Road race routes will be in Mission Viejo, the 4-man team trials on the Artesia Fwy (CA 91).*

Santa Barbara
San Gabriel Mountains
405
5
Cal State Dominguez Hills
San Diego
Distance from Coliseum: 16 miles (26km)

The 7 contests of 1984 include the first Olympic women's cycling event, a 70km (43.49mi) road race. The events are:

Track racing: 1000m (1093.6yd) match sprint, 1000m individual time trial, 4000m (4374.4yd) individual pursuit, 4000m team pursuit, 50km (31mi) points race.

Road racing: 100km (62mi) team time trial, 175k (108.7mi) individual road race, women's 70km (43.49mi) race. Road races begin from a massed start.

Pursuit races: Either individuals or 4-man teams vie for position in this 4000m (4374.4yd) race. The object is to pass the opponent. If no passing is executed, the fastest time wins.

Team Time Trial: At a grueling 100km (62mi), members of 4-man teams ride as a unit, alternately pacing and creating slipstream. Teams begin the approximately 2hr race at 2min intervals.

Watch for special cycling maneuvers, such as drafting, designed to reduce wind resistance.

Classic event: The most prestigious medal to be won comes in the 1000m (1093.6yd) match sprint. This will be 3 laps around the 333.33m (1094′) oval. A series of matches whittles the field down to 2 finalists. Positions in elimination heats are decided by seeding entrants off the past year's international results.

This is anything but the all-out dash to the finish line that you'd expect. Instead, it is a *cat-and-mouse* duel of split-second timing. Riding on single-speed, brakeless bikes, the cyclists ride slowly for the first 600 or so meters, or about 2 laps. ***They may stop entirely*** (but not back up) as they jockey for position until the finish is relatively close. Each waits for the other to make a break for the finish line. Whoever breaks first must open up a wide gap to win, otherwise his opponent will be able to ***draft*** behind him, taking advantage of his windstream and conserving energy for a final burst. Because of the unusual strategy of the sprint race, only the final 200m are timed. Speeds up to 40mph (64k/hr) are reached when at last the racers go all-out for the wire.

In 1972 a Greek racer crashed into a carriage and spilled—but got up and won the gold medal.

Two Danish riders collapsed in the smothering heat of the 1960 Games in Rome; one died.

Road bike

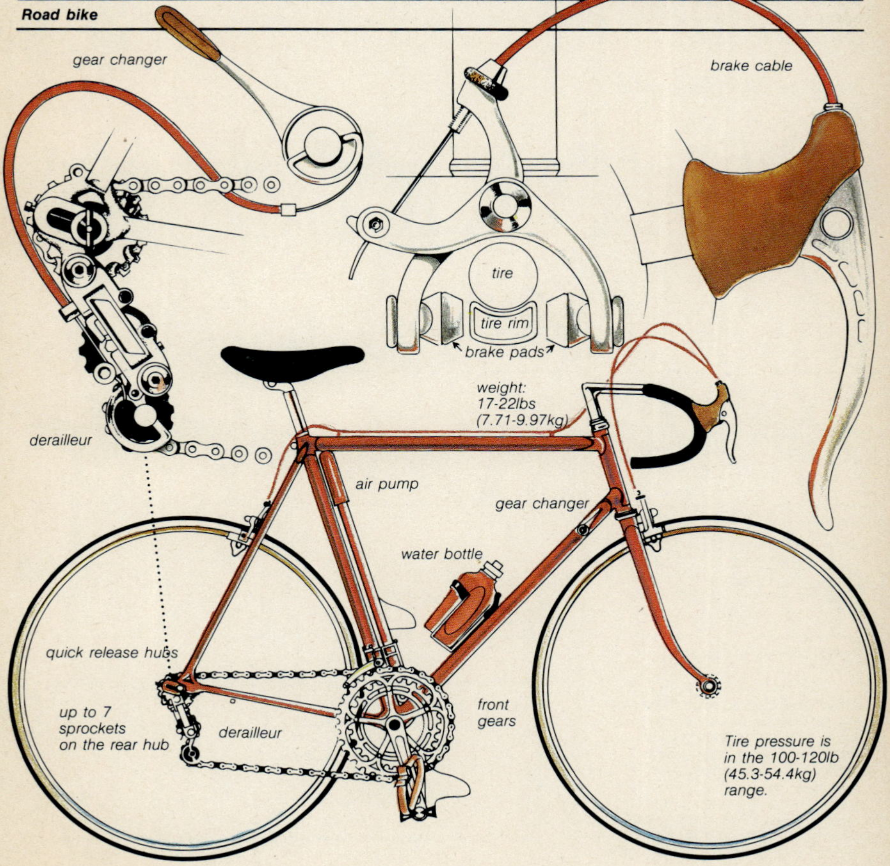

gear changer
brake cable
tire
tire rim
brake pads
derailleur
weight: 17-22lbs (7.71-9.97kg)
air pump
gear changer
water bottle
quick release hubs
up to 7 sprockets on the rear hub
derailleur
front gears
Tire pressure is in the 100-120lb (45.3-54.4kg) range.

EQUESTRIAN EVENTS

1980 Olympic Champions
***Grand Prix Dressage:* Elisabeth Theurer,** AUT (aboard *Mon Cherie*)
***3-Day Event:* Federico Euro Roma,** ITA (aboard *Rossinan*)
***Grand Prix Jumping:* Jan Kowalczyk,** POL (aboard *Artemor*)
***Team Grand Prix Dressage:* USSR**
***Team 3-Day Event:* USSR**
***Team Grand Prix Jumping:* USSR**

At the Los Angeles staging of the Games in 1932, **Lieutenant Charles Ferdinand Pahud de Mortanges** of the Dutch hussars was a one-man sensation. De Mortanges had won the demanding 3-Day Event in the previous Olympics aboard a beautiful palomino named **Marcroix.** He'd won at the 1924 Games. Now, at Los Angeles, still riding Marcroix, the Dutchman triumphed once more. "This," he said, "is not enough. The horse remains sound." And so, in the 1936 Olympics at Berlin, the 17-year-old palomino carried De Mortanges to the all-time standout record. Middle-aged iron man, fabulous mount.

The multiple-event Olympic program of **Dressage, Grand Prix Jumping,** and **3-Day** (cross-country, dressage and jumping) is the fiercest set of tests for horse and rider yet invented. It will be a TV highlight in '84 as 30-odd masters of equitation vie for honors.

Santa Barbara · *San Gabriel Mountains* · *Coliseum* · **Santa Anita Park** · 11 · 5 · *Long Beach* · *Distance from Coliseum: 19 miles (30km)*

Not only are grace, courage, endurance, harmony, speed and split-second timing on parade, but so is courage; these events can be very dangerous. Six-foot fences, walls-and-rails, triple bars and water jumps are among the many hazards.

Even the best-trained thoroughbreds will refuse a jump, break rank, or lose their footing, as the following shows:
In the 1960 Games, **Bill Roycroft** of Australia crashed and broke his clavicle.
In 1964, **Michael Bullen** of Great Britain had the worst of many falls, breaking several bones.

Events:
Individual Grand Prix Jumping
Team Grand Prix Jumping (Nation's Cup)
Individual Grand Prix Dressage
Team Grand Prix Dressage
Individual 3-Day Event
Team 3-Day Event

Each nation may enter 4 riders plus 1 reserve and 6 horses in Dressage; 5 riders plus a reserve and 8 horses in the 3-Day and Jump competitions. Only the maximum number of entrants allowed may be sent to Los Angeles.

***Horses** of any breed and a minimum of 6 years old may be entered.*

Half pirouette

Dressage: One of the finest aesthetic pleasures of the Olympics. Training their own horses, using English hunting-type saddlery and double bridle, riders lead their mounts through a complicated drill of maneuvers which test control, pace, seat, regularity and ease of movements. Riders (3 from a nation) are judged on a scale of 0-10 in various categories. Horses must be a minimum 14.2 hands (4'8"or 1.4m) tall. **Watch for smoothness and rhythm** in transitions between movements. Alert, balanced confidence marks winners; raised tails, tossing and hesitation are signs of trouble.

Dressage exercises include:

Flying change of leg canter

***Other Dressage executions** include the **Serpentine** (a weaving course the length of the 60x20m arena), the **Reinback** (walking the horse backwards), the **Piaffe** (highly cadenced, majestic trot, done from one spot) and the **Passage** (a sort of extended and slow-motion Piaffe). **Turning** requires an even bend along the entire length of the horse's spine.*

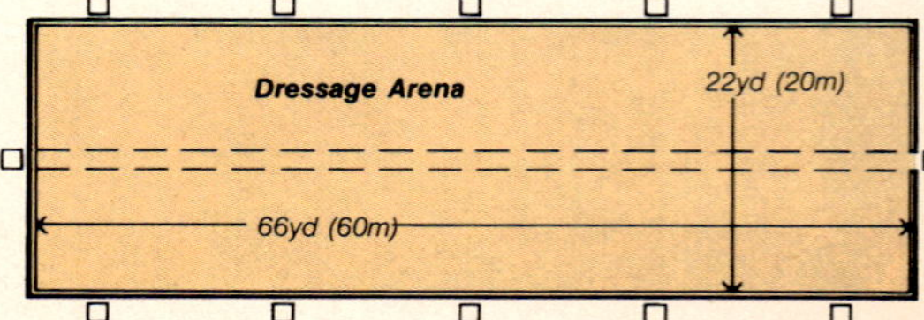

Uprights (jumps with a single vertical plane to clear)

Spreads (double or triple planes in one jump)

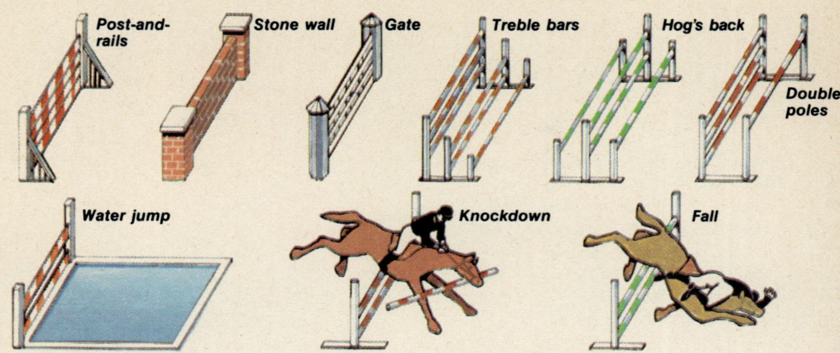

*A typical course might be as diagrammed below. **Uprights** and **spreads** (above) of various kinds dot the field; horse and rider must follow a set sequence through the barriers. **4a** and **4b** are **combination jumps** as are **9a** and **9b**.*

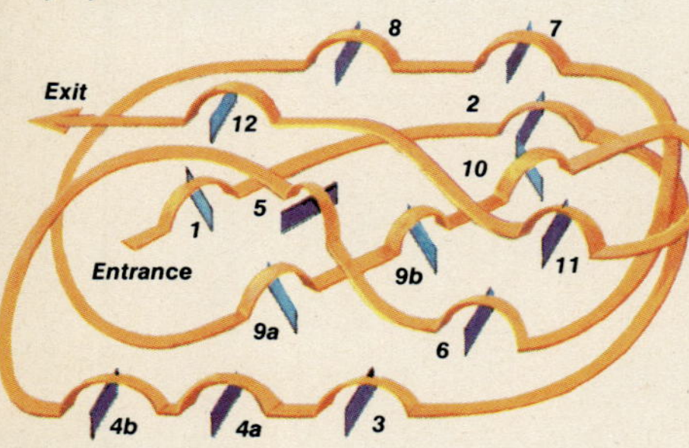

***Uprights:** This jump results in a high, rounded arc. If the horse takes off too near or too far from the obstacle a knockdown occurs (below left).*

***Spreads:** Jump arc is flatter. Again, jumping from too far or too near results in a knockdown (below right).*

***Riders and horses** do not get a chance to practice Olympic courses. A rough sketch is sent to competing national teams only **30 days** before the Games. The actual course is officially shown the day of competition.*

Grand Prix jumping: A spectacular display, jumping is over a 765½-984¼yds (700-900m) arena course with 12-15 obstacles, some of fearsome dimensions. The Olympics usually features 5-6′ (1.5-1.8m) high upright planks, parallel poles, treble bars, stone walls and a 16′5″ (5m) water jump. Horses splashing water cost penalty points, and with such a distance to clear, it's a difficult challenge. Each entrant covers the course twice. Medalists are determined by a combination of faultless execution and time in which the course is covered. A medal is awarded the competitor, not the horse or its owner.

Watch the combination jumps for a good display of equestrian skills. Stride length and timing precision make horse-and-rider teamwork critical here.

***Penalties** include:*
1st refusal** by horse: **3 faults
Knockdown** of an obstacle or **failure at the water jump: 4 faults
2nd disobedience: 6 faults
Fall** by horse or rider: **8 faults

*A **time factor** calculated at a speed of 400m (437yds) per minute is involved and penalties are invoked for exceeding it.*

3-Day Event: The 3-Day is a combination of events. **Dressage** on the first day is similar to Grand Prix Dressage. The second day is a **Cross-country run** in various phases, such as the 13.3mi (21k) gallop over roads and trails and a steeplechase over obstacles spotted about every 3280′ (1000m). It's an endurance and horsemanship challenge where the victors are those with the least penalty and most bonus points. On the third day comes **Jumping** over 10 to 12 tough obstacles.

Some event obstacles:
a. Log pile
b. Ramp
c. Water jump

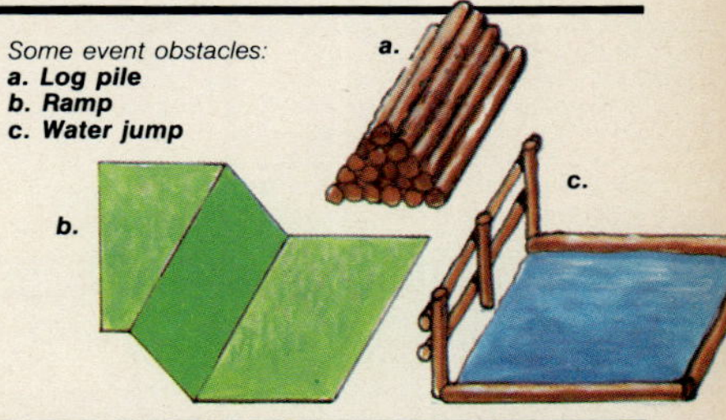

***Clothing** for Dressage as shown. Hardhats and looser clothing for riders and boots for horses are added for the jumping events.*

***Tack:** horse's gear*

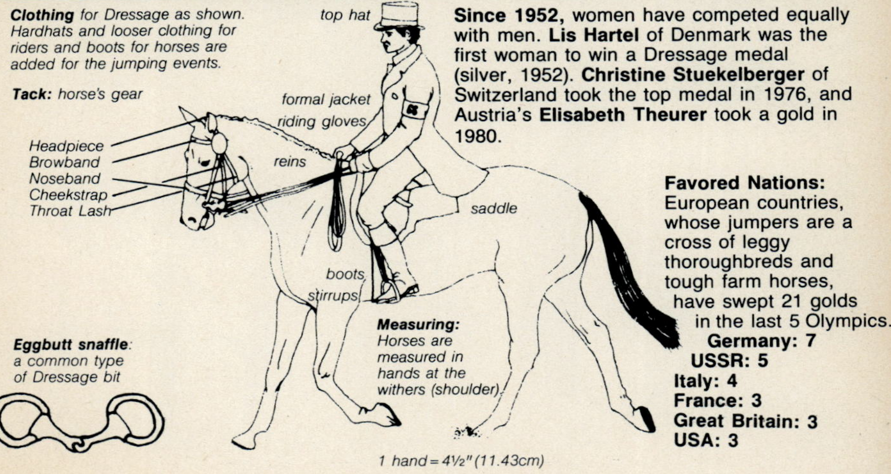

***Measuring:** Horses are measured in hands at the withers (shoulder).*

1 hand = 4½″ (11.43cm)

***Eggbutt snaffle:** a common type of Dressage bit*

Since 1952, women have competed equally with men. **Lis Hartel** of Denmark was the first woman to win a Dressage medal (silver, 1952). **Christine Stuekelberger** of Switzerland took the top medal in 1976, and Austria's **Elisabeth Theurer** took a gold in 1980.

Favored Nations: European countries, whose jumpers are a cross of leggy thoroughbreds and tough farm horses, have swept 21 golds in the last 5 Olympics.
Germany: 7
USSR: 5
Italy: 4
France: 3
Great Britain: 3
USA: 3

FENCING

Field of play: *Fencers in foil events duel on a strip of metallic mesh 46' (14m) long called the* ***piste.*** *In épée and saber, the field of play is 59' (18m) long.*

Fencing piste

1980 Games Olympic Fencing Champions

Men's Foil: **Vladimir Smirnov**, USSR

Men's Epée: **Johan Harmenberg**, SWE

Men's Saber: **Viktor Krovopuskov**, USSR

Women's Foil: **Pascale Trinquet**, FRA

If **Errol Flynn,** the king of movie swordsmen, were here today, he wouldn't last 5 minutes in this show of lightning reflexes, timing, feinting, parrying, riposting and speedy footwork. Fencing masters from Hungary, the USSR, France, Poland, Sweden and Italy have advanced an ancient art to the stage where electronic registering of *hits* is required. *Foils* and *épées* flash faster than any judge's eye can follow. Of all Olympian endeavors, this is one of the most difficult for spectators to follow—but they can enjoy the showmanship, dexterity and panther-like moves of contestants.

Procedure: Men cross weapons in individual and team contests in ***foil, épée*** and ***saber.*** Women meet only with ***foils*** in the Olympics, with individual and team titles at stake.

Nations may bring 22 fencers, 3 for each of the individual events plus 4-member men's and women's teams and a substitute for each team. Individual entrants are placed in ***pools*** where they face all other competitors in a round-robin elimination. The number of entrants in an individual event ranges between 60 and 75, with up to 30 countries represented.

Electronic judging: *Viewers will note that fencers at foil and épée have a body wire attached to the weapon at the guard that runs through the sword arm and is connected at the fencer's back to a reel wire, which, in turn, is connected to the scoring box. The reel wire runs off a spool, letting out or taking up slack as the fencers advance and retreat. When a hit is made, contact between the blade's point and an opponent's jacket closes the electric circuit and colored lights flash on, indicating a valid or non-valid hit. The scoring box allows a hit to be accurately determined since a pressure of only 500g in foil and 750g in épée is all that is needed to register a hit made against an opponent. As complicated as this apparatus is, it is essential to determining a winner, due to the speed of the action. The saber is not electronically judged.*

Distance from Coliseum: 23 miles (37km)

Weapons: *The* ***foil*** *is a thrusting weapon. Only* ***hits*** *scored with the blade point on an opponent's torso are valid. It is 3'6" (110cm) long at maximum, cannot weigh over 17 5/8oz (.5kg) and has a tapering quadrangular blade measuring 3' (90cm). It's made of fine steel.*

The ***épée,*** *based on dueling weapons of European noblemen, is the same length as the foil but heavier at 27 1/8oz (770g) due to a larger hand guard. It is a thrusting or stabbing weapon. Legal target is any part of the body, from head to toe.*

The ***saber*** *is both a cutting and thrusting sword, derived from the 18th-century cavalry saber and the Middle Eastern scimitar. It weighs almost the same as the foil, but is about 1" (2.5cm) shorter. Saber hits may be made with the blade's front edge or the last ⅓ of its back edge (cuts), as well as with the point. The target area is from the bend of the hips upwards, derived from cavalry days when fighting was done on horseback.*

Special rule: *In épée, when fencers hit simultaneously, each has a hit scored against him. But in foil and saber there are no double touches. Only the fencer who has the* ***right of way*** *(takes the initiative by launching an attack or blocking the attack) receives credit.*

Jacket— *a double thickness of heavy-duty lamé cloth with an undergarment, called* ***plastron,*** *made of hempcloth or nylon*

Mask— *made of wire mesh with 2.1mm spacing and usually constructed of stainless steel*

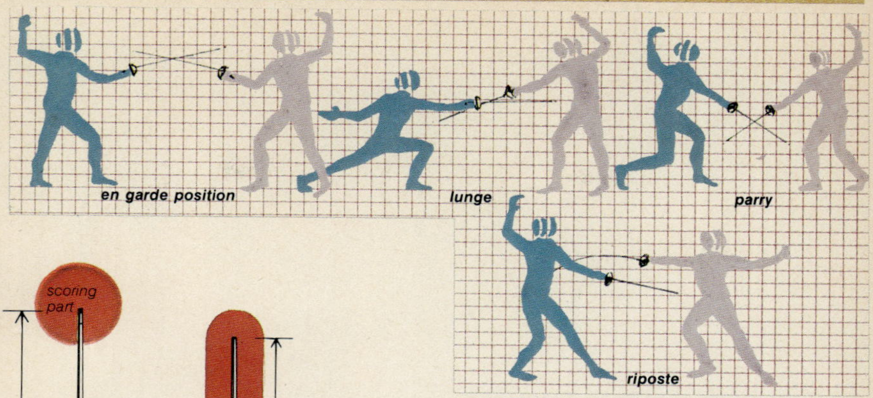

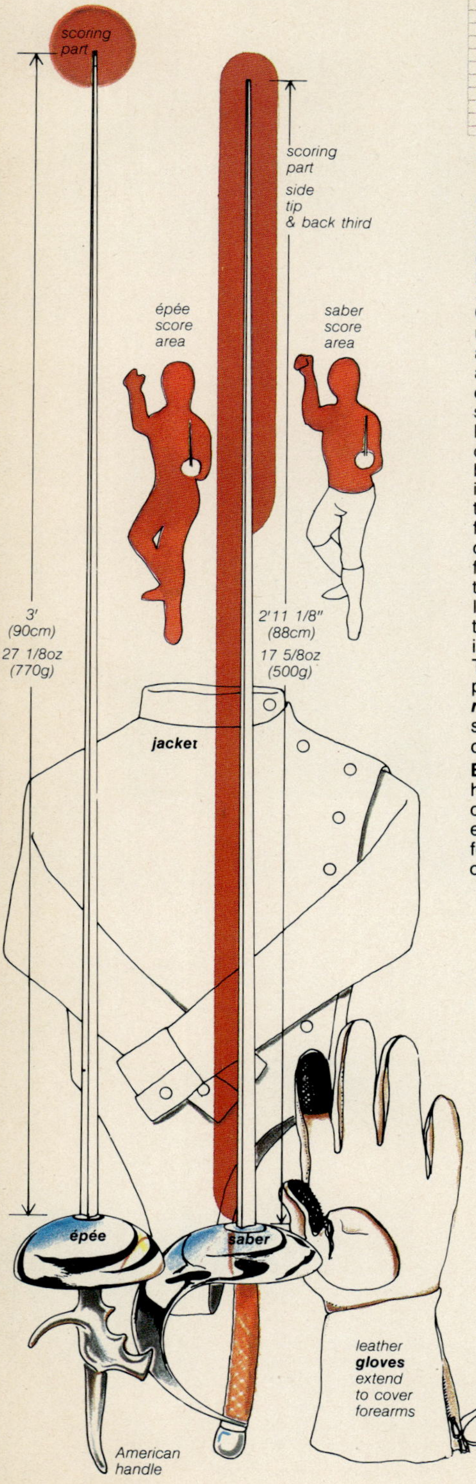

What to watch for: Pick a point between contestants. Then, as for boxing, concentrate on the ebb and flow of the action. Aggressiveness counts in fencing—but many a bout has been lost through overexcitement and disregard for defense basics.

Combat Techniques: Bouts begin with unmasked opponents ***saluting*** each other and officials by raising the blade to the chin and dropping it. Duelers then assume the ***en garde,*** masked position, standing sideways to the opponent to present the least target area. Weight is evenly distributed and the rear arm curled up for balance. The ***attack*** varies by event, but it is generally a ***thrust*** or ***lunge.*** In the lunge, the attacker moves forward by extending his front leg. In a thrust, the sword blade is quickly extended, the rear leg being used for balance. A short jump, called a ***balestra,*** toward the target may be combined with a lunge. The ***flèche*** is a short, quick run toward the opponent. A ***compound attack*** is one made with several blade movements. To recover from a lunge and continue pressing the attack is called ***reprise.*** A ***riposte*** is an offensive action following a successful ***parry,*** or blocking move, of the opponent's attack.

Bout duration: Generally, bouts last until 5 hits are made against an opponent, or 6min of actual bouting have elapsed. In direct elimination rounds, the number of hits is 10 for men and 8 for women with a time limit of 10min for men and 8min for women.

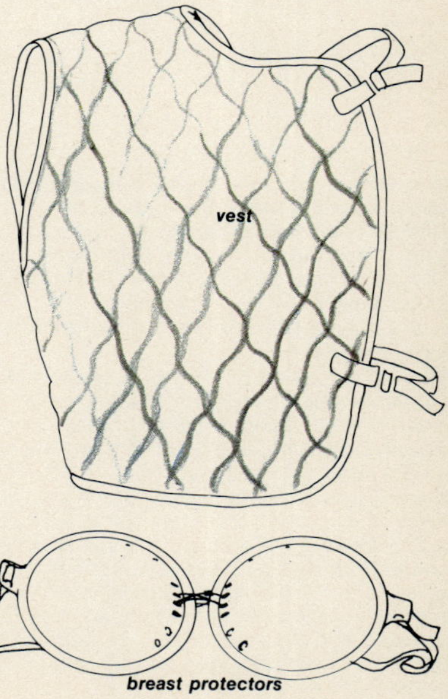

5yds (4.6m)
Side Line
5yd line
100yds (91.4m)
Striking circle
5yds (4.6m)
16yds (14.6m)
Center line
10yds (9.14m)
Goal
60yd (54.9m)
4yds (3.7m)
Goal
Penalty spot
25yd line
25yd line
Goal line
25yds (2.29m)
25yds (2.29m)
25yds (2.29m)
25yds (2.29m)
Corner flag
Center flag
Field Hockey field

1980 Olympic Field Hockey Finals
***Men:* IND 4, ESP 3**
***Women:* ZIM 8, TCH 7**

When **Zimbabwe's** women's field hockey team defeated powerhouse Soviet and European teams for the 1980 Olympic gold medal, it drove home a point about the game. Field hockey is one of the few endeavors in which small nations consistently knock off the Goliaths. Zimbabwe, in southeast Africa, has a population of 8 million; the USSR has 273 million.

1984 Olympic field: A dozen national teams selected after worldwide eliminations will reach Los Angeles; each team will have 16 members. Field hockey is largely unknown in the USA, yet it is the grandfather of all stick-and-ball games, traced to the early Persians and Egyptians. It was played in England as far back as 1175, and is the basis for the **shinty** of Scotland, **bandy** in Wales and **hurling** in Ireland. The French long ago dubbed it **hoquet,** meaning a shepherd's crooked stave, from which comes **hockey.**

***Red, below, is offside** because: **a**) he is within his opponent's half when the ball is played by a teammate further from the goal than he is; **b**) there are fewer than 2 opponents between himself and the goal. An offside is penalized by a free hit at the spot where it occured.*

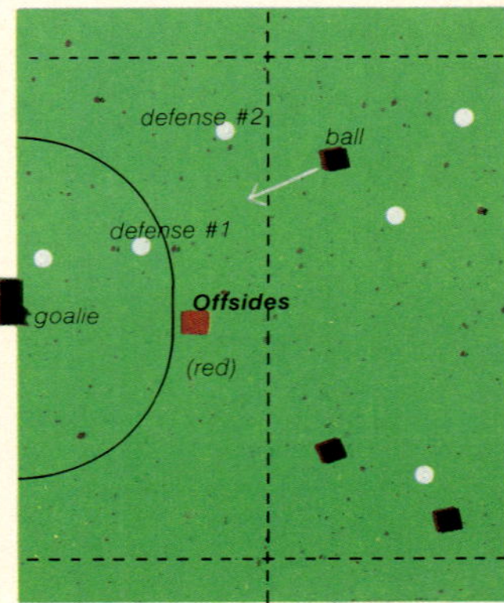

The Game: It's been called ***soccer with a stick.*** Rules of the 2 games bear a similarity. Like American football, it's played with 11 men to a side on a field measuring 60yds×100yds (54.9m×91.4m). The goals, at either end of the field, measure 7′ (2.13m) high by 4yds (3.7m) wide and are guarded by a goalkeeper.

The object—using 3′ (1m) long sticks with curved wooden heads—is to advance a small ball by hitting it, passing it to a teammate or dribbling it with the stick while on the run.

Field hockey teams: 11 players make up a team. Two of the most common formations are: 5 forwards, 3 halfbacks, 2 backs and a goalie (Pakistan and Australia); and 3 defenders, 3 midfielders, 3 strikers (main scorers), 1 sweeper and a goalkeeper (Holland and West Germany). In general, the strikers are attackers and the other players are defenders.

***Stick:** India pioneered the stick, with a tightly curved bend (head) made of mulberry wood, that is widely used today. The shaft or handle is of cane with cork or rubber inserts.*

Tape

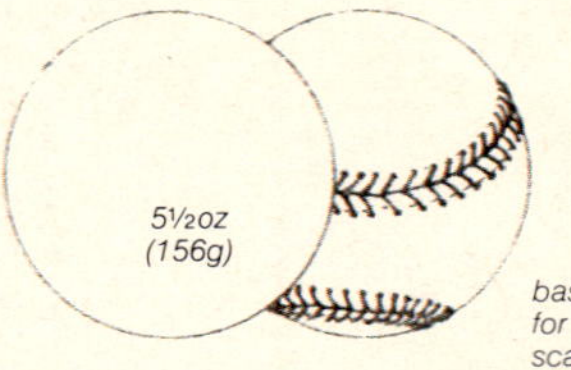

***Ball:** White leather over a cork-and-twine center, weighing just under 6oz. 8 1/5-9¼″ (20.8-23.5cm) in circumference, it's slightly larger than baseball, and very hard. Flying balls, swinging sticks and crashing bodies make field hockey a punishing game.*

FIELD HOCKEY

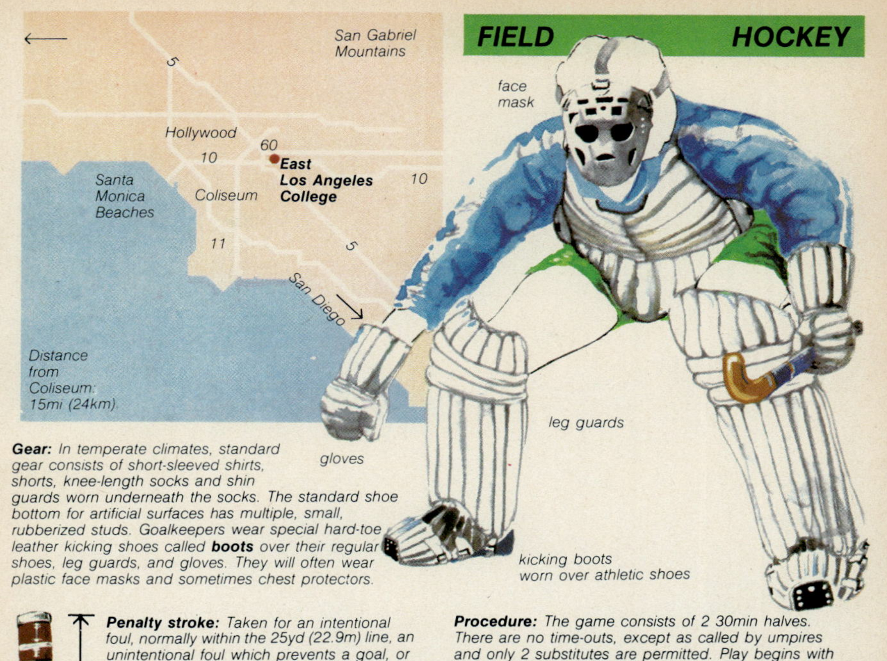

Gear: *In temperate climates, standard gear consists of short-sleeved shirts, shorts, knee-length socks and shin guards worn underneath the socks. The standard shoe bottom for artificial surfaces has multiple, small, rubberized studs. Goalkeepers wear special hard-toe leather kicking shoes called* **boots** *over their regular shoes, leg guards, and gloves. They will often wear plastic face masks and sometimes chest protectors.*

Penalty stroke: *Taken for an intentional foul, normally within the 25yd (22.9m) line, an unintentional foul which prevents a goal, or continued deliberate position infringements at penalty corners. Only the goalie and the player taking the penalty stroke may stand inside the 25yd line.*

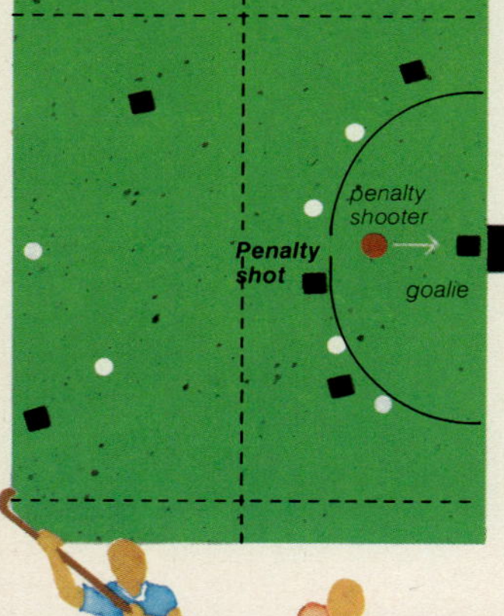

Procedure: *The game consists of 2 30min halves. There are no time-outs, except as called by umpires and only 2 substitutes are permitted. Play begins with the team winning the coin toss hitting the ball backward from midfield to a teammate. If a game ends in a tie, a penalty stroke competition or* **shootout** *will be held, where groups of 5 from each team will alternate shots until there is a result.*

Scoring: *A goal, worth 1pt, can only be scored by putting the ball over the goal-line between the goal posts and under the crossbar and* **from within the shooting or striking circle.** *The striking circle is an area marked by a white line 16yds (14.6m) from the goal-line and curving in a semi-circle around to meet the goal-line. Goals may be scored in 3 ways:* **1**) *from open play,* **2**) *from a penalty stroke and* **3**) *from a penalty corner or fixed play.*

Stick use: *Only the flat (left) side of the stick may be used to play the ball; the rounded (right) side may not be used at any time. The stick may not be raised over the shoulder if this leads to dangerous play or, in the umpire's opinion, produces an advantage. There are 2 umpires to control the play. There is a also a technical delegate plus 2 judges at the side of the field who keep time, keep score and monitor substitutes.*

Ball must be hit with the **flat** *side of the stick, not the rounded side.*

3' (1m)

Fouls: *Main offenses are* **obstructions** *(moving the body between the ball and opponent),* **offsides** *(there must be at least 2 players between pass receiver and goal when ball is hit),* **foot stop, dangerous play** *(hitting the ball into a group or in a dangerous manner), or* **standing too close** *(an opponent must be at least 5yds (14.6m) away from player taking a hit).*

A **penalty stroke** *is awarded when a major foul occurs. a* **free shot** *is taken on goal from 7yds (6.4m) in front of the goal by the fouled team. The defending goalie may not move his feet until the ball is played.*

Use of body: *Players other than the goalie are not allowed to use any part of the hand or body to propel the ball. No longer, under revised rules, are they permitted to catch the ball, even if it is immediately released and dropped to the field into play. The goalie may use hands, stick or body to stop shots and is the only person allowed to kick the ball.*

The most unusual reason for **not** *staging the Games was that for Rome's 1906 pull-out. The eruption of* **Mt. Vesuvius** *that year, with widespread damage, was so costly to the Italian government that Rome, awarded the 1908 festival, was forced to withdraw.*

What to watch for: ***Passing.*** The team which can maintain possession of the ball and keep passes under control has a great advantage. Note **fakes** and **feints**—these are vital tools in a hockey player's passing repertoire.

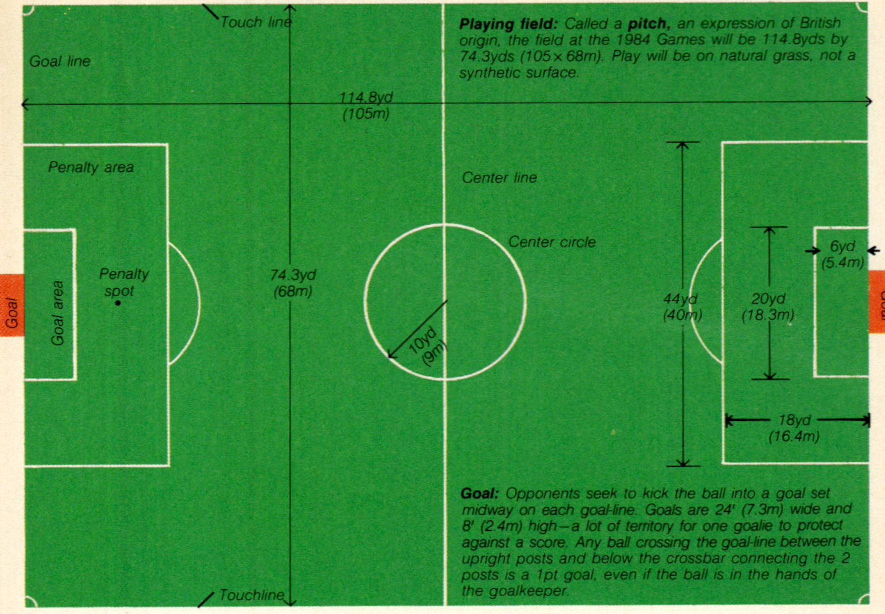

1980 Olympic Football Champion: **TCH**

Olympic Champions: In the formative years, 1900-28, the Games title went to Great Britain 3 times, Uruguay twice and once each to Canada and Belgium. From 1936 through 1980, progressively, victors have been: Italy, Sweden, Hungary, USSR, Yugoslavia, Hungary, Hungary, Poland, East Germany and Czechoslovakia.

Most Olympic Wins: **Hungary** (3)

Association football, or soccer, is the most widely played game in the world. It thrives on every continent and enlists more than 25,000,000 participants. Little that goes on at the Olympics draws more live fans (647,683 watched the 23 matches at the '76 Montreal Games) or has more fireworks attached.

"Soccer is at its craziest in the Olympics," experts observe. Belgium and Czechoslovakia were locked in deadly combat in a Games final when the entire Czech team walked off the field and refused to play any more in a rules dispute. Belgium won on a forfeit.

There's the question of amateur status. It's said by many that a truly amateur team hasn't triumphed in the Olympics since Sweden won in 1948. State-supported stars and pseudo-amateurs—many who play in World Cup competition for their nations—are entered, leading to much bitterness. In Europe, subsidized footballers perform as a unit year-round, leaving non-subsidized teams' members frustrated.

One of the saving graces of Games football competition is that many a small nation makes a terrific showing against traditional winners such as East Germany and the USSR. Denmark, Poland, Austria, Holland, Bulgaria and Yugoslavia all have taken home Olympic medals—win, place or show.

Procedure: For more than 15 months before the Games—ending in May, 1984—a worldwide elimination competition is held to reduce a field of 100 nations to just 14 teams. These 14 national squads, plus teams from the host (USA) and defending champion (Czechoslovakia) reach the Olympics. They will fight it out through 32 matches and 14 days for the gold.

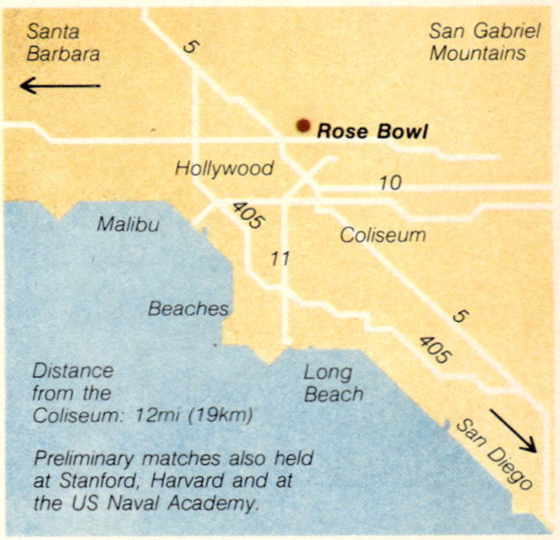

The **sublime 16** are geographically representative: **4** from Europe, **3** from Africa, **3** from Asia/Oceania, **4** from the Americas/Caribbean, plus the USA and 1980 Games champ.

When the 16 are named, the Games field is divided into groups, or ***pools,*** of 4 teams each. They play each other 1 time each, a round-robin. Sites other than the Rose Bowl will be Stanford and Harvard stadiums and the US Naval Academy. The 2 emergent victors in each group move to the quarter finals. Eventually, it gets down to the semifinals of 4 teams. The survivors meet for the gold medal. The Rose Bowl in Pasadena, scene of the final events, will provide more seating than any Olympic stadium yet—for about 105,000 people.

Action: Soccer football's tremendous popularity is based in the fact that action is continuous. There are no time-outs or delays for platooning or injection of special teams, as in USA/Canadian football. Whereas in the North American game the ball is actually in play for 12-15min during the game, here there are 90 full minutes of action.

Periods: There are 2 halves of 45min each, with a 10min halftime break.

Goal: A goal is worth 1pt and there is no other scoring method in the game.

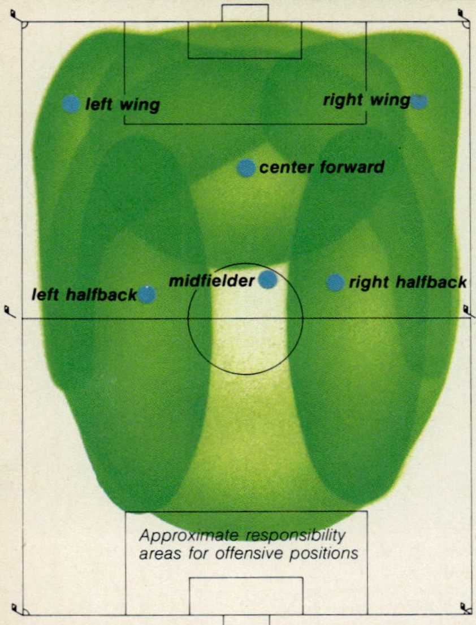

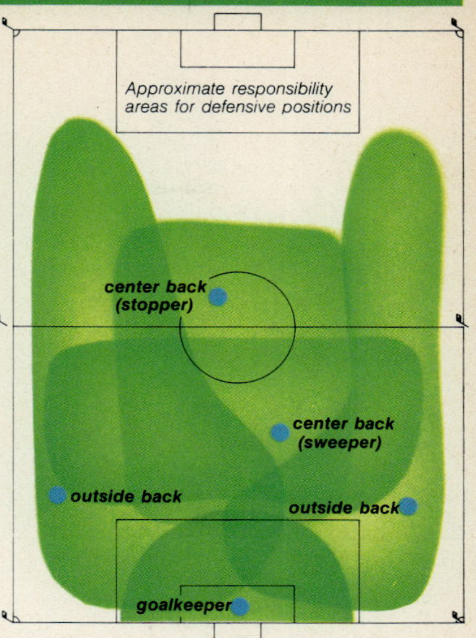

Teams: There are 11 men to the side, with 2 substitutes per match. If a player is replaced, he may not return to the game. Besides the goalie, teams consist of 4 defenders, 3 midfielders and 3 forwards; or 4 defenders, 4 midfielders and 2 forwards.

Use of hands: Only the goalie, within the penalty area, may use his hands. Other players must propel the ball with their feet, heads, chests or other parts of their bodies.

The Game: The 114.8yd (105m) side boundaries are called ***touchlines.*** At midfield a line 5″ (12.7cm) wide is drawn across the field. In the line's center is the ***center circle*** with a 10yd (9m) radius. At the beginning of each half, and after every goal, the ball is kicked off from this circle by one team or the other. Defending players must stay outside that circle until the ball is kicked into play.

Two rectangular zones are marked on the field in front of the 8yd (7.3m) wide goal. The smaller area is the ***goal area,*** 20yds (18.3m) wide and 6yds (5.4m) deep out from the goal line. Other players may enter this space, but can't charge or contact the goalie so long as he doesn't have the ball. The larger rectangle, extending 18yds (16.4m) out from the goal and 44yds (40m) wide, is the ***penalty area.*** A rules infraction here can be fatal to a defending team. A major foul within this area gives the offense a ***penalty kick***—good for 1pt if the ball goes into the net.

Ball: *A bit smaller than a basketball, the football is spherical, cased in leather and 27″(68.58cm) in circumference. Inflated weight at the game's start must be 14-16oz (397-453g). The ball's 30-odd black and white panels enable players to judge its speed and direction of spin while in motion.*

Positions of offensive players at kickoff:
Center forwards, 2 players also called ***strikers,*** work as a pair. One, usually the right-most, kicks the ball into play. After play begins, only the goalie has a fixed lineup position. All other players roam freely as the attacking strategy dictates.

Wings, one to the right and one to the left, range near the touchlines and are key attackers.

Left halfback and ***right halfback,*** sometimes called ***linksmen,*** are positioned behind the center forward. They function chiefly as playmakers, those who set up scores, but are also important as defenders.

Center backs play in tandem, the front-most called the ***stopper*** and the one nearer the goal called the ***sweeper.*** They defend the area in front of the goal.

Left and ***right outside backs,*** also defensive specialists, stand at either end of an area called the ***penalty zone,*** flanking the goal.

Goalie: A 6′ (1.83m) tall goalkeeper is estimated to be able to protect 20′ (6m) of the goal mouth—leaving 4′ (1.2m) or more he often can't reach. His main advantage is that he's the only member of the team allowed to use his hands. His techniques include:

tipping the ball above the crossbar

diving left or right to make a ***save***

coming out of the goal to meet a single attacking enemy, narrowing the space-angle of his shot

2-handed punching of the ball out of danger

The net guards are such ball hawks that scoring is usually low, in the 3-4pt range at the Olympics as a total for both teams. The final championship match score at the last 3 Games was: 1972: POL **2**, HUN **1**
1976: GDR **3**, POL **1**
1980: TCH **1**, GDR **0**

What to watch for: The goalie is a play*maker* as well as a play-*saver.* From his unique position, the goalie can see the whole field. Watch him place the ball with precision and speed after an offensive rush.

Referee: A law unto himself, the football referee has complete control, maybe the most powerful mandate of any sports official. Working alone, except for 2 ***linesmen,*** he can eject a player at will, determine all penalties and can only be approached by the team captains.

Penalty kick: *Upon a foul, a designated kicker blasts the ball on a goal from a small circle 12yds (11m) from the goal. Only the goalie stands between him and a score. And, because penalty kickers are so skilled, a point results a high percentage of the time.*

Fouls: *There are many, the worst being:*
tripping
striking or shoving
charging *a man from behind*
handling *(use hands on) the ball*
ungentlemanly conduct *(the referee decides)*
knocking down *a dribbler by charging into him on a* **tackle** *(trying to take the ball away from an opponent with footwork)*

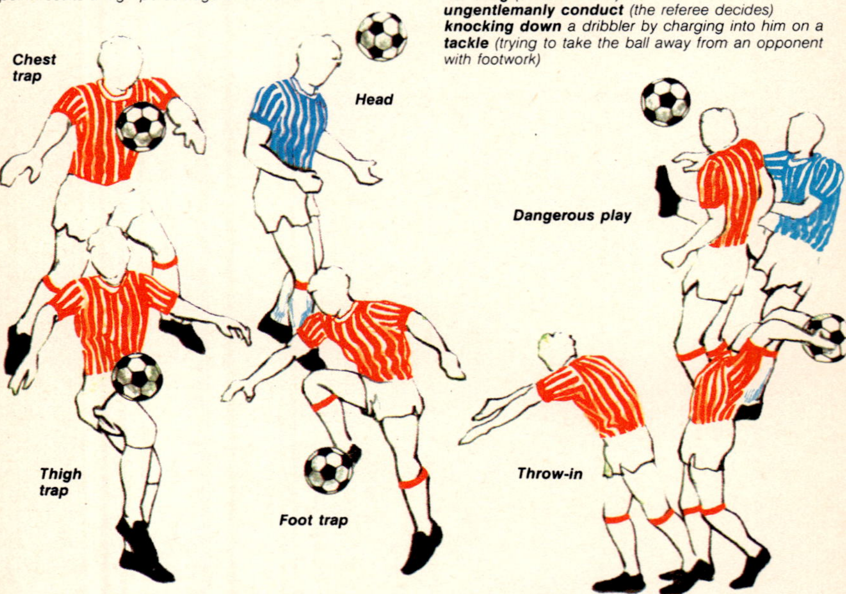

Offside: *This rule baffles newcomers. It states that at all times there must be 2 opponents between an attacker and the defense's goal. But there are exceptions to this. Chief exceptions are that there's no offside when a player is in his own half of the field or when he receives the ball from a goal kick, corner kick or throw-in.*

Throw-in: *When a ball goes over the sideline, the team that did not last touch it gets a* **throw-in.** *This must be done with both feet on the ground and with both hands; the ball is thrown over the head.*

Goal kick and corner kick: *In each corner of the field is a* **quarter-circle** *with a 1yd (.91m) radius, with a 5' (1.5m) flag marking the exact corner. If the ball goes over the goal line without a score being made and was last touched by a defending player, the attacking team gets a* **corner kick.** *This kick is made from the quarter circle and returns the ball to attacking play. If the ball was last touched by an offensive man before going out-of-bounds, the defense gets the corner kick. Usually, a goalie does the booting and booms the ball far downfield.*

Wall: *The closer a free kick is to the goal, the greater the danger that the kicker will be able to score from a direct shot. When the free kick is within 30yds (27m) of the goal or so, a* **human wall** *is built to help narrow the area the goalie has to protect. The moment the free kick has been made, the defenders disperse once again to their positions. A wall is* **not** *allowed when a penalty shot is being taken.*

The world today knows Artistic Gymnastics as a discipline of supple beauty and strength melded with breathtaking excitement—an exploration of the ultimate limits of the body. Who could forget **Olga Korbut,** (USSR), the elastic, childlike pixie in ecstasy (and at times in tears); the disciplined elegance of a maturing **Ludmilla Tourischeva** (USSR), 1972 Olympic All-Around Champion; or **Nadia Comaneci** (ROM), 1976 Olympic All-Around Champion, the mysterious, machine-perfect *10* personified? There was also the awesome strength and boldness of **Sawao Kato** (JPN), the ingenuity of **Nikolai Andrianov** (USSR) and the precision of **Alexander Ditiatin** (USSR), 1980 Olympic All-Around champion, performing stunts that appeared to be death-defying, even to the gymnastics fan.

Tickets for this sport have always been in high demand by Olympics-goers. Gymnastics transforms movement into art and the competitive arena into a theater of thrills. There's an illusion of danger in this complex sport, but in reality, gymnastics' difficulties are technically analyzed to the utmost and performed thousands of times in the practice gym with safety precautions before any attempt is made at executing them in the competitive arena.

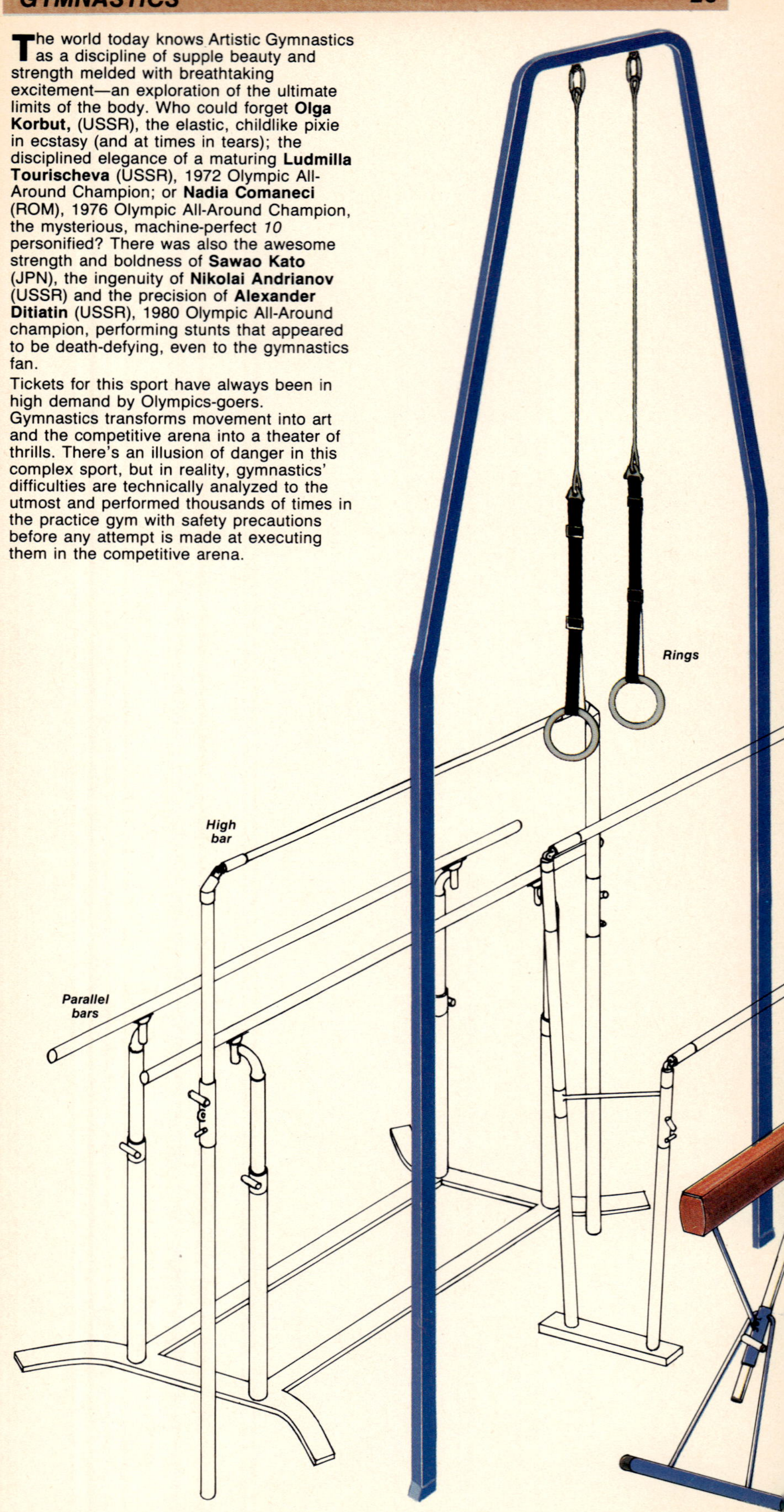

The ***Federation Internationale de Gymnastique*** (FIG), formed in 1881, governs the sport worldwide. At the first Games of 1896 in Athens, 75 male gymnasts from 5 countries competed. Growth was slow—at the 1932 Los Angeles Games, only 46 athletes from 7 countries took part.

Women fought against their exclusion from the Games for a quarter century—and finally won. In 1928 at the Amsterdam Olympics, they were allowed to compete in a few exercises as teams, but not as individuals. Not until 1952 did female gymnasts break through as full-scale competitors.

At Los Angeles in 1984, 192 of the best gymnastic performers on the globe will be in action in 10 ***Artistic Gymnastics*** events. Recently, the International Olympic Committee added ***Rhythmic Sportive Gymnastics*** to its Olympic program. Los Angeles will be the first site in history to host this new discipline. The sport came from Eastern Europe, where the first National Championships were held in Russia in 1948. The FIG recognized Rhythmic Sportive Gymnastics in 1962 and the first official World Championships were held in Budapest, Hungary in 1963.

Women's artistic gymnastics involves 4 events: vaulting, uneven bars, balance beam and floor exercise. **Men's artistic gymnastics** includes floor exercise, pommel horse, rings, vaulting, parallel bars and high bar. All moves are judged in terms of difficulty: **A** (least difficult), **B** (moderately difficult) and **C** (most difficult).

Two sets of routines are performed:
Compulsory: FIG-required routines judged on exactness, execution and amplitude of elements.
Optional: Individually created routines that characterize personal style and follow the required FIG guidelines. The apparatus used for both compulsory and optional exercises are identical.

Traditionally, *gymnastics honors gymnasts that execute original stunts for the first time in international competition by naming the stunt after the performer. For instance:* **Tsukahara** *was the first athlete to perform his roundoff back tuck in international competition. At that point the* ***Tsukahara vault*** *was born. Other common moves named after famous gymnasts include the* ***Geinger, Krieskehre, Comaneci, Barani, Kasamatsu, Thomas flairs, Diamadov, Deltchev, Cuervo*** *and* ***Stalder***

Uneven bars

Balance beam

Pommel horse

Women's Vaulting horse

Women's Events (in Olympic order):

Women's vaulting *is similar to the men's long horse vault, with the difference that women do stunts across the width of the apparatus and males work longwise. The horse is leather-covered, fixed to a steel base and 47" (120cm) high. It is very heavy, weighing in at 384lbs (174kg).*

All vaults are executed from a running start with a takeoff from the springboard, and with the hands having to touch the horse. The approach may include tricks performed on the springboard for takeoff, with the feet having to leave the board last. A good vault will be very high off the hands with flight away from the horse. For both compulsory and optional vaults, the gymnast has 2 tries, with the best vault score being counted. Vaults are given values, much like diving, with the FIG setting up the norms. Up and coming vaults include multiple twists and flips off the horse.

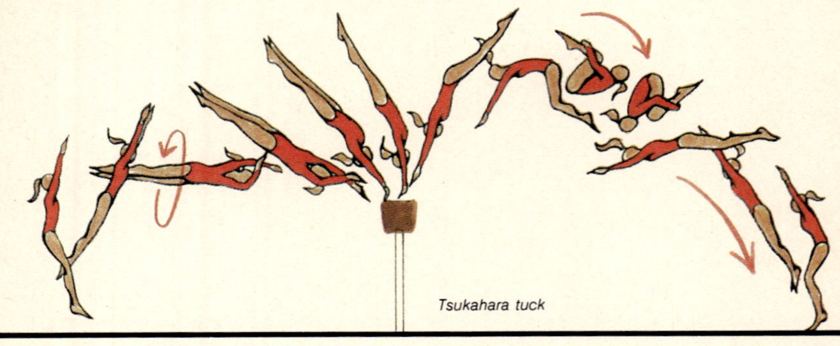

Tsukahara tuck

Front tuck over low bar to high bar

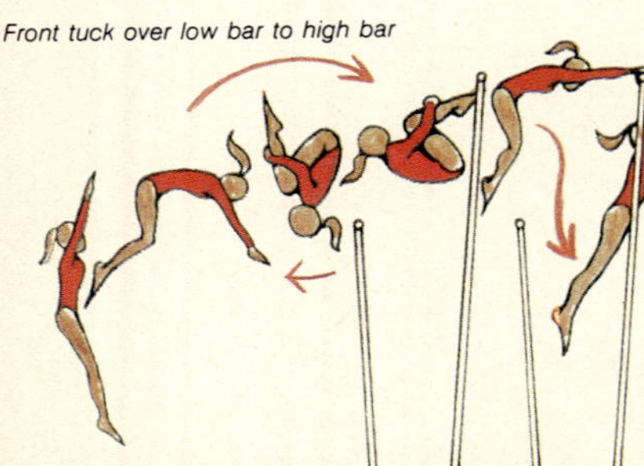

The bars are flexible and aid the gymnast in keeping her swing flowing rhythmically through her routine. The gymnast works with the 2 bars in continuous action, moving through the high bar and low bar. No stops and no more than 5 maneuvers in a row on one bar are permitted, with 10 total moves being the minimum FIG requirement.

Uneven parallel bars *competition features one high bar at 7'2½"-7'10½" (2.2-2.4m) and one adjustable at 4'7"-5'3" (1.4-1.6m). The rails are oval shaped, made of fiberglass with a wood veneer, and adjusted to fit the gymnast.*

Stalder to handstand

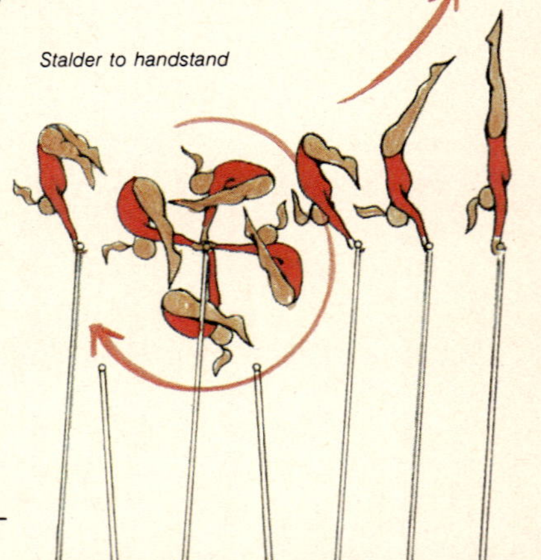

Rhythmic Events (Women only):

An individual All-Around Rhythmic gymnast will perform routines with 4 of the 5 apparatuses. The 5th apparatus is used for the group exercise. Each routine must contain at least 2 moves of superior difficulty and at least 6 of medium difficulty.

Ball *is seen rolling, bouncing, being thrown and caught with lots of body waves and circumduction.*

Rope *is measured in length according to the individual gymnast's height. In this event you will see movements performed by throwing, catching, swinging and circling with the rope open or folded.*

Hoop *weighs 10½oz (300g) and is more flat than round. The audience will see turning, swinging, throwing and catching. The gymnast gives this apparatus a personal flair with rotations on the floor and around her hands or body.*

Balance beam *is 47" (120cm) in height and 16'5" (5m) long. It is padded with foam and covered with vinyl or leather.*

A contestant may mount from a running or stationary start or from a springboard takeoff. She must execute dance moves, acrobatic moves, tumbling moves and a dismount while using the entire length of the beam, and demonstrate ultimate control, flexibility and strength—all within the 1:10-1:30 time limit. No stops are allowed. Time begins when the competitor's feet leave the floor and ends when her feet leave the beam. A warning is given 5sec before overtime is charged.

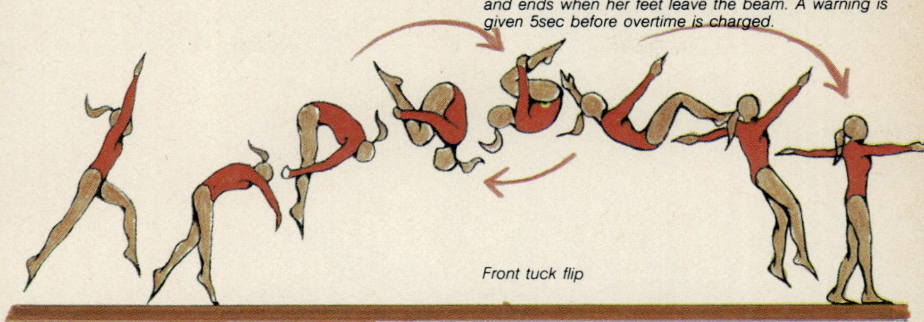

Front tuck flip

Floor exercise *is performed on a mat 40'x40' (12×12m) square lined with springs underneath and a 1" (2.5cm) layer of foam covered with carpet. This event combines grace, balance, rhythm, advanced dance movements, flexibility, dynamic changes, strength and a personal interpretation of the music through the gymnast's style. All these elements are combined and highly technical tumbling movements are used for transition. The winning gymnast will play to the audience like an actress, with proper body carriage and plenty of facial expression and eye contact. All of these qualities must be fitted to the music she has chosen and harmoniously blended within 1:10-1:30min. Timing begins with the gymnast's first move and ends with her last move. She does not need to start or finish with the music.*

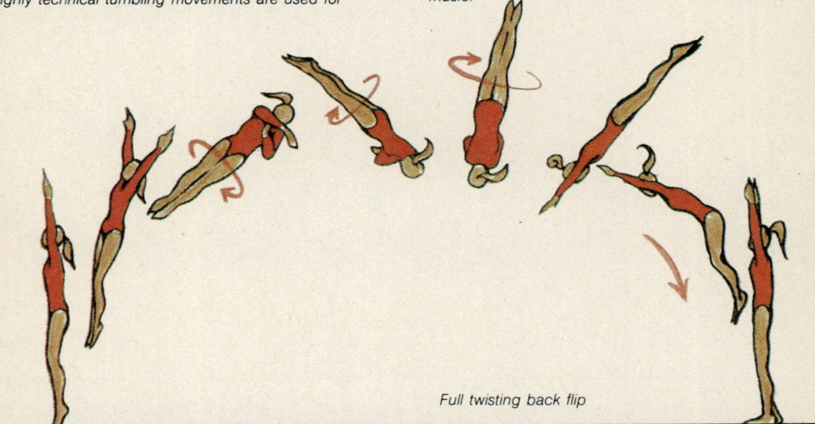

Full twisting back flip

What to watch for: Don't look for gymnastic tumbling skills in this sport. Rather, watch for flamboyant acrobatic movements integrated with ribbons, clubs, balls, hoops and ropes. Olympic-level rhythmic requires flexibility, balance, expression, highly perfected dance techniques and, most importantly, movement of the body and the apparatus as one.

Clubs *must weigh about 5¼oz (150g) and are balanced. Audiences will especially enjoy the rhythmic tapping of the clubs. The spectator will also see large and small circles, throwing, catching and swinging.*

Ribbon *is one of the most spectacular rhythmic events to watch. Its length and color add to the sport's beauty. Forms include flowing* ***spirals, snakes, throws*** *and* ***catches,*** *plus making large and small circles.*

Men's Events (in Olympic order):

Floor exercise: *Men's floor exercise is one of the most daring and sensational gymnastic events to watch, the trend heading toward highly acrobatic dance and floor skills, and curving floor patterns covering the entire floor space. The gold-medal gymnast will demonstrate front, back and, although not required, sideward tumbling involving multiple twists and somersaults with clean transitional movements displaying balance, flexibility and strength. He should flow rhythmically with precision in form and technical execution. There is a time limit of 50-70sec with a 10sec warning at the 50sec minimum and again at the 70sec maximum time. There is great emphasis in men's floor exercise on* **landing** *skills without any loss of balance—in this way the gymnast demonstrates full control to the judges.*

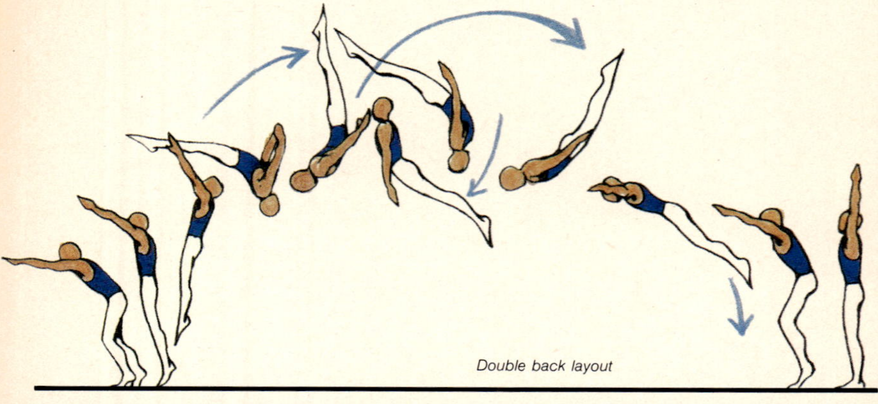
Double back layout

Pommel horse *is a leather-covered form supported by 4 legs on which 2 curved pommels are mounted to divide the surface into 3 parts. The pommels are flat with a width of 16″ (410mm) and can be adjusted between 16″-17⅓″ (40.64-44mm).*

A pommel horse routine should cover both ends and the center, with lots of circling, scissoring and single legwork—and with continuous, fluent swing. Many fans feel that this event requires the most strength because the gymnast is supported by the arms throughout the event without the possibility of much swing for help. In the near future, audiences will see more unique handstanding work in this event.

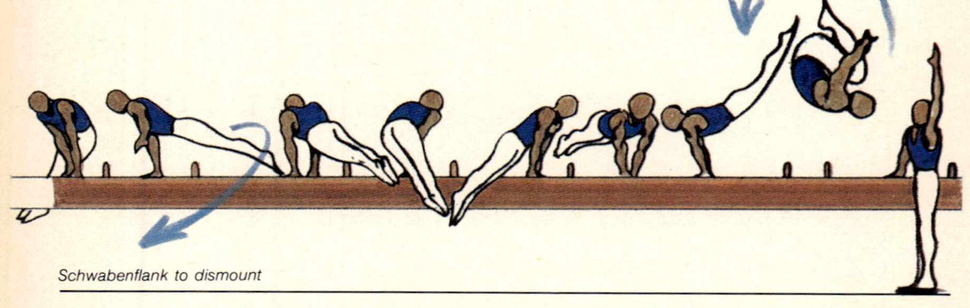
Schwabenflank to dismount

Still rings *consist of 2 wooden or fiberglass rings suspended from long straps 8′2″ (2.5m) off the ground. Holding the rings, the gymnast uses the strength of his arms to execute a series of movements, lifting and swinging his body. Requirements include swinging and pressing to handstands and holding a position stationary for 2sec.*

What to watch for: Work on rings should be done with straight arms, good swing technique and precise form. The rings must remain stationary, with a deduction for sway during the routine.

Pike double back dismount

Horse vault *consists of a steel base, leather covered and facing longwise. It stands approximately 4⅓' (1.3m) high. Vaulting is an expression of speed and flight. Recognizing a good vault takes split-second judgment. It must have a high degree of difficulty, include* ***virtuous*** *height and distance from the horse, and be executed with precision so that the landing can be* ***stuck*** *without a wobble. Only one vault is allowed except in optional finals when 2 different vaults are required.*

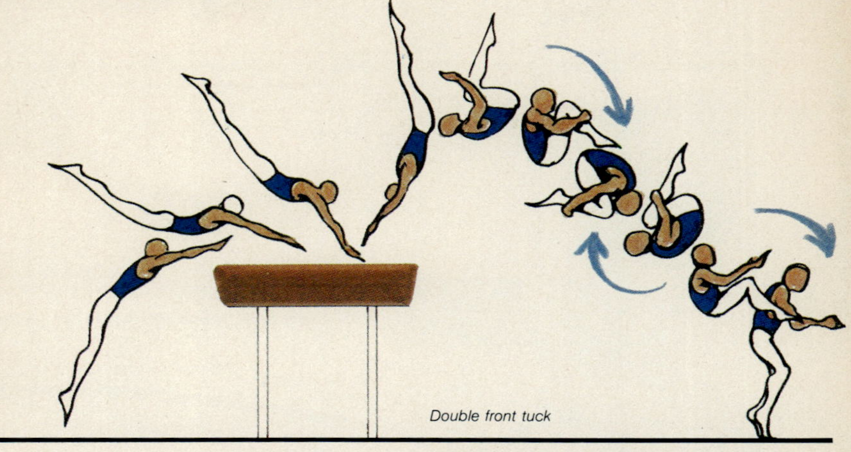

Double front tuck

Parallel bars *feature 2 oval wooden or fiberglass bars, each 5'10" (1.78m) long and approximately 5'8¾" (1.75m) above the floor. The parallel bar is an unusual rhythmic exercise. The athlete moves from full stop to swing and back again with flowing movement. This dynamic event includes pressing and swinging to a handstand, 2sec holds, elements of flexibility, balance and particularly strength, and very difficult and spectacular dismounts.*

Diamadov with added quarter turn

High bar *is a hollow, flexible single steel bar raised approximately 8'4" (2.54m) above the floor and supported by steel cables at each end. Once the contestant grasps the bar and begins, he can never stop as he progresses from swinging to changes of grip and direction, to release moves and finally to his difficult dismount. These movements are connected with turns and hops requiring the utmost flexibility, strength and timing. Spectacular release moves are now being done singularly and consecutively, along with technically difficult one-arm work.*

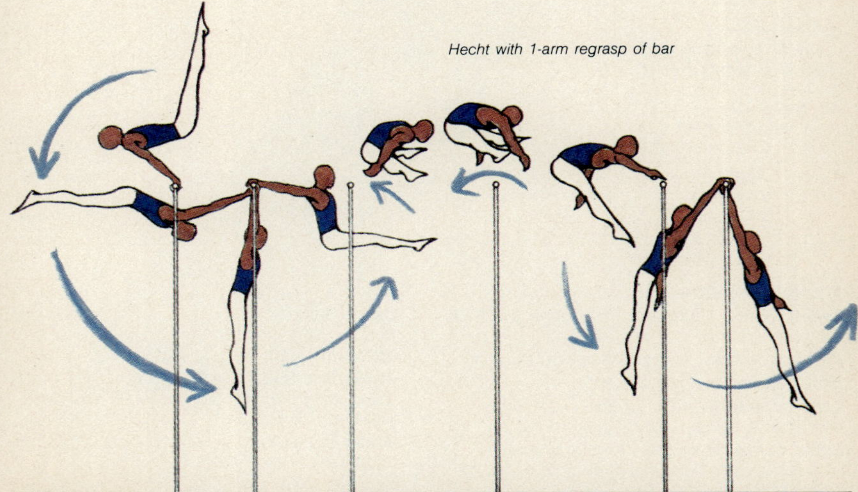

Hecht with 1-arm regrasp of bar

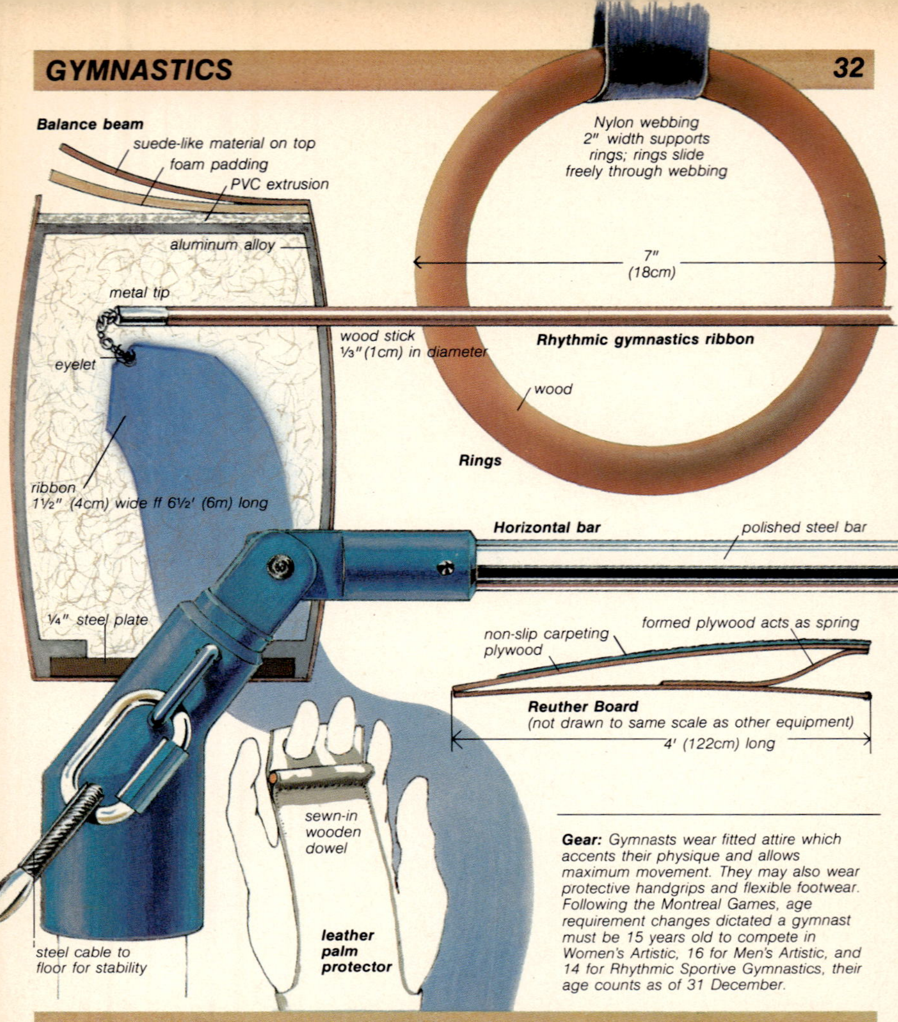

Gear: *Gymnasts wear fitted attire which accents their physique and allows maximum movement. They may also wear protective handgrips and flexible footwear. Following the Montreal Games, age requirement changes dictated a gymnast must be 15 years old to compete in Women's Artistic, 16 for Men's Artistic, and 14 for Rhythmic Sportive Gymnastics, their age counts as of 31 December.*

Artistic Gymnastic Events

Competition I	Competition 2	Competition 3
Team	All-Around	Individual Apparatus
1st session— individuals qualifying but not belonging to national teams 2nd session— teams ranking #9-12 from World Championships 3rd session— teams ranking #5-8 from World Championship 4th session— teams ranking #1-4 from World Championship	Top 36 competitors (maximum 2 competitors per country) from Competition 1 compete on all apparatuses Scores from Competition 1 and Competition 2 are combined to determine winners	Top 6 competitors on each apparatus from Competition 1 compete on one apparatus
Team medals awarded	Individual medals awarded	Individual medals awarded

Artistic penalties *(medium and major):*

Falling *from an apparatus or during a skill on the floor exercise*

Balance losses, *major, minor and slight*

Bent legs *or arms, small-large*

Lack of extension *or stretch in all skills, acrobatic and gymnastics movements*

Extra swinging *needed for support or impetus to get through an element, considered as serious as a fall*

Rhythmic penalties:

Dropping apparatus *from a minor (.1) drop to a major (.5) drop where the gymnast or apparatus leaves the boundaries*

Apparatus continually touching *the body out of control, such as the ribbon always loose and falling on the performer*

Break in pattern *of apparatus, such as the hoop wobbling in the air*

Lack of extension *and amplitude in skills*

Aerial—a stunt in which the gymnast turns completely over in the air without touching the apparatus with the hands

Apparatus—one of the various pieces of equipment used in gymnastics events

Arch position—a position in which the body is curved backwards

Compulsories—Predesigned routines that contain specific movements, required of all competing gymnasts

Kip—movement from a position below the equipment to a position above the equipment

L-position—90° forward bend at the hips

Layout position—straight or slightly arched body position. May be seen during a movement or a still position

Optionals—Gymnast-designed routines using movements that show the athlete to best advantage

Pike position—body is bent forward more than 90° at the hips while the legs are kept perfectly straight

Rip—a piece of skin torn away from the palm of the hand

Routine—a combination of stunts displaying a full range of skills on one apparatus

Trick—a movement, skill, or stunt

Tuck position—a position in which the gymnast tucks the knees to the chest and holds them tighty in place with the hands

Virtuous—movement performed to the fullest limit

Handspring—springing off the hands by putting the weight on the arms and using a strong push from the shoulders. It can be done either forward or backward, usually a linking movement,

Twist—rotation of varying degrees, on the long axis unsupported in the air, usually done with a straight body

Flip—turning over one full rotation. Performed either forward, backward or sideward, done in the air without the support of the arms

Straddle—legs straight and feet apart in varying degrees. Hips can be straight or bent

Chalk—used on hand and feet for most apparatus to aid in gripping and prevent slipping

Springboard—board used to aid in flight to apparatus

Amplitude—complete and fullest stretch and extension; extent of heights reached (as in a leap)

Cast—straight body swing to initiate momentum into Gymnastic skills, done on apparatus

---

Competition 1 (Team artistic competition) *consists of 5 scores using 6 competitors. Twelve men's and 12 women's Artistic Gymnastics teams qualify for Olympic competition from World Championships with an allotment of 6 competitors and one substitute allowed for each team. Additionally, 4 groups of 6 competitors from countries without national teams but meeting minimum FIG requirements may participate in this competition. The team medals are awarded here.*

Competition 2 (Individual artistic competition) *is in all 4 events for women and all 6 events for men for a total All-Around score. In the Olympics, 36 men and 36 women qualify for the finals after the team competition (with a maximum of 2 per country).*

Six groups of 6 competitors each are formed among the men and 4 groups of 9 competitors each among the women for team, individual and finals. Each score is a combination of 25% Competition 1 compulsories, 25% Competition 1 optionals, and 50% the Competition 2 score. Gold, silver and bronze in All-Around are awarded here.

Competition 3 (Artistic or Apparatus final competition) *in the Olympics includes 6 men and 6 women on each apparatus qualifying from the team competition (Competition 1). In these finals, gold, silver and bronze medals are awarded for each apparatus.*

Individual rhythmic competition, *as in Artistic gymnastics, is a combination of all 4 events ending with a total All-Around score. There will be 2 competitors and one substitute allotted per country in 1984. Los Angeles will host 20-35 countries sending approximately 50 rhythmic competitors. Because Rhythmic is new, there will only be 2 gold medals awarded to the top All-Around finishers from an anxious group of 20.*

Group rhythmic competition *involves a 6-woman team which incorporates one apparatus designated by the FIG into a routine. The apparatus alternates every 2 years. There will be no group routine performed in this first Olympics. A combination of the hoop and rope was chosen for the 1983 World Championships.*

Scoring: *After Nadia Comaneci's perfect 10 score in Montreal, women's scoring was altered to provide a greater challenge—female gymnasts now begin with a 9.5, males a 9.4. There is still a chance of achieving a perfect 10. However, the routine must be exeedingly more difficult,* ***virtuous,*** *original, or sensational.*

Gymnasts are judged on a scoring scale of 10pts that breaks down into a variety of categories. As an example:

Women:

3.0 difficulty
2.5 combinations, construction of exercise
4.0 execution and amplitude
.5 bonus for virtuous, original or spectacular difficulty

Men:

3.4 difficulty
1.6 combinations
(for a 5.0 actual value of an exercise)
4.4 execution (minor breaks)
.6 bonus for virtuous, rare or spectacular difficulty

Rhythmic:

5.0 difficulty
3.0 execution and amplitude of elements
.5 general impression
1.0 composition
.5 rhythm synchronization

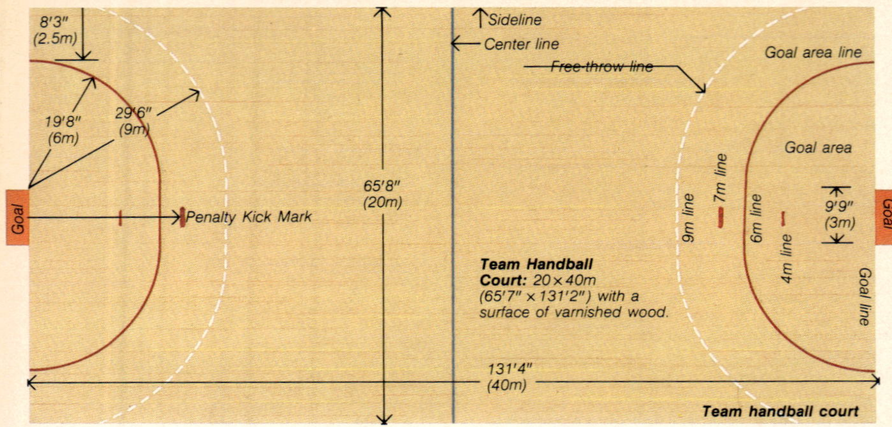

Team handball court

1980 Olympic Team Handball Champions
***Men:* GDR**
***Women:* USSR**

Team handball is a fast and furious court game admitted to the Olympics on a permanent basis for men in 1972 and for women 4 years later. It's contested on a large court with 7 athletes to a side, and although it has elements of basketball and soccer, handball is distinctly different. You will need quick eyes to follow the canteloupe-size ball as it is jostled back and forth between a set of netted goals.

1984 Olympic Field: After international qualifying tournaments, 12 men's and 6 women's teams will compete at Los Angeles. Team handball is one of the Olympic sports where play is conducted on every day of the Games. There will be 12 straight days of competition, ending the day before closing ceremonies.

The game's modern version was invented as an outdoor sport, called ***field handball,*** in Central Europe during the early 1900s. Each team's aim is to propel a stitched-leather ball similar to a small soccer ball through a goal measuring 9'9" (3m) wide and 6'7" (2m) high. Play is on an indoor court similar to a basketball court, but longer and narrower. Team handball is a rigorous sport with a high level of physical contact—and lots of action. The ball is thrown at high speeds (50mph or more) by the human arm. Goalies are especially depended upon for quick reaction time and bold plays.

The most significant line on the court is the **goal area line,** a semicircle extending out 6m from the goal-line. The area enclosed by the 6m line is called the **goal area** or **circle.** Only the goalie is allowed to stand inside the goal area. Offensive and defensive players must remain outside of this area. However, any player may be in the air over the circle as long as he or she made their take-off from outside the goal area line and releases the ball before touching the ground. In addition, a 7m line, or **penalty line,** is drawn and used for a major penalty. A dotted 9m line (**free throw line**) is drawn from the goal and used for minor penalties.

Playing the ball: Players are allowed to run for 3 steps with the ball or to hold it for 3sec either in their hands or holding the ball against the floor. They can stop, catch, hit or throw the ball with their hands (open or closed) or with arms, head, torso, thighs and knees. They may play the ball while kneeling, sitting or lying on the court.

A player may not:
Touch the ball more than once, unless it has touched the ground or another player.
Dive for the ball when it is stationary or rolling on the ground (exception: goalkeeper).
Touch the ball with any part of the leg below the knee.

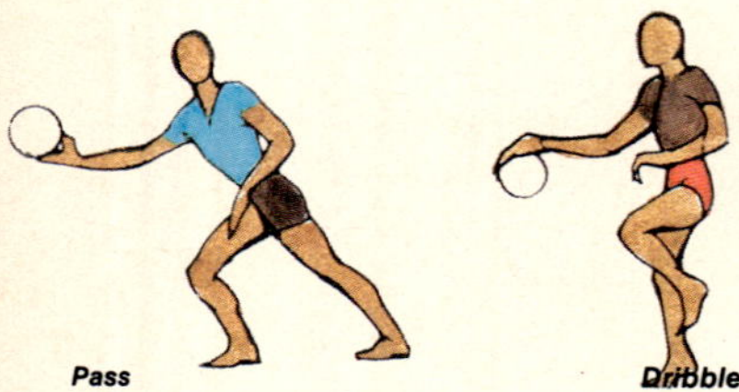
Pass Dribble

Goal Defense Hit

Basic objective: to outmaneuver the opponent by passing the ball deftly and quickly, then hurling it past the goalie to score. Passing requires little wind-up, but rather a quick flick with the wrist. A goal counts 1pt.

Strategy: As in soccer or basketball, a basic strategy hinges on a **fake rush,** and unexpected **pass** to an unguarded teammate and a subsequent **attack** from a surprise quarter.

Ball: *23" (58.4cm) in circumference and 16oz (453.6g) in weight for men; 21½" (54.6cm) in circumference and 13oz (368.5g) for women. The ball is multi-paneled, of a single color and has a non-slip surface.*

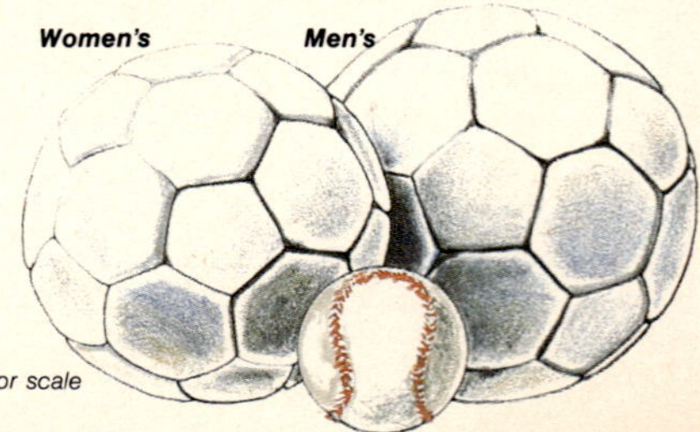

baseball for scale

Jump shot

Teams: 6 court players and 1 goalkeeper per team. Unlimited substituting is allowed and there are 5 subs per team, for a total of 12 to a team (in both men's and women's play).

Duration of play: 2 30min halves with a 10min intermission (for both men and women).

Time-outs: None, except for injuries.

__Classic attack shots:__ the __jump shot__ (high in the air), the __set shot__ taken at head or shoulder level, the __dive shot__ and the __reverse shot__ (facing away from the goal, whirling around).

Player positions: There are ***backcourt players, wing players, circle*** or ***pivot players*** and ***goalkeepers. Shooters*** are the key pointmakers and they range from 6′3″-6′9″ (1.9-2m) in height.

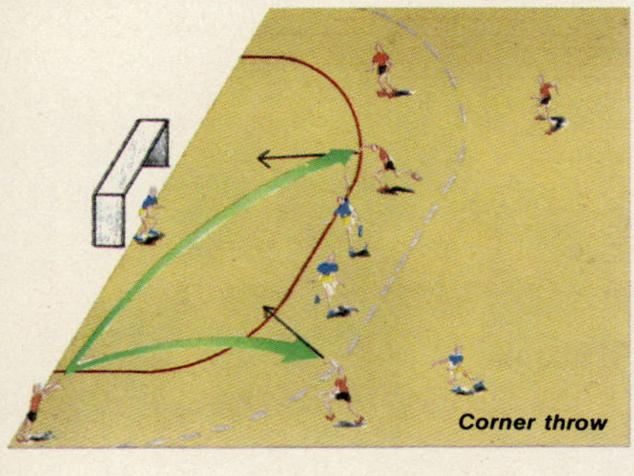
Corner throw

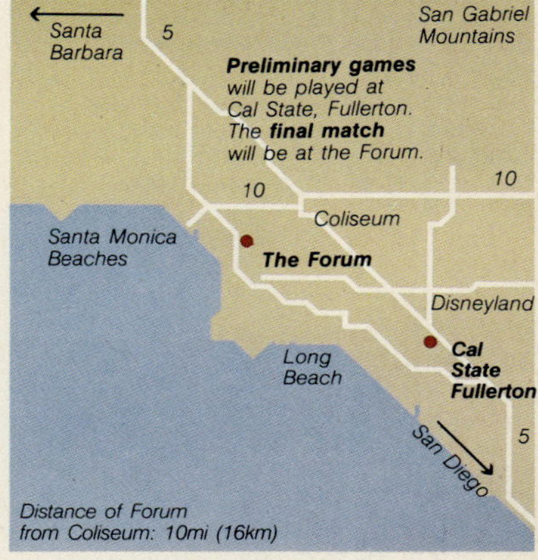

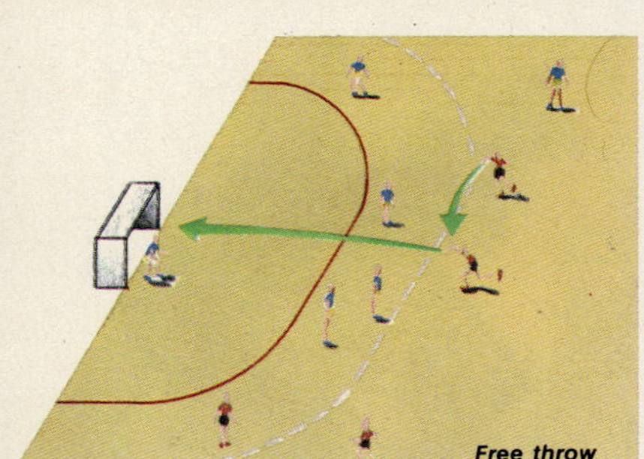
Free throw

__Penalties: A free throw__ is given for minor violations, taken from the point where the foul occured and with the defense remaining 3m away. A __penalty throw__ is given for fouls in the act of shooting and is shot at the goal from the 7m penalty line within 3sec of the referee's signal. A 2min suspension is given for serious personal fouls.

__Officials:__ 2 in number, they are the __goal-line referee,__ who works behind the defensive team, and the __court referee,__ who works behind the attacking team.

Illegal block Legal block

Penalty throw

Instead of following the ball, choose one player to watch. For instance, pick a wing forward and note his strategy for setting up passes to teammates, or note how he changes from offensive to defensive techniques as the ball's possession passes from team to team.

__There is no limit on dribbling__ (bouncing) the ball. But, as in basketball, a __double dribble__ is a violation. Opponent gets a free throw. In other words, a handballer may, in a single series of actions: 1) take 3 steps with the ball, 2) dribble as many times as desired, 3) take 3 steps, and 4) pass or shoot, but not dribble again.

Throw-off

JUDO

Almost nothing on the Games program will be more difficult for Western viewers to understand than 300 or so skilled **judokas** practicing their ancient art. They move with lightning physical and mental speed, following a complex set of rules.

Judo is an Olympic sport derived from ***ju-jitsu,*** one of the most famous of medieval Japanese fighting skills. Today judo is considered the most efficient of all unarmed self-defense techniques. Sleight of body and mastery of the *physics of applied force* are its basic principles. Swift, clever movement—not violence—is the key to overcoming an opponent. However, maiming another fighter is very much frowned upon. The idea is to take advantage of the opponent's moves to overcome stability and execute a throw.

The principle of ***ju*** translates into the ***gentle*** or ***soft way*** in English. For many of the elite practitioners of judo, the skill is less a sport than a way of life. A true judoka devotes himself religiously to his discipline.

Olympic Judo

The referee calls 2 opponents to the competition mat. One wears a red belt, the other a white one. For further identification, thin red and white tapes are fastened around their wrists.

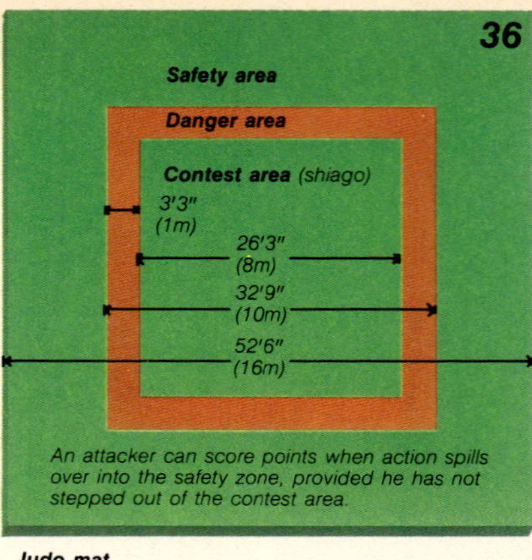

Judo mat

The fighters assume a standing position about 13′ (4m) apart at mat's center. Both then perform the ritual ***ritsurei*** (bow) to the referee and each other. ***Hajime!*** cries the official—and the battle begins.

The contest may end abruptly with a winning throw, but the minimum length is usually 3min. Matches may extend to as much as 20min or so when a clear victory hasn't been decided. Most Olympic and international matches are 5-10min.

Koshiwaza *(hip throw)* ***Kouchigari*** *(foot and leg technique)*

Hip throws, foot and leg techniques, arm locks, strangle techniques, sacrifice and combination techniques and **groundwork** are the main position/throw categories. Basic throws can be divided into 5 categories. Each of these has many variations; more than 40 maneuvers are listed in the **Gokyo,** or manual of judo. But all depend on swift contact, timing, understanding of the human balance-center and methods of destroying stability.

__In the Koshiwaza (hip throw),__ for instance, the fighter grasps an opponent's lapels, pulls him off balance into the hip and rotates him over the hip onto the mat. The __Osotogari__ is a big power throw to the rear. This is done by maneuvering an opponent onto one leg. Then the attacker strikes behind the thigh with his own leg, sweeping the opponent over backwards. The __Ukiotoshi__ is a spectacular move, a 2-handed grab and pull which results in the opponent flying through the air and landing on his back. In __groundwork,__ a specialty of some judokas, __armlocks, elbow joint locks, strangle__ and __choke techniques__ are employed to render a fighter __hors de combat__—without serious damage.

Scoring: Matches are won by the athlete who first scores an ippon. Points are scored with a variety of throws, each meeting a certain standard of quality for points scored.

Point Scoring Values

Ippon: *This move can win a match. It is awarded to the fighter who forcibly dumps his opponent on his back, pins his opponent for 30sec, or checks or arm-bars him into submission (usually signified by 2 quick taps on the mat). An __ippon__ scored means victory.*

Waza-ari: *Almost an __ippon,__ it is given for a not-quite perfect throw or for immobilizing a man for 25 but less than 30sec. Two __waza-aris__ equal an __ippon,__ or a win.*

Yuko: *A throw which is less than a __waza-ari,__ it is given for a hold lasting 20sec but less than 25sec.*

Koka: *Almost a __yuko,__ it is given for a hold lasting 10sec but less than 20sec, or when the opponent is knocked down to his hips.*

Osotogari

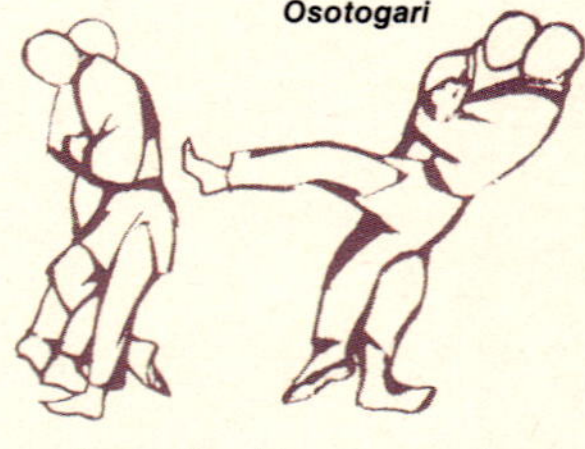

Points and penalties: *The __referee__ calls points and penalties. Two __judges__ sitting off the mat in the safety area hold red and white flags and immediately review the referee's decision. If they disagree on the call, while agreeing between themselves, the judges may overrule the referee. In the Olympics, such a dispute can cause angry exchanges, but not from the fighters, who cannot protest.*

A wide range of penalty calls are subtracted from the fighters' scores at the contest's end. (Most points scored wins the match unless the match is won by an ippon.)

Penalties include:

__throwing__ an opponent with __1 leg entwined__ around his leg

__applying joint locks__ other than on the elbow joint

using the __arm__ or __hand on an opponent's face__

__straying outside__ the contest area

__grabbing__ the bottom of an __opponent's trousers__

applying any hold which might injure the __neck__ or __spinal vertabrae.__

__Kicking__ and __hand-slashing__ are prohibited, along with a number of restraints, but any part of the body may be grabbed. Repeated serious breaches of the rules bring a __hansoku make,__ or disqualification. The referee stops the match, the judges are notified, and the offender kneels for public dishonor by the officials. Nowhere in the world of sports is there a more humiliating penalty. Judo has one of the highest codes of honor anywhere.

Repechage: *This is a series of contests staged before the various weight finals to decide the winner of a bronze (3rd place) medal. Those eligible for repechage are fighters who were defeated en route in the elimination tournament by a finalist.*

JUDO

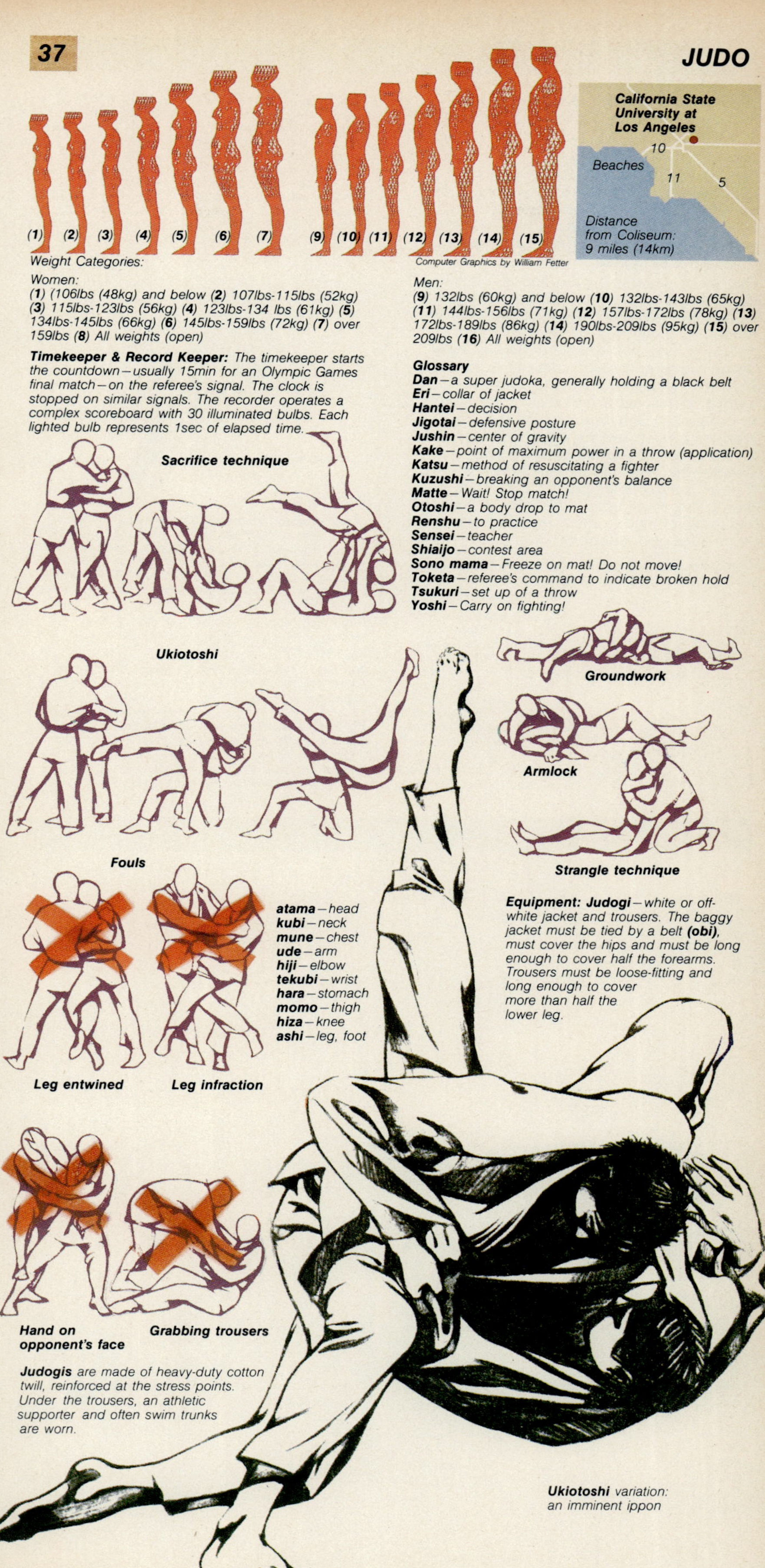

Computer Graphics by William Fetter

Weight Categories:

Women:
*(**1**) (106lbs (48kg) and below (**2**) 107lbs-115lbs (52kg) (**3**) 115lbs-123lbs (56kg) (**4**) 123lbs-134 lbs (61kg) (**5**) 134lbs-145lbs (66kg) (**6**) 145lbs-159lbs (72kg) (**7**) over 159lbs (**8**) All weights (open)*

Men:
*(**9**) 132lbs (60kg) and below (**10**) 132lbs-143lbs (65kg) (**11**) 144lbs-156lbs (71kg) (**12**) 157lbs-172lbs (78kg) (**13**) 172lbs-189lbs (86kg) (**14**) 190lbs-209lbs (95kg) (**15**) over 209lbs (**16**) All weights (open)*

***Timekeeper & Record Keeper:** The timekeeper starts the countdown—usually 15min for an Olympic Games final match—on the referee's signal. The clock is stopped on similar signals. The recorder operates a complex scoreboard with 30 illuminated bulbs. Each lighted bulb represents 1sec of elapsed time.*

Glossary
***Dan**—a super judoka, generally holding a black belt*
***Eri**—collar of jacket*
***Hantei**—decision*
***Jigotai**—defensive posture*
***Jushin**—center of gravity*
***Kake**—point of maximum power in a throw (application)*
***Katsu**—method of resuscitating a fighter*
***Kuzushi**—breaking an opponent's balance*
***Matte**—Wait! Stop match!*
***Otoshi**—a body drop to mat*
***Renshu**—to practice*
***Sensei**—teacher*
***Shiaijo**—contest area*
***Sono mama**—Freeze on mat! Do not move!*
***Toketa**—referee's command to indicate broken hold*
***Tsukuri**—set up of a throw*
***Yoshi**—Carry on fighting!*

***Equipment: Judogi**—white or off-white jacket and trousers. The baggy jacket must be tied by a belt **(obi)**, must cover the hips and must be long enough to cover half the forearms. Trousers must be loose-fitting and long enough to cover more than half the lower leg.*

***Judogis** are made of heavy-duty cotton twill, reinforced at the stress points. Under the trousers, an athletic supporter and often swim trunks are worn.*

***Ukiotoshi** variation: an imminent ippon*

MODERN PENTATHLON

1980 Modern Pentathlon Champions
***Individual:* Anatoly Starostin** (USSR) 5568pts
***Team:* USSR,** 16,126pts

There are those who claim that the modern pentathlon—not the track & field decathlon—is the supreme test of the world-class athlete. What we have here are not variations on a single sport, but **5 totally different disciplines.**

Pentathlon is based in Europe and it was dreamed up for its 1912 Olympic debut by **Baron Pierre de Coubertin,** founder of the Modern Games. His format was the following scenario: A military courier takes off by **horse** and has it shot out from under him. He fights off his enemies with his **sword.** When the sword breaks, he resorts to his **pistol.** Shooting his way out, he reaches a river, **swims** it and escapes. For a finale, he runs **cross-country** and delivers his message. Sweden, with a great 2-time Olympic champion in **Lars Hall,** has won 9 individual gold medals in 15 Games pentathlons held to date. **Russia** holds 4 team titles and **Hungary** holds 3.

Competition: *The 5 contests take place over a 4-day period at* ***Coto de Caza,*** *California.*

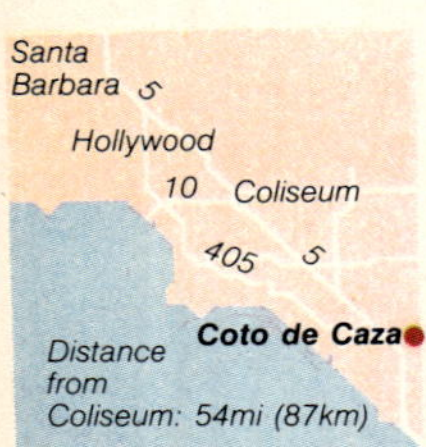

Scoring: *Complicated scoring tables exist for each sport. Generally, scoring is based on a standard 1000pt system (in some events 1100pts). Total points accumulated in the 5 tests are added to determine the winner, both individually and on a team basis. Nations can enter 4 men in the pentathlon, but only 3 are allowed to compete.*

1 ***Riding*** *is over a half-mile (600m) course with 15 obstacles, including a water jump and a double and triple jump. The horses do not belong to the competitors and are supplied by the Organizing Committee. Drawn by lot, mounts are strange to their riders, although selected for equality of performance. There are tough rules against cruelty to horses in their handling. The obstacles are a maximum of 4' (120cm) high and 15 in number, topped by a hedge-fronted water jump of 10' (300cm). A bell is rung to start the jumping and each round must be completed in 3:26.*

Penalty points *are severe. It's a penalty of 60pts if horse, rider, or both fall. It costs 30pts for 1st refusal of a barrier, 60pts for 2nd refusal, 90pts for 3rd refusal. Other penalties are assessed for knocking down a barrier or the horse's foot in the water. For each second taken beyond the 2min course time limit, 2pts are deducted.*

Rider *must wear safety headgear and dress in hunt uniform or national uniform including jacket, collar and tie, and britches.*

Saddles *of the English type are used, blinkers and hoods are prohibited and spurs with rowels or cutting edges are prohibited.*

2 ***Fencing*** *uses electrically wired épées. Contestants must score* ***hits*** *under the presssure of a 3min time limit on each bout. This contest is conducted under the same general rules as regular Olympic swordplay (see* ***Fencing*** *section).*

OBSOLETE OLYMPIC SPORTS

	American Football	**Archery**	*Fixed bird targets (large bird)*	*Moving bird target*	**Art**	*Town planning*	*Medals and badges*	*Compositions for one instrument*	**Australian Football**	**Canoeing**	*Folding kayak, 1000m singles*	**Cricket**	**Croquet**	**Cycling**	*2000m (1.25mi) tandem*	*12-hour race*	**Equestrian**	*Figure riding*	**Fencing**	*Single sticks*	**Field Handball**	**Gliding**	**Golf**	**Gymnastics**	*Swedish exercises*	*Team exercises with portable apparatus (women)*	*Calisthenics*	*Tumbling*	*Rope climbing*	*Club-swinging (men's Indian club)*
1896																●													●	
1900												●	●										●							
1904																				●			●						●	●
1908															●															
1912						●																			●					
1920			●	●		●									●			●							●					
1924						●									●														●	
1928						●	●	●							●															
1932	●					●	●								●													●	●	
1936						●	●	●			●				●						●	●								
1948						●	●	●							●												●			
1952															●											●	●			
1956									●						●											●				
1960															●															
1964															●															
1968															●															
1972															●															
1976																														
1980																														
1984																														

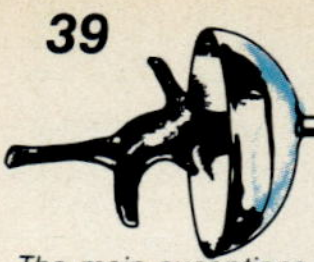
épée

The main exceptions are that only a single **hit** is needed to win a bout and bouts are 3min long. Each pentathlete must face all fencers in the competition. If the 3min time limit expires without a winning hit, both fencers are counted as hit and a defeat is scored against both.

Winning 70% of bouts counts 1000pts for a fencer. Above or below 70%, victories mean added or deducted points.

The épée is closely regulated as to size, weight and structure.

3 Shooting is with a .22 caliber pistol at silhouette targets at 25m range, with a 3sec time limit per shot. Contestants work under roofed stations, protected from weather. Screens separate them so that hot lead spattering from a pistol or ejected hot shells will not injure anyone. Twenty shots are fired in 4 series of 5 shots each by each man with pistols of controlled weight. Only 1 hand may be used. The same weapon must be used in all series. Bullets must be of lead or lead alloy. Correcting lenses on the firearm's sights are barred.

rapid-fire pistol

At 25m (40km) distance, pivoting silhouette targets are 63" (160cm) high and 17½" (45cm) wide and black with a white edge. The shooter has 3sec in which to fire as the target rotates into view, after which the target vanishes for 7sec. A second backup target is used to help judge doubtful shots.

Shooters must score 194pts out of a possible 200 to receive 1000pts. A bonus of 22pts is given for each point over 194 and subtracted on the same scale.

Two gun malfunctions per series of 20 shots are allowed without penalty; after that, it's a 2pts per target penalty.

freestyle stroke

4 Swimming is a 987¼' (300m) race against the clock. Done in heats, there is no final race. Points and finishing positions are decided strictly by elapsed time. The magic time is 3:54 for the 300m race, worth 1000pts. Each half-second faster or slower than 3:54 is worth 4pts plus or minus.

If 2 false starts occur, the starter warns all competitors that the race will proceed on the 3rd attempt, even if there is a further infringement. Any swimmer who causes a 3rd false start is penalized 5sec of time.

5 Cross-country run takes place over hill and dale, including climbs as high as 328' (100m), for 2½mi (4000m) with a time limit. Runners in the final event start individually according to their position after 4 events. The leader starts first and each contestant starts thereafter, according to how many points he is behind the leader. Thus the first man to cross the finish line at the end of the cross country run is the winner of the modern pentathlon competition. He may not have the fastest running time, but will have the highest point total overall. The route starts and finishes at the same point. Tapes of bright color mark both sides of the course for its full 4000m length.

The starter's signal is of the countdown type: **5-4-3-2-1-Go!** During the race, no refreshment of any kind is offered. The use of short-range radio transmitters to offer information is forbidden. Going the route in 14:15 is worth 1000pts. Each second faster or slower than that is worth plus or minus 3pts. Times just over 12:00 flat have been made in the **cross,** good for 1300pts and more.

running shoe

Lacrosse
Lawn Tennis
Motorboating (40 sea miles)
Pelota (jai alai)
Polo
Racquets
Rowing
Fours, inriggers with coxswain
Roque (a kind of croquet)
Shooting
Dueling pistol
Army gun
Running deer
Live pigeon
Swimming & Diving
Plain high diving
Plunge for distance
100-meter freestyle for sailors
200-meter obstacle race
Underwater
Track & Field
56lb (25.4kg) weight throw
16lb (7.3kg) shot put, both hands
Discus, both hands
Javelin, both hands
Tug-of-war
10mi (16km) walk
Standing hop-step-and-jump
Weightlifting
1-hand
Yachting
10-20 ton (9072-18,144kg)

Dating to 1900 as a Games event, rowing is a visually striking sport. In perfect synchronization, 8 tall men send a svelte shell—which they outweigh by 1400lbs (635kg) or so—skating over water. A tiny ***coxswain*** steers the boat, planning the team's strategy as he or she watches for tell-tale signs from opponents. Oars flash: 34 strokes per minute! 38! 40 or more! At the finish—utter exhaustion. Contests between single rowers—or 2- and 4-man teams—are no less dramatic.

Two rowing styles are employed. In ***sweep rowing,*** oarsmen handle one oar with both hands. In ***sculling,*** 2 oars are used, one in each hand.

The single sculls—a 1-person, head-to-head confrontation—is regarded as the most difficult division. The 8-oared shells are the fastest, most visible and most glamorous.

Technique, strategy: Teamwork is a major factor: the 2-, 4- or 8-man crew must match rhythm and movement precisely. And they must trust the coxswain to operate as the team's brain (statistician) and eyes. Remember, the cox is the only team member facing forward! Of the various strategies, a favorite involves trying to outguess rivals on how much oar should be extended from the oarlock for best efficiency in varying weather.

The start: In coxed events, the *coxswain,* weighing 100-105lbs (45kg-47kg), sits facing the ***stroke oar*** and steers. The stroke oarsman sets the pace. The crew bursts into furious motion at the starter's command and nearly a ton of bodies, fiber and fittings moves from a dead stop to a speed of 13-14mph (21-22.5km/hr)—in 10 strokes.

Women's rowing: Added to the Games in 1976, this event is so new that little history exists. East German women have won 8 of 12 gold medals in the past 2 Games, in single sculls, coxless pairs, coxed pairs, coxed quadruple sculls, coxed fours and eights. Bulgaria, Romania, and the USSR have been the East Germans' only competition.

Watch for precision and smoothness. At the beginning of each stroke the oars should catch the water quickly and uniformly; at the finish of a stroke, all oars should leave the water together without splashing. The more effortless the rowing looks, the better the crew or sculler.

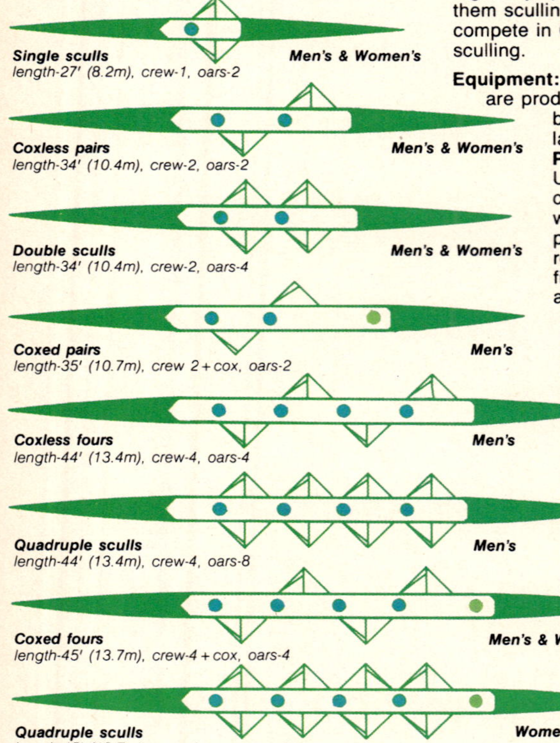

Rules: *Men's races are 1mi 427yds (2000m). Women's races measure 1094yds (1000m). Qualifying heats and races begin with boats in respective marked lanes and with bows exactly on the starting line. The starting official warns all crews or single oarsmen to be ready, then shouts* ***partez!*** *(French for* ***go!****) and drops a flag.*

In case of a false start, *a bell rings, a red flag drops and contestants are recalled to start again. The recall must be done within the first 328′ (100m) rowed.*

Straying from a lane *is punishable. An umpire on the officials' launch warns of any impending collision (to collide out-of-lane can mean disqualification).*

The winner is the boat whose bow touches the finish line first. If a rower falls out of a boat, *the crew still can win, if they're good enough. But if a coxswain hits the drink, the boat is disqualified because of the loss of the cox's weight. Electronic photo-timing is made of all races and a tie finish means a re-row.*

Eight Olympic races are held—3 of them sculling events and 5 rowing. Women compete in 6 contests—3 rowing and 3 sculling.

Equipment: Finely crafted shells and sculls are produced worldwide. A top-line 8-oar boat costs $8500 or more. The late, famous shell-builder, **George Pocock** of Seattle, Washington, USA, constructed boats composed of seven different woods. Western cedar was the primary wood used. But today's rowers prefer shells of carbon fibre or plastic. Eight-oar shells are tippy because they're only about 2′ wide—23½″ to 24½″ (59.7-62.2cm)—yet at 62′ (18.9m) or more in length, are nearly as long as a World War II PT boat. Boats may be of any dimension, and designers seek to reduce the amount of boat surface contacting the water—a goal which reduces friction, but sacrifices stability. Eight men averaging about 6′3″ (1.9m) and 210lbs (95¼kg) make up the rowing crew.

Oars: Racing oars are hollow to reduce weight. Size and shape are unrestricted. The blade has a pronounced curve to improve its grip on the water. Oars are connected to boats by adjustable outrigger devices with an oarlock. The largest ***sweeps*** are 12-13′ (3.65-3.96m) in length, much longer than the 9½-10′ (2.89-3m) sculling oars. The modern trend is to the ***spade blade,*** a shorter, wider oar thought to have better propulsion quality.

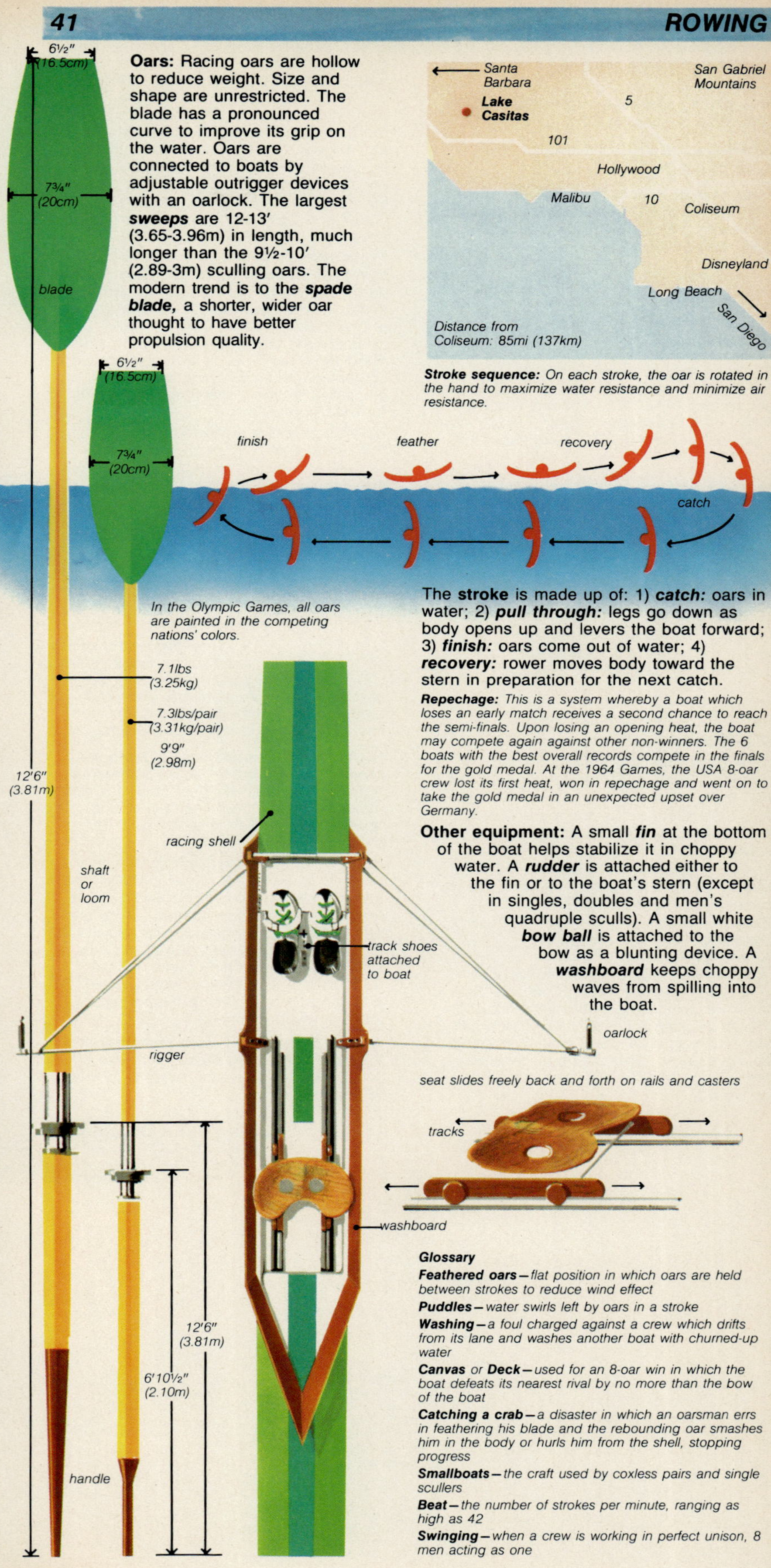

Stroke sequence: *On each stroke, the oar is rotated in the hand to maximize water resistance and minimize air resistance.*

In the Olympic Games, all oars are painted in the competing nations' colors.

The **stroke** is made up of: 1) ***catch:*** oars in water; 2) ***pull through:*** legs go down as body opens up and levers the boat forward; 3) ***finish:*** oars come out of water; 4) ***recovery:*** rower moves body toward the stern in preparation for the next catch.

Repechage: *This is a system whereby a boat which loses an early match receives a second chance to reach the semi-finals. Upon losing an opening heat, the boat may compete again against other non-winners. The 6 boats with the best overall records compete in the finals for the gold medal. At the 1964 Games, the USA 8-oar crew lost its first heat, won in repechage and went on to take the gold medal in an unexpected upset over Germany.*

Other equipment: A small ***fin*** at the bottom of the boat helps stabilize it in choppy water. A ***rudder*** is attached either to the fin or to the boat's stern (except in singles, doubles and men's quadruple sculls). A small white ***bow ball*** is attached to the bow as a blunting device. A ***washboard*** keeps choppy waves from spilling into the boat.

Glossary

Feathered oars—*flat position in which oars are held between strokes to reduce wind effect*

Puddles—*water swirls left by oars in a stroke*

Washing—*a foul charged against a crew which drifts from its lane and washes another boat with churned-up water*

Canvas *or* ***Deck***—*used for an 8-oar win in which the boat defeats its nearest rival by no more than the bow of the boat*

Catching a crab—*a disaster in which an oarsman errs in feathering his blade and the rebounding oar smashes him in the body or hurls him from the shell, stopping progress*

Smallboats—*the craft used by coxless pairs and single scullers*

Beat—*the number of strokes per minute, ranging as high as 42*

Swinging—*when a crew is working in perfect unison, 8 men acting as one*

Olympic Shooting Record

Free pistol: **Aleksandr Melentyev,** USSR, 1980 (581 of possible 600)

Rapid-fire pistol: **Norbert Klaar,** GDR, 1976 (597 of 600)

Rifle, prone: **Karoly Varga,** HUN, 1980; **Hellfried Heilfort,** GDR, 1980; **Karlheinz Smieszek,** FRG, 1976; **Ho Jun Li,** PRK, 1972 (tie at 599 of 600)

Rifle, 3-position: **Viktor Vlasov,** USSR 1980 (1173 of 1200)

Trap shooting: **Angelo Scalzone,** ITA, 1972 (199 of 200)

Skeet shooting: **Josef Panacek,** TCH, 1976; **Eric Swinkels,** HOL, 1976; **Romano Garagnani,** ITA, 1968; **Konrad Wirnhier,** FRG, 1968; **Yevgeniy Petrov,** USSR, 1968 **Luciano Giovanneti,** ITA, 1980 (tie at 198 of 200)

Running game target: **Thomas Pfeffer,** GDR, 1980; **Igor Sokolov,** USSR, 1980 (tie at 589 of 600)

Shot and shells will fly in record numbers at the 1984 Games as sharpshooters vie in pistol, rifle, shotgun and air rifle competitions. Over 1100 shooters representing 80 countries are expected in Los Angeles, a field of unprecedented size. Included for the first time will be a women's shooting division. Europeans hold almost all Olympic shooting records, although the USSR and USA have turned in strong showings.

Procedure: Shooters work from roofed stands or ***stations*** which are platformed and screened-off individually, except for skeet. The ***ranges*** are set up with the sun at the shooter's back. ***Targets*** are numbered to correspond with firing stations. ***Wind flags*** set at 33′ (10m) intervals aid the competitors in judging the wind effect. An elapsed-time clock gives the time remaining for each contestant.

No team prizes are awarded, only ***individual*** ones.

Nations may enter **2 contestants** per event. ***Officials*** include: Results Jury, Jury of Appeals, range officers, target operators, scorers, markers, firearms inspectors.

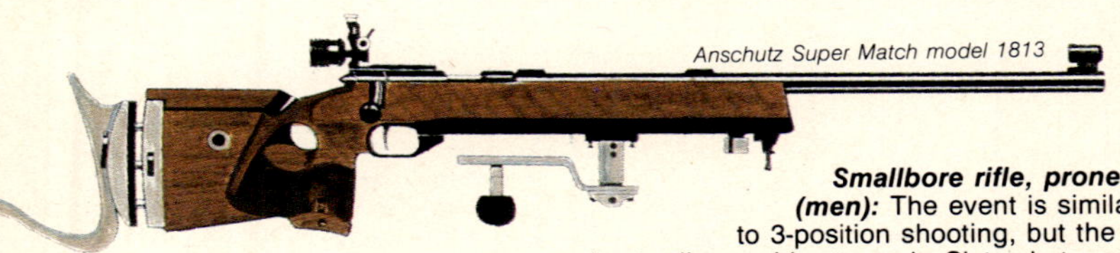

Anschutz Super Match model 1813

Smallbore rifle, prone (men): The event is similar to 3-position shooting, but the shooter lies on his stomach. Sixty shots are fired in 10-shot strings within a 2hr time limit. The target is 164′ (50m) distant.

Standard rifle, smallbore, 3 positions, (new event, women): Unlike the men's 3-position contest, with set times for each position, women must finish in a block time of 2hrs, 15min. Range of target is 164′ (50m).

Running game target (men): In this exotic contest, employing a .22cal (5.6mm) rifle, the only telescopic sights allowed in Olympic shooting are needed. Thirty shots are loosed at a slow-moving target and 30 at a fast-moving target. Moving on rails, a simulated boar, painted black, covers 32′9″ (10m) in 2.5sec at fastest speed. At a distance of 164′ (50m), this requires instantaneous reaction.

Air rifle (new event, men & women): Women take 40 shots and men take 60. An 11lb (5kg) gun is used. Target is 32′9¾″ (10m) distant.

Rifle Events

Smallbore rifle, 3 positions (men): The gun is a .22cal long rifle weighing 14-15lbs (6.4-6.8kg). The German-made Anschutz precision rifles are generally the favored models and cost $1500 apiece with accessories.

In this competition, 120 shots are fired at a target 164′ (50m) distant. Position, number of shots and time limit are:
Prone: 40 shots/1hr, 15min
Standing: 40 shots/1hr, 45min
Kneeling: 40 shots/1hr, 30min
The target's inner ring, the *bullseye,* is .448″ (12.4mm) in diameter, smaller than a dime. No telescopic devices are allowed; maximum sling width is 1½″ (40mm). The same rifle must be used in all 3 positions. A bullseye earns 10pts; value of concentric rings range from 9-1pts away from the bullseye.

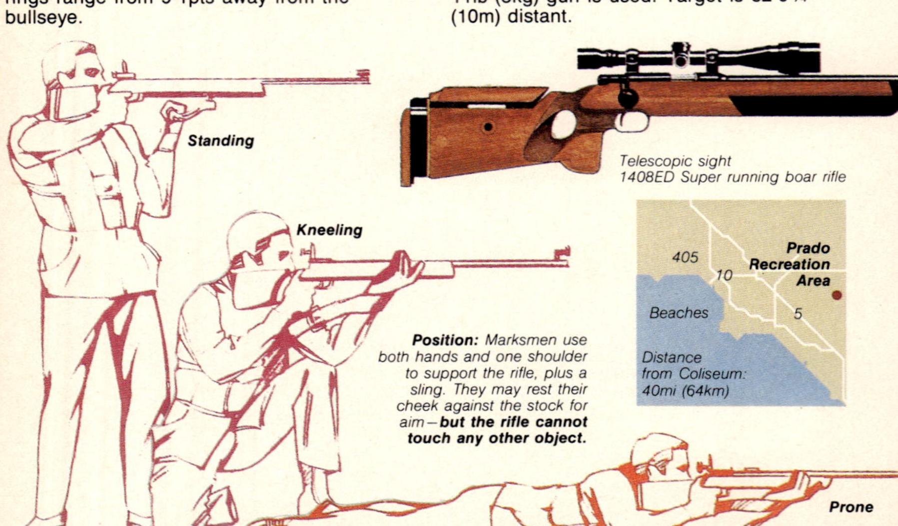

Telescopic sight
1408ED Super running boar rifle

Position: *Marksmen use both hands and one shoulder to support the rifle, plus a sling. They may rest their cheek against the stock for aim—* ***but the rifle cannot touch any other object.***

Pistol Events

Typical free pistol Hammerli

Free pistol (men): Only one hand can be used, calling for the finest muscle control in the firing of shots at a range of 164′ (50m). The small targets have 1-10pt scoring rings; the 10pt ring is 1.97″ (50mm) in diameter. Time limit for the event is 2.5hrs. The gun's bore must be .22″ (5.6mm). No extra support grips are allowed and optical sights are banned.

Rapid-fire pistol (men): A 5.6mm pistol is used. The marksman takes 60 shots at 5 targets at an 82′ (25m) range. When he calls ***ready,*** 5 targets pop up simultaneously; one shot is made at each target. In the first 2 series, 5 shots must be fired within 8sec; in the next 2 series, within 6sec; in the final series, within 4sec.

Smith & Wesson model 41

Smallbore sport pistol, (new event, women): Target range is 82′ (25m). Contestants shoot 30 shots on the ***free pistol*** target (precision) and 30 shots on the ***rapid fire*** pistol target (duel).

Oscar Swahn *of Sweden not only took 6 medals in shooting events, but between 1908 and 1924 he competed with his son,* **Alfred,** *who won 9 medals. The 15 gold, silver and bronze medals collected by the Swahns may be the ultimate Olympic achievement by members of a single family.*

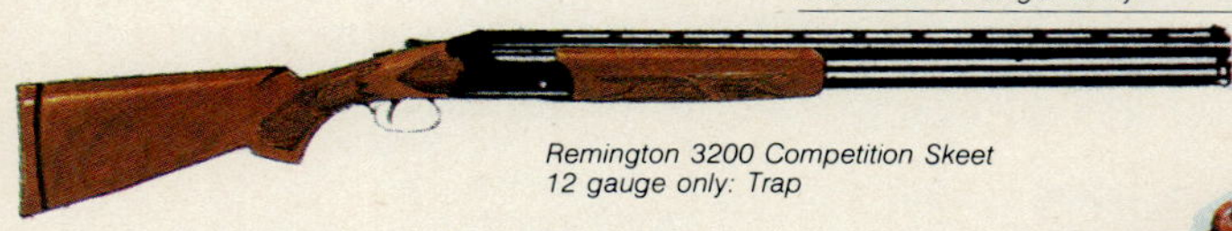

Remington 3200 Competition Skeet 12 gauge only: Trap

Trap and Skeet Events

In both trap and skeet shooting, clay pigeons measuring 4⅓″ (11cm) across and moving at flashing speed are the targets.

Trapshooting (mixed): The marksman loads 2 cartridges into his 12 gauge shotgun (he's allowed a second shot if the first misses) and faces 5 trap pits 49′3″ (15m) away. The gun is held at the shoulder. When the shooter says ***pull!,*** his voice activates a releasing device and a ***clay disk*** leaves a trap at 125mph (201km/hr). Target direction varies and first hits need to be made within about 1.5sec.

Targets, *called* ***clays*** *or* ***birds,*** *are 4⅓″ (11cm) in diameter and less than 1″ (25-26mm) thick. The 3.7oz (105g) saucers come in a variety of bright, highly visible colors, but* ***the same color must be used throughout a contest.***

Skeet (mixed): The gun is held belt high. Targets are thrown up from 2 trap-houses and the shooter moves about to 8 shooting stations. Unlike trapshooting, the competitor has no idea when the targets will be released. Skeet ***birds*** have a 90mph (145km/hr) velocity.

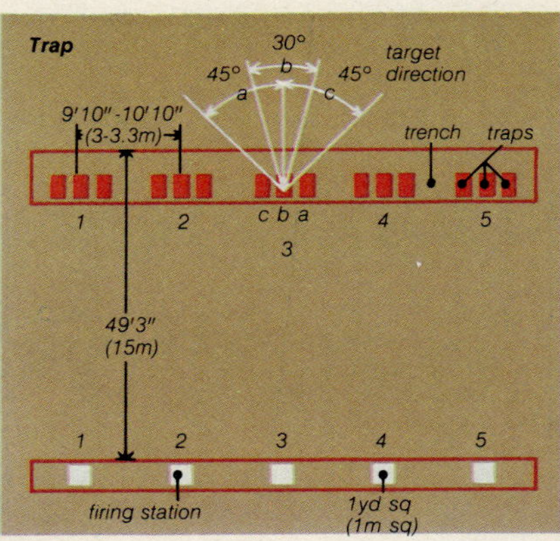

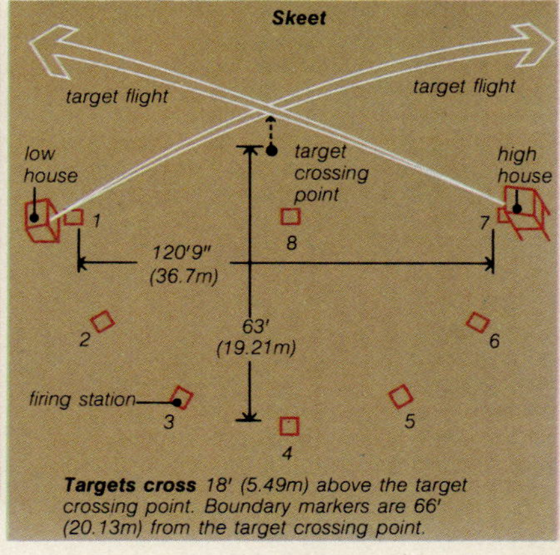

Targets cross *18′ (5.49m) above the target crossing point. Boundary markers are 66′ (20.13m) from the target crossing point.*

Olympic Shooting Event Summary:

Event	distance	perfect score	current Olympic record	maximum diameter #10 ring (bullseye)
Men				
Smallbore free rifle, prone	164′(50m)	600	599	.448″ (12.4mm)
Smallbore free rifle, 3-position	164′ (50m)	1200	1173	.448″ (12.4mm)
Air rifle, standing (indoor)	32′9″ (10m)	600	new	.039″ (1mm)
Free pistol	164′ (50m)	600	581	1.97″ (50mm)
Rapid fire pistol	82′ (25m)	600	597	3.937″ × 5.905″ (100mm×150mm)
Running game target	164′ (50m)	600	589	2.36″ (60mm)
Women				
Smallbore standard rifle, 3-position	164′ (50m)	600	new	.448″ (12.4mm)
Air rifle, standing (indoor)	32′9″ (10m)	400	new	.039″ (1mm)
Smallbore pistol	82″ (25m)	600	new	1.97″ (50mm) & 3.937″ × 5.905″ (100mm×150mm)
Mixed				
Trap	varies	200	199	4.33″ (110mm) clay target
Skeet	varies	200	198	4.33″ (110mm) clay target

8'2" (2.5m)

False Start Line

Backstroke Turning Line

Swimming pool

1972-1980 Games/National Gold Medals

Swimming (men): **USA, 21; USSR, 7; SWE, 4; GBR, 2; JAP, 1; HUN, 1**

Swimming (women): **GDR, 22; USA, 9; AUS, 6; JAP, 1**

Diving (men): **ITA, 2; USSR, 2; USA, 1; GDR, 1**

Diving (women): **USA, 2; USSR, 2; SWE, 1; GDR, 1**

Water Polo (men only): **USSR, 2** (1972, 1980); **HUN, 1** (1976)

Concentrated weightlifting, gymnastics training, increased endurance swimming, faster modern pools, sleeker swim suits—these are the main reasons for the incredible aquatic sports record-smashing of the last decade. Nowhere is this more emphasized than in the Olympics. Records are made and broken so quickly that televiewers may, in 1984, expect to see more Olympic and world records set in the water than in almost any other sport.

Training: National coaches push their Olympic contenders in training for the gold. Daily routines include ***training swims,*** up to 9.3mi (15km) per day, with the emphasis on keeping a predetermined pulse rate throughout the workout. Combined with this are several hours of weightlifting and more hours of ***practicing turns,*** the big time-saver in aquatic racing. ***Drills*** focus attention on the technical aspects of the swim, further whittling more seconds from a racer's time.

Some countries even employ poolside psychiatrists, whose job is to calm, inspire and relax the stars before and during meets.

Olympians today are bigger than ever in musculature and height: **Vladimir Salnikov** of the USSR, who broke the *unbreakable* 15min barrier in the 1500m freestyle at the 1980 Games and has set numerous world records, stands 6'6" (1.98m) at 160lbs (72.5kg).

1984 Program: There will be 15 swimming events each for men and women on the roster. Each sex competes separately, and there is little difference between their programs. Both sexes compete at:

100m freestyle
200m freestyle
400m freestyle
100m backstroke
200m backstroke
100m breaststroke
200m breaststroke
100m butterfly
200m butterfly
400m individual medley

The exception to ***even distances*** for men and women is that ***men*** swim a ***1500m freestyle*** while ***women*** swim an ***800m freestyle.***

Team relay events:
Men: **4×100m medley relay; 4×100m freestyle relay; 4×200m freestyle relay**
Women: **4×100m medley relay; 4×100m free relay**

New events:
Men: **200m medley, 4×100m relay**
Women: **200m medley, synchronized swimming**

With the 2 diving events—*springboard* and ***platform***—and ***water polo,*** this comprises the most ambitious swimming schedule in Games history. A field of more than 900 competitors is expected, 2nd only in number to track and field's estimated 2000. Each nation is allowed 33 men and 30 women swimmers and divers, including members of relay teams.

Starting platforms: *Raised 29½" (75cm) above the water surface and coated with non-skid material, the blocks from which swimmers take off are numbered on all 4 sides for easy identification of contestants.*

Lanes are separated *by lane ropes extending the course's length and fixed to anchor brackets. Lane ropes consist of floats placed end-to-end and with a minimum diameter of 4'3" (1.29m). At each end of the pool, 16' (5m) from the walls, a distinctively colored float is positioned as a guideline to swimmers putting on a finishing burst.*

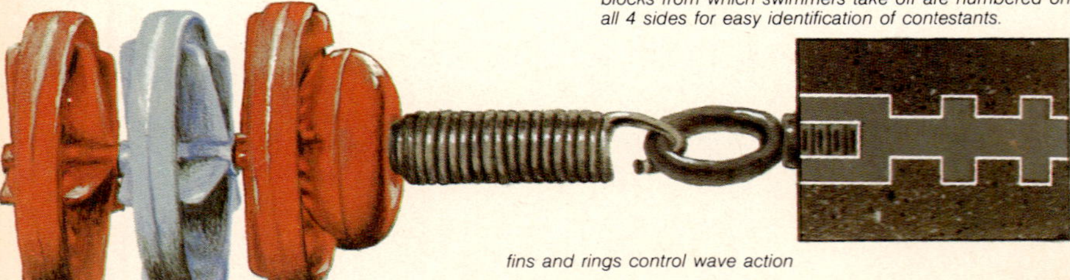

fins and rings control wave action

Olympic pool: Pools have improved vastly from early Games when swimmers had to brave the chill waters of open-sea racing or compete on courses laid out in the middle of rivers and lakes. The 1984 facility may be the best ever built. Located on the University of Southern California campus, the $7 million project will have everything from a continuous feed system to keep water level constant, to electronic touch-timing panels and water heated to a steady 77°F (.25°C).

The pool measures a long-course 55yds (50m) in length, 25yds (22.8m) wide and has a minimum water depth of 6′6″ (1.98m). It is divided into 8 lanes, each 8′2″ (2.5m) wide and marked for the swimmer with a dark line running down the lane's center at pool bottom.

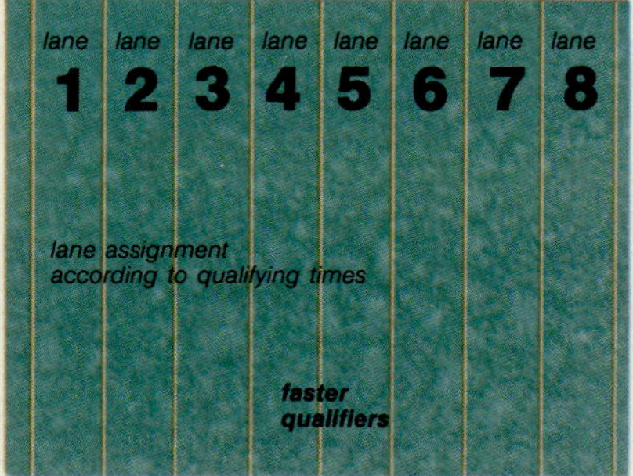

Lane assignments: Swimmers file entry forms with officials certifying their fastest competitive times up to the Games. The fastest swimmer or relay team is placed in the center lane (Nos. 4 or 5); the next-fastest alternate in lanes left and right of the center lanes. This covers trial heats. Fastest times in heats determine lane placings in accordance with the above procedure.

Start and timing: After a second false start, ***anyone causing a 3rd false start is disqualified***—even if they were innocent in the initial 2 instances. The field is recalled after a false start by either a gunshot or dropping a rope. ***Timing*** is completely electronic, and accurate to 1/1000 sec, but times recorded and displayed on the scoreboard are shown only to 1/100th sec for fairness, because variability in pool construction can mean centimeter differences in lane length. This difference, compounded by each lap of a race, can add up to a ½″-¾″ (1-2cm) difference in total length, or several thousandths of a second on the clock. Timing devices covering each lane are activated by a direct hookup with the starter's gun, and record elapsed time and relative finishes when swimmers touch contact pads fixed in the walls at the pool's end. The pads have a 1″ (2.54cm) black border and are sensitive to a light hand-touch, but not to water turbulence. Videotapes of races are also made to aid in judging finishes.

Starting dive

University of Southern California McDonald's Swim Stadium is near the Coliseum.

Officials: Nowhere in the Games are they more numerous. The ***referee*** has full control of all officials, including the ***chief timekeeper, lane timekeepers, starter, stroke judges, turning judges, finish judges, recorder*** and ***clerk.*** Along with the starter, these 2 officiating groups are especially important:

Turning judges—Called ***inspectors,*** they make sure that competitors comply with the rules on turns, beginning with the last armstroke before touching contact pads and ending with completion of the first armstroke after turning. They also keep count of the number of laps completed and inform swimmers of the remaining laps to be made by displaying large ***lap cards*** bearing numbers.

Stroke judges—They make sure that the rules governing each style of swimming are being observed and report any infringement.

Turning and general strategy: The ***flip*** or somersault turn was introduced in the early 1960s but was banned at the Tokyo Olympics in 1964. In it the swimmer twists completely around on himself, going into a somersault a 1yd (.91m) or more from the pool's end and touching only with the feet as he powerfully pushes off with the legs. The ***Federation Internationale de Natation Amateur,*** the worldwide governing body of swimming, accepted the somersault in 1965. The result in Mexico City in 1968 was 13 Olympic and 9 world records set by men and women, combined.

Strategy is limited in the short, sprint events, where swimmers go full blast from the gun. In longer events, such as those at 800m and 1500m, a shrewd assessment of rival swimmers is needed before a racer decides how to pace himself, when to turn on the speed and when (as swimmers say) to "listen to your body." Tactically, the ***racing dive*** at the start can gain a substantial advantage. The dive is a long, flat, on-the-belly maneuver, with arms thrust out in front and legs shoving off the starting block with full power. Momentum achieved here translates into the first strokes taken.

Swim Styles

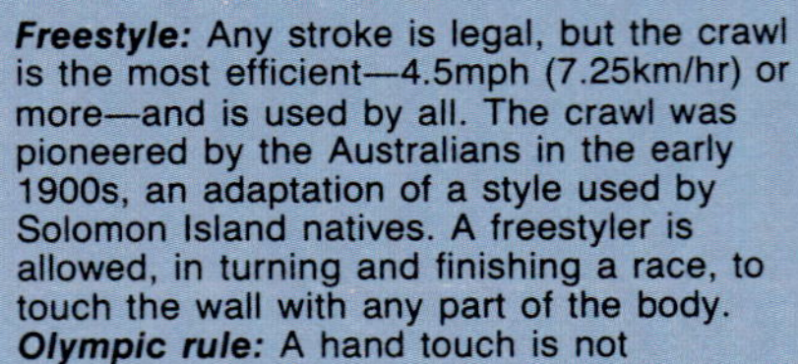

Freestyle: Any stroke is legal, but the crawl is the most efficient—4.5mph (7.25km/hr) or more—and is used by all. The crawl was pioneered by the Australians in the early 1900s, an adaptation of a style used by Solomon Island natives. A freestyler is allowed, in turning and finishing a race, to touch the wall with any part of the body.
Olympic rule: A hand touch is not obligatory.

Backstroke: While on their backs, swimmers combine alternating arm movements and ***flutter kick*** to splash through the water at about 4.03mph (6.48km/hr). Ancient Egyptians are said to have invented the style. Backstroke is the only swim contest where entrants begin from a position in the pool, rather than diving from starting blocks. They hang on to starting grips until the gun is fired.

Olympic rules: Swimmers must be immobile at the start. No bending of toe over the gutter's lip is permitted. On turns, a somersault turn is legal, but the entrant must return past the vertical to a supine position before feet have broken contact with the wall.

Breaststroke: In the slowest of the 4 swimming styles, competitors move both arms and both legs simultaneously, keeping the entire body on the same horizontal plane, parallel to the water's surface.

Olympic rules: Arms and legs must be in the water at all times. Hands must be pushed forward together from the breast and brought back under water. In the leg kick, no vertical, up-and-down movement is legal. Feet must be turned outwards in the backward movement. Part of the head must break the water's surface except at the start and turns, where one arm stroke is allowed.

Butterfly: This stroke is the result of an overlooked loophole in breaststroke regulations. Original rules did not specify whether the arms were to be thrust forward in or out of the water after they had been pulled back. Thus German swimmers had the idea of lifting arms above the water while using the breaststroke leg-scissors movement. The stroke calls for the arms to be flung away from the torso.

Olympic rules: Arm action must be simultaneous—**both** arms moving forward or both moving back together. The feet must also be in action simultaneously. When touching at a turn or the race's finish, the touch must be with both hands at once at the same level.

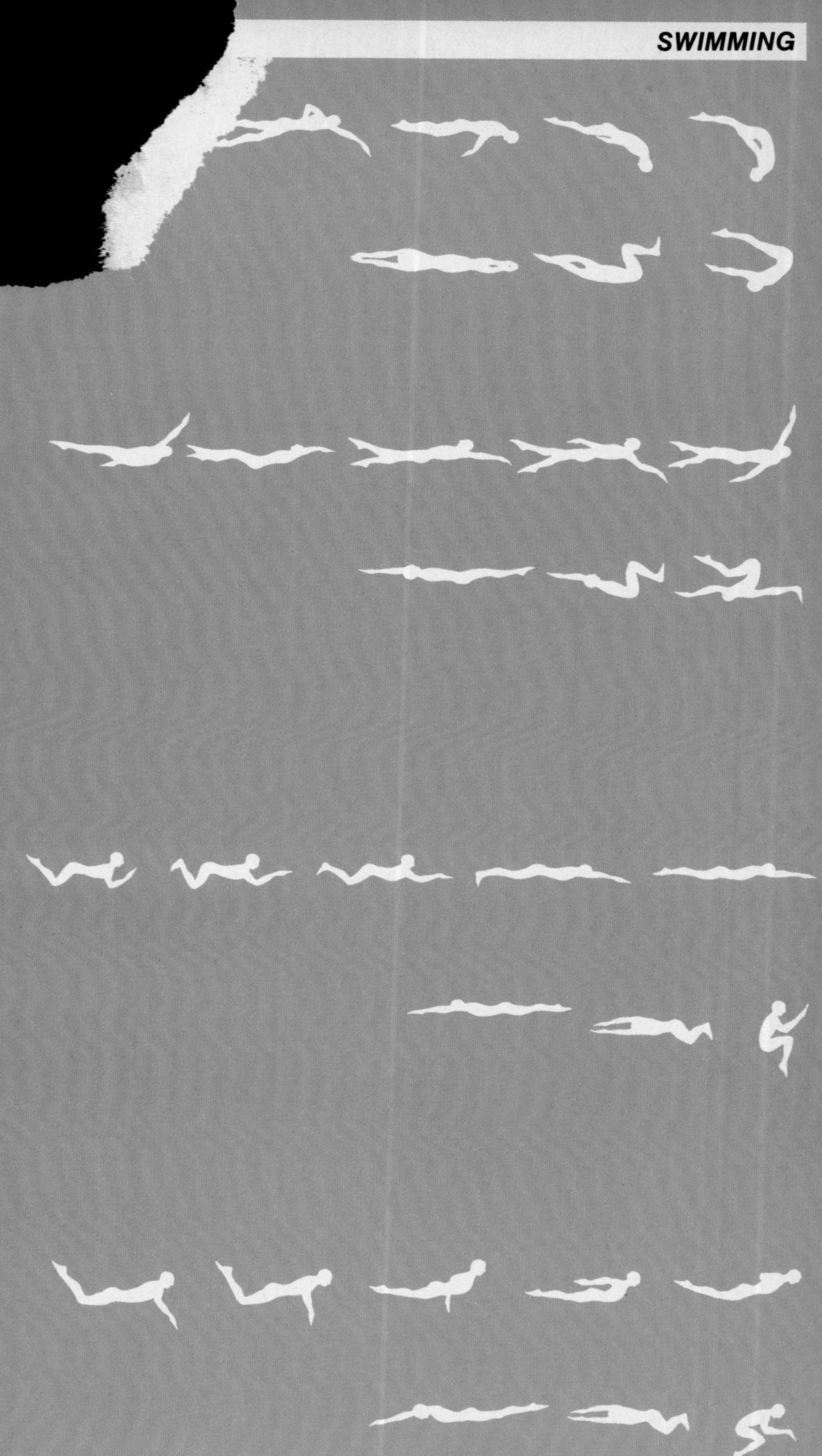

Medley events: In individual competition, athletes swim an equal distance with each of 4 strokes, in this order: butterfly, backstroke, breaststroke, freestyle. In medley (team) relays, each of 4 swimmers swims, in order: backstroke, breaststroke, butterfly, freestyle.

DIVING

1980 Olympic Diving Champions
Men's Springboard: **Alexsandr Portnov,** USSR

Women's Springboard: **Irina Kalinina,** USSR

Men's Platform: **Falk Hoffman,** GDR

Women's Platform: **Martina Jaschke,** GDR

Perhaps diving's allure is the technical precision of its practitioners. Or perhaps it is the graceful display of these primed human bodies. But probably most will agree that the biggest thrill is the suspenseful split-second these daredevil athletes hang suspended in the air, combining that precision and grace, before sliding effortlessly into the water. This category of contests was added to the Games' roster in 1904, when it was called **fancy diving.** That name is even more apt today as divers continue to add to the complexity of their mid-air twists, spins and turns.

Diving is punishing. **Mic** medalist at the Munich Ga broken arm when she crash The great 4-time Olympic winn **McCormick** (USA) cracked ribs, fingers, split her scalp and lacerat feet and elbows, typical career inju estimated that in some dives, a spe more than 50mph is reached before the water.

Reverse 2½ somersault

Inward 1½ pike

Straight back dive, pike position

Dives:
Forward dives *with body facing water and dive made forward*
Backward dives *with back to water and rotating away from the board or platform*
Reverse dives *with the diver facing forward, but rotation back to the board*
Inward dives *with back to water and rotating inwards toward board or platform*
Twisting dives *made from either starting position and body twisting in the air*
Armstand dives *made from the platform only; the diver begins the maneuver from a motionless handstand on the platform's edge*

Within these groupings, FINA—aquatics sports' governing body, the ***Federation Internationale de Natation Amateur****—lists 82 different types of dives which may be performed, with various degrees of difficulty.*

Basic body positions:
Tuck*—body is bent at the knees and at the hips, with knees held together and drawn to the chest*
Pike*—the body is bent at the waist, with legs straight*
Straight*—the body remains straight*
Free*—combination of 2 or more above body positions*

Required Dives are divided into 2 categories:

Voluntary dives with degree-of-difficulty limits: On springboard, the degree of difficulty limit is 9.6. Divers must perform 5 dives—one from each style except armstand—whose individual degrees of difficulty do not add up to more than 9.6. From the platform, divers choose 4 dives from the 6 styles and do not exceed a degree-of-difficulty total of 7.6.

Voluntary dives without degree-of-difficulty limits: On springboard, women perform 5 and men make 6 dives. From the platform, women dive 4 times and men 6. There is no limit to total degree-of-difficulty.

No dives are ever repeated from any category.

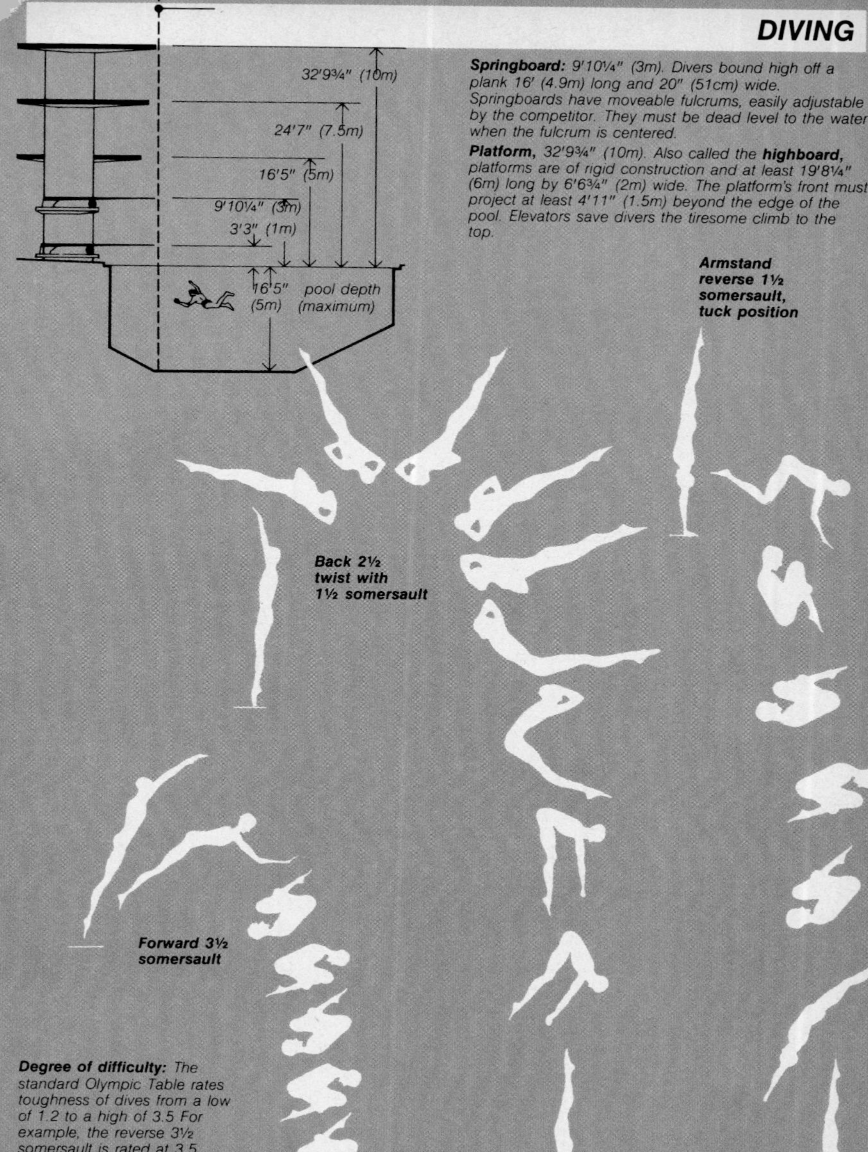

Springboard: *9'10¼" (3m). Divers bound high off a plank 16' (4.9m) long and 20" (51cm) wide. Springboards have moveable fulcrums, easily adjustable by the competitor. They must be dead level to the water when the fulcrum is centered.*

Platform, *32'9¾" (10m). Also called the* ***highboard,*** *platforms are of rigid construction and at least 19'8¼" (6m) long by 6'6¾" (2m) wide. The platform's front must project at least 4'11" (1.5m) beyond the edge of the pool. Elevators save divers the tiresome climb to the top.*

Degree of difficulty: *The standard Olympic Table rates toughness of dives from a low of 1.2 to a high of 3.5 For example, the reverse 3½ somersault is rated at 3.5 degree-of-difficulty, the highest for any springboard dive. While watching Olympic diving, be alert when the next dive attempted is announced by commentators. Watch for these wild, high-scoring acrobatics:* ***forward 3½ somersault, forward 1½ somersault with 3 twists, back 1½ somersault with 2½ or 3½ twist, armstand cut-thru reverse 1½ somersault, reverse twister with back 2½ or 3½ twist.*** *You'll see human pinwheels in action, and there's no more impressive sight in sports.*

Judging: *In this very delicate matter, a panel of 7 judges awards points on this basis:*
Failed dive—0 points
Unsatisfactory—½-2pts
Deficient—2½-4½pts
Satisfactory—5-6pts
Good—6½-8pts
Very good—8½-10pts
The procedure for arriving at a consensus of the 7 judges is as follows: After each judge registers his score on large card-displays, the highest and lowest marks are thrown out. The remaining 5 scores are multiplied by a factor of 3/5 and by the listed degree of difficulty of the particular dive.

Dive:
Starting position must be fully erect, relaxed and confident, with arms straight forward, to the sides or over the head.
Run to takeoff must be smooth, straight and leading into the hurdle, which is a springing action in the board to gain upward propulsion.
Takeoff by world-class divers can go up to 7-8' (2-2.4m) with a strong hurdle. The takeoff must be bold and high to score big points and it must clear the board by an ample safety margin.
Execution of the dive's components from any of the tuck, pike, straight or free positions must be performed crisply, with flair and control, and held long enough in flight to clearly identify them.
Entry, according to the Olympic rulebook, "shall in all cases be vertical, or nearly so, with body straight, feet together and toes pointed." In a head-first entry, arms are extended overhead with hands together; in a feet-first entry, arms are held tightly against the sides for ***streamlining.*** The less splash the better.

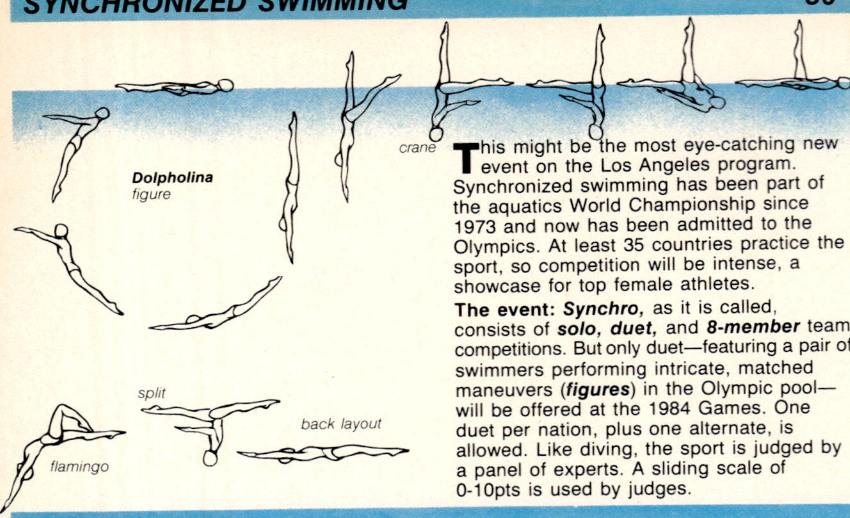

This might be the most eye-catching new event on the Los Angeles program. Synchronized swimming has been part of the aquatics World Championship since 1973 and now has been admitted to the Olympics. At least 35 countries practice the sport, so competition will be intense, a showcase for top female athletes.

The event: *Synchro,* as it is called, consists of ***solo, duet,*** and ***8-member*** team competitions. But only duet—featuring a pair of swimmers performing intricate, matched maneuvers (***figures***) in the Olympic pool—will be offered at the 1984 Games. One duet per nation, plus one alternate, is allowed. Like diving, the sport is judged by a panel of experts. A sliding scale of 0-10pts is used by judges.

WATER POLO

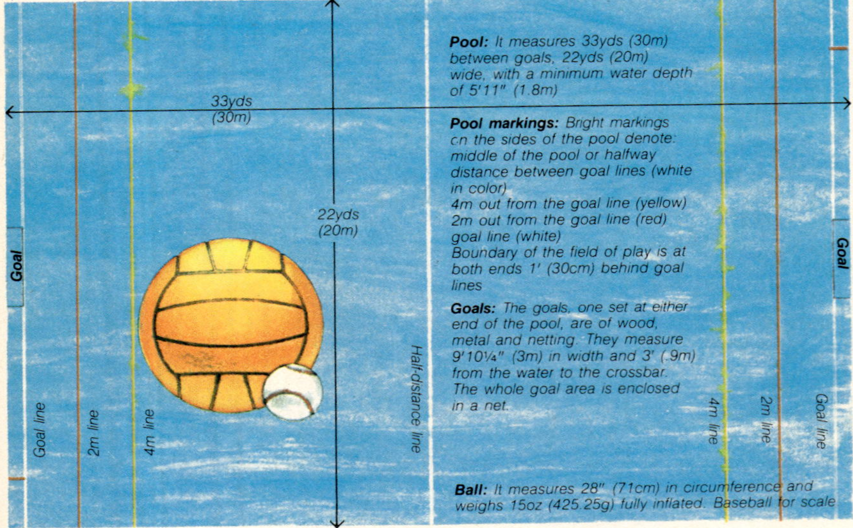

1980 Water Polo Champion
***Men only:* USSR**

For those not initiated to this most physical of aquatic contests, water polo is played by 7-man squads, or teams, in a relatively small area. The aim is simple, although the rules are not: to put an inflated ball through a small goal while preventing your opponent from doing the same. Some of the game's fine points:

It's against the rules for anyone but the goalkeeper to touch pool bottom, and international competition pools are usually too deep for that to happen. For 4 periods of play, battling for possession of the ball, players do nothing but ***swim.***

The ball must be propelled with 1 hand only and cannot be hit with a closed fist by anyone other than the goalie.

Advancement: Teams meet in a round-robin tournament, never meeting a team they have played previously. For each game, winners receive a score of 2pts; tieing teams are given 1pt; losers earn 0pts. Point total determines final standing.

With all the splashing that goes on, it won't be easy for televiewers to identify the various international stars. Exceptions to this may be such famed figures as **Gianni de Magistrio,** the Italian superstar, who has played in the last 3 Olympics.

Players: Six field players plus a **goalkeeper** make up a team. While each man is a specialist, all share scoring and defending responsibilities. ***Shooters*** specialize in scoring points. ***Holemen*** are the key members of a 6-man offensive formation, like the pivot-man in basketball. They operate directly in front of the enemy's goal and are under more physical attack than any other player. ***Drivers*** are the team's quickest swimmers, and they continually move, trying to get open for a shot at the goal. There are also ***defensive specialists.*** A team is allowed 6 substitutes.

As in other sports, the water polo referee's whistle stops the clock—but it certainly doesn't stop the action. Watch the burst of activity as the offense attempts to make a defensive player foul. For instance, an offensive player might try to capture a position closer to the goal, forcing the defender to foul while trying to protect this goal area. During this ***dead time*** (when the clock is stopped), a foul by the defense results in a 45sec ejection of the guilty player, beginning at the time the clock starts again. An offensive foul during dead time results in a personal foul being scored against the fouling player, but no ejection; ball possession goes to the other team.

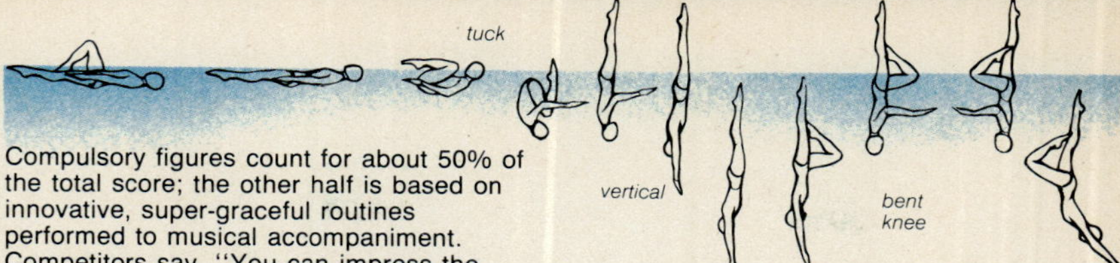

Compulsory figures count for about 50% of the total score; the other half is based on innovative, super-graceful routines performed to musical accompaniment. Competitors say, "You can impress the judges with your choreographed routines, but without doing as well or better in the compulsory figures, you don't win."

Water maneuvers: *Each of the figures has a name, such as* ***swordfish, porpoise, heron, albatross, catalina, castle*** *and* ***flamingo.*** *One of the most difficult maneuvers is a mixture of various basic figures called a* ***hybrid twist/spin.*** *This calls for a 360° spin followed by an 180° to a stop, then another 180° to a stop—with twists woven in to fill the breaks in action. And this is done with heads underwater at all times.*

Since synchro may require a swimmer to hold her breath for 30-40sec in some strenuous and difficult underwater moves, athletes do not like the comparison often made with ballet. The sport is better compared to figure skating and gymnastics. As much as half of the routine is performed upside-down in the pool, requiring the durability of a water poloist. Toughness must match beauty of body motion.

Rules: *Competitors cannot touch the bottom or sides of the pool at any time. Compulsory figures must be done without music. Any lack of grace or inability of duet swimmers to duplicate each other's actions (the* ***mirror*** *effect) counts against the team.*

Technique: *Treading water in the usual manner is not used, but a rotary kick, often called an* ***eggbeater,*** *borrowed from water polo, keeps the athletes afloat. For propulsion, sculling with the hands and with back muscles locked is used.*

WATER POLO

Santa Barbara ←
San Gabriel Mountains
5
Pepperdine University
Malibu
10
Coliseum
405
5
Long Beach
Distance from Coliseum: 32mi (51km)
San Diego ↘

Play: Only the goalie may handle the ball with 2 hands. Players must advance the sphere by ***carrying*** it in 1 hand while swimming, by ***passing*** or by ***dribbling*** (pushing the ball along the water's surface by creating waves with the head or chest). On a goal shot, any part of the body may be used except the clenched fist; passing has the same restriction.

Players don't merely tread water while never touching the bottom, but use an alternating breast stroke kick called the ***eggbeater.*** This enables them to rise up out of the water and, for a split-second, ***stand*** at hip height to the surface. Goalies, with a 3m goal to protect, may—within the 4m area in front of the goal—stand, walk or jump from the floor of the pool.

Substitutions may only take place after a goal, after a 3rd foul, or at the interval between periods.

Game duration: *4 periods of 7min each are played, with 2min rest intervals between periods. Teams change ends of the pool before starting a new period.*

Officials: 2 **referees** work each game, along with one **goal judge** at each goal, **timekeepers** and **secretaries.**

Fouls

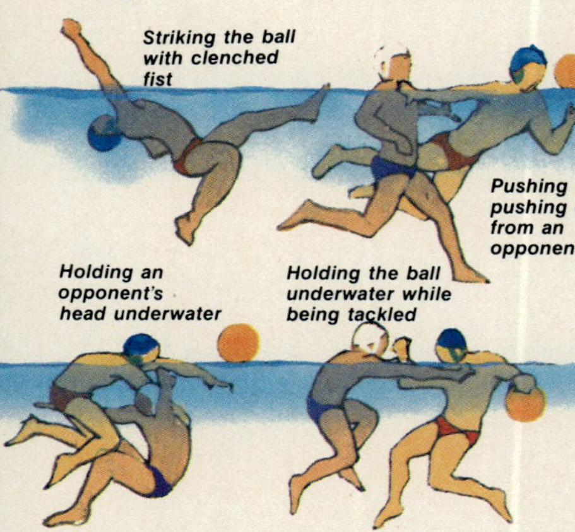

Other fouls: *wasting time, faking a foul, touching ball with 2 hands.*

Equipment: *One team wears blue caps and the other white caps. The 2 goalies wear red caps with a No. 1 designation. Caps of the others are numbered 2-13 (teams are allowed to carry 6 reserves). Caps are fitted with malleable ear protectors and tied under the chin to guard the eardrums from the damaging combination of a waterfilled ear canal and a blow to the head. Double (2 sets) of trunks are worn. Grease or any other oil on the body is banned.*

Shot clock: *Water polo has a time limit—a team can't retain possession of the ball for more than 35sec without making a goal-shot try. If the rule is violated, the opposing team is awarded a free throw from the point of foul.*

Penalties: *Hard to detect because of their often submarine nature, fouls are classified as* ***ordinary*** *or* ***major.*** *Ordinary fouls include impeding or preventing free movement of an opponent, unless he's holding the ball; standing on the bottom of the pool; striking the ball with a clenched fist; splashing an opponent in the face. Major violations, including kicking, clubbing, holding, sinking (submerging) and elbowing, can earn a player 45sec in the penalty area, ejection from the game with substitution for* ***disrespect****—or ejection from the game with no substitution in the case of* ***brutality*** *fouls.*

Penalty throws: *These are awarded when an opponent illegally:*

kicks or strikes *a man within the 4m area*
commits a brutal act *inside the 4m area*
commits a foul *within the 4m area and prevents a goal*
pulls down a goal
uses 2 hands *to defend*

Watch for defenders to continually switch off the opponents they are covering. This is because persistence in ordinary fouls (usually fouling a man 3 or more times in a row) results in ejection from the game. Trading coverage prevents defensive players from being called for this penalty.

THE TRACK

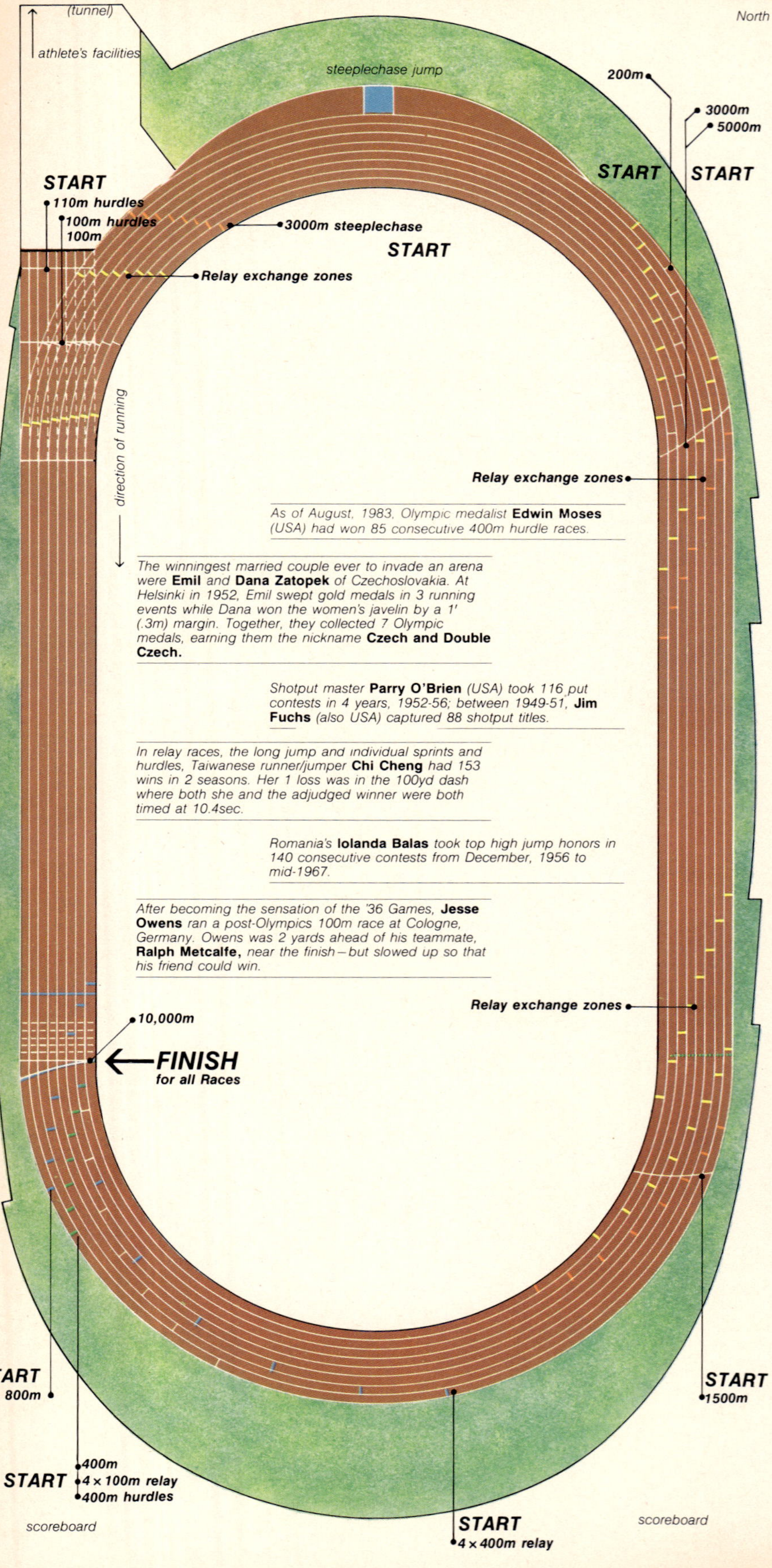

(tunnel)

athlete's facilities

North

steeplechase jump

200m

3000m

5000m

START

START

START

110m hurdles

100m hurdles

100m

3000m steeplechase

START

Relay exchange zones

direction of running

Relay exchange zones

As of August, 1983, Olympic medalist **Edwin Moses** *(USA) had won 85 consecutive 400m hurdle races.*

The winningest married couple ever to invade an arena were **Emil** *and* **Dana Zatopek** *of Czechoslovakia. At Helsinki in 1952, Emil swept gold medals in 3 running events while Dana won the women's javelin by a 1' (.3m) margin. Together, they collected 7 Olympic medals, earning them the nickname* **Czech and Double Czech.**

Shotput master **Parry O'Brien** *(USA) took 116 put contests in 4 years, 1952-56; between 1949-51,* **Jim Fuchs** *(also USA) captured 88 shotput titles.*

In relay races, the long jump and individual sprints and hurdles, Taiwanese runner/jumper **Chi Cheng** *had 153 wins in 2 seasons. Her 1 loss was in the 100yd dash where both she and the adjudged winner were both timed at 10.4sec.*

Romania's **Iolanda Balas** *took top high jump honors in 140 consecutive contests from December, 1956 to mid-1967.*

After becoming the sensation of the '36 Games, **Jesse Owens** *ran a post-Olympics 100m race at Cologne, Germany. Owens was 2 yards ahead of his teammate,* **Ralph Metcalfe,** *near the finish—but slowed up so that his friend could win.*

Relay exchange zones

10,000m

FINISH
for all Races

START
800m

START
400m
4 × 100m relay
400m hurdles

START
1500m

START
4 × 400m relay

scoreboard

scoreboard

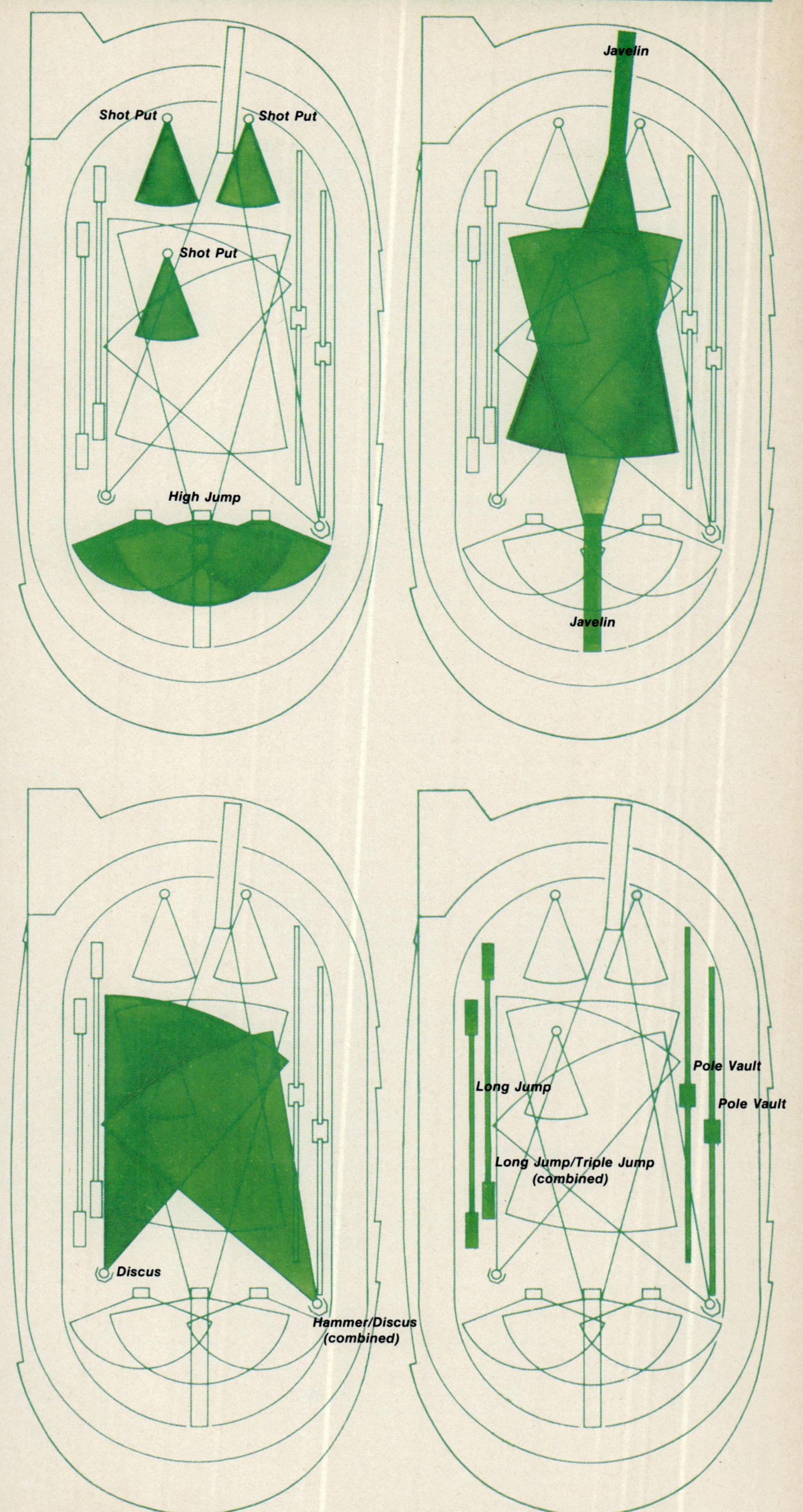
Shot Put
Shot Put
Shot Put
High Jump
Javelin
Javelin
Discus
Hammer/Discus (combined)
Long Jump
Long Jump/Triple Jump (combined)
Pole Vault
Pole Vault

SPRINTS

Olympic 100 Meter Record
Men: 9.95sec (**Jimmy Hines,** USA, 1968)
Women: 11.01sec (**Annegret Richter,** FRG, 1976)

So tightly matched are the earth's fastest mortals that most Olympic *centuries* are decided by a few inches. At top speed, athletes move at 27-plus mph (43 or more km/hr). Although **Jimmy Hines'** 9.95, set in Mexico City's thin air, remains the Olympic record, **Bob Hayes'** 10.0 at the 1964 Tokyo Games is rated superior. Hayes also ran 9.9 in a Tokyo heat.

"Sprinters can't get much faster," scientists say. Yet they said that in 1956 when **Bobby Morrow** of Texas was Olympic champ with a time of 10.5. Faster tracks, paper-light shoes and the advent of *human bullets* from the tropical nations of Trinidad, Jamaica, Cuba and Panama—as well as those from the USA and USSR—have surpassed Morrow's mark.

Olympic 200 Meter Record
Men: 19.83sec (**Tommie Smith,** USA, 1968)
Women: 22.03sec (**Barbel Wockel,** GDR, 1980)

Similar to the 100m, the *Olympic furlong* differs in that it is run around a turn from a staggered start so that all runners cover the same distance.

Strategy: *Time lost on the curve is calculated at .4sec per 100 meters. To save ground, sprinters run as close to the inside of their 4' (1.22m) lanes as possible. They also lean inward to counteract the centrifugal force generated around a turn. The 200m racers need more stamina than their 100m colleagues, although 7 men have won the 100m and 200m in the same Games. The finish burst occurs at about 40m from the tape.*

Parts of the race: *the* ***start, acceleration, stride*** *and* ***finish.*** *Of these, the start is the most important—but the finish, or* ***gather,*** *is a close second.*

Placement of feet *in starting blocks varies by individual preference and leg length. The shortest spacing between front and back footplates is 11" (28cm); the longest is 21-26" (53-66cm). A* ***bunch*** *start clears the blocks sooner, but a longer spacing is thought to deliver more leg drive and early velocity.*

The starter gives 2 verbal commands *with sufficient spacing between them to accommodate all runners:* ***On your mark! Set!*** *He then fires his pistol. On false starts, the recall starter, a backup official, fires a gun to stop and return the field to the starting line. One false start (beating the starter's gun) brings a warning; 2 such starts mean disqualification.*

The start *combines powerful rear-leg thrust with an upwhipping action of the opposite arm. Body lean is extreme until full acceleration is reached after about 20 strides.*

Acceleration *is all high knee action, with arms pumping to chin height and a lessened body lean. Maximum velocity is reached about 6sec after the start.*

Full stride *is a shifting of gears. The sprinter is more erect, increases on-the-toes knee lift, and is powered by rear-leg drive. (An 8' stride—2.43m—has been attained by the fastest tall sprinters.) The racer is on his toes at all times.*

The ***gather*** *or finish begins about 15yds (13m) from the finish line. The stride is slightly shortened, lean is accentuated, arm-churn increased and chest and shoulders hurled forward in the final strides.*

Starter's gun: *The popular model is a revolver that uses loud-fire .32 caliber blanks. An electronic sound-sensing device, mounted on the gun, reacts to the sound of the starting shot, as do the athletes, and activates the timing system for the race.*

Cheat detector: *Sprinters are prevented from anticipating the gun and starting a split second before the gun's crack by sensing devices placed in the starting blocks. An electric switch is held open by the normal pressure of the runner's feet. If he exerts more pressure—as he would in a false start—before the starting group, an electronic beeper in the starter's headsets signals the irregularity.*

Starting blocks: *Made of aluminum or other metals, the blocks have a measuring gauge to allow the runners to place them precisely according to their tastes, and a lock-in gadget to immobilize them. Cost: $65 to $75.*

Shoes: *Little more than ballet slippers with spikes in the soles, they weigh about 6oz (170g) and are made of calfskin, glove leather or kangaroo hide. Spikes are limited to ⅓" (8.4mm) in length. Soles cannot exceed ½" (13mm) thickness, heels cannot exceed soles in thickness by more than ¼" (6mm). Racers may compete barefoot—but seldom do.*

Electronics: *Obviously, accurate timing mechanisms are critical in sprints and other events. Signals from video cameras at the finish line start their own race—through computers, recording devices, electronic and fiber-optic transmitters, through encoders and decoders, even to satellites in orbit and back—to be seen on screens around the world in less time than it takes to win the 200m (see below).*

Determining winners: Photo-finish cameras help judges decide how runners have finished. International Amateur Athletic Federation Rule 162 (Olympics Rules 12) states: ***"Competitors shall be placed in the order in which any part of their bodies (i.e. torso, as distinguished from the head, neck, arms, legs, hands or feet) reaches the vertical planes of the nearer edge of the finish line."*** It is the torso—chest to waist—which is the decisive factor. The man whose upper body first reaches the ***vertical plane*** is the victor. Getting a shoulder (***shrug*** finish), a head or neck across first does not beat the torso-first principle. Watch for extreme upper-body lean.

Precision timing, *from starting blocks to photofinishes, has added a new dimension to sports. When* ***G. Drat*** *(FRA) took the 1976 110m hurdles by 3/100sec over* ***A. Casanas*** *(CUB), instruments showed that Drat had started 135/1000sec after the gun; Casanas took 223/1000sec to react. Casanas actually covered the distance faster, but Drat's quick start gave him the winning edge.*

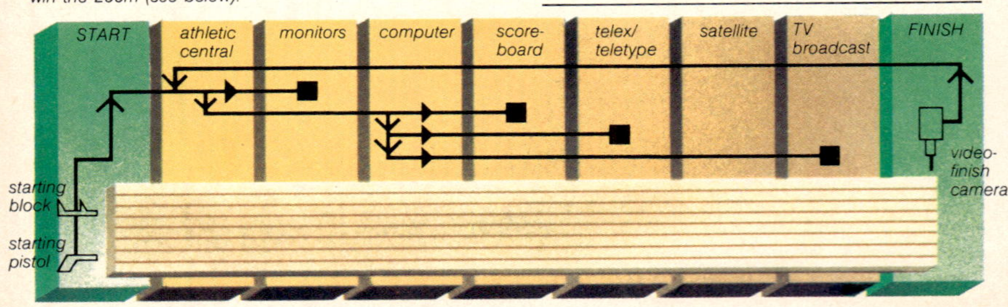

Olympic 400 Meter Record
Men: 43.86sec (**Lee Evans,** USA, 1968)
Women: 48.88sec (**Marita Koch,** GDR, 1980)

An ***endurance sprint,*** the 400 meter may be the most demanding of track contests. In the days when a 47sec clocking would win, the 400 was considered a middle-distance event. But taller men who could go full blast for a full lap of the track turned the 400 into a continuous dash with no ***float*** or breather along the way. The old sprint-float-sprint pattern fell before such greats as **Arthur Wint** and **George Rhoden** (JAM), **Otis Davis** (USA) and other great runners in the 1940-60s.

Only 1/500th of a second *separated gold medalist* **Otis Davis** *(USA, 44.9) from silver medal winner* **Carl Kaufmann** *(FRG, 44.9) in the 1960 400m final. Deciding with the aid of an electric timing device, judges awarded the medal to Davis.*

Strategy: *The 400 is run from* ***staggered starts.*** *The first 50-60yds (46-55m) are spent in acceleration. Momentum is sustained while racing is as relaxed as possible, at a speed just below that of 200m flat speed for the first half of the race. The decisive test comes at 300m, when the mythical* ***bear*** *jumps on the racer's back as fatigue sets in.*
From there on, it's a matter of courage in dealing with that animal for the final 100 meters.

Knee lift is lower *and arm-whipping less pronounced than at 100m and 200m.*

Most 400 runners *hope to draw lanes* ***1, 2,*** *or* ***3.*** *This places them on the inside of the track, behind those in the outer lanes, and they can see the field* ***coming back to them*** *as the stagger effect takes place. It's more difficult to pace yourself from the front lanes without your opponent as a point of reference.*

Speed: *The aim is to run the 1st and 2nd 200m in close to the same time. However, the first half is usually covered 2-3 seconds faster than the last half—due to the effects of the bear.*

HURDLES

Olympic 100 Meter Hurdles Record
Women only: 12.56sec (**Vera Komisova,** USSR, 1980)

Olympic 110 Meter Hurdles Record
Men only: 13.24sec (**Rod Milburn,** USA, 1972)

Hurdlers don't just jump the barriers in their way—they *step* over them with such fluid grace that great champions cover the 100m and 110m in only 2 seconds more than it takes to sprint the distance without hurdles. They spend only about 1/5sec over each barrier.

IAAF officials dropped the 80m hurdles for women after 1972, replacing the event with the 100m hurdles. Female hurdlers clear 10 33″ (83.82cm) fences; males must maneuver over 10 42″ (106.68cm) barriers. Otherwise the races are alike.

These events are famous for exciting finishes. The USA's **Lee Calhoun** and **Jack Davis** were both timed at 13.5sec in one year's Olympic final. In another Games final, **Guy Drut** of France lost to **Rod Milburn,** USA, by a margin of .1sec (13.24 to 13.34). Nowhere are photo-finish judges kept busier.

Olympic 400 Meter Hurdles Record
Men: 47.64sec (**Edwin Moses,** USA, 1976)
Women: New event

To win the 400m, runners must cruise an approximate quarter-mile over 10 flights of 36″ (91.44cm) hurdles—and they must do it at a speed not much over 400m flat dash running. In 1984, women will join men in running this grueling race, a specialist's event which demands ability to hurdle with either lead leg as well as top speed.

Technique: *With body leaning low, the hurdler fires his flexed lead leg over the barrier while the folded-flat trailing leg begins to move past the lead leg. Lead leg is snapped down sharply to the ground, saving time; arms are both forward.*

Running between hurdles: *A sprint action is resumed after clearance and repeated after each hurdle is surmounted. Arms pump.*

Power finish: *Quick recovery after the last hurdle determines how fast a man can burst into a true sprint to the wire.*

Watch heads and shoulders. Hurdlers who keep their ***center of gravity*** flat and even are using energy efficiently.

Procedure: *From* ***staggered starts****, the race is in lanes all the way, including 2 turns of the track. Runners in inside lanes (****1, 2*** *and* ***3****) have an unavoidable advantage since they can judge their pace by the runners in front of them.*

Clearing the hurdle *is almost the same in style as in the other 2 hurdle events, except there is less body lean. In a crouch start, the trailing leg is placed in the front block. From 15 to 21 strides are needed to reach the first obstacle. After that,* ***13 to 15 strides between hurdles is average.*** *A 13-stride pattern of 8′ (2.43m) to the stride has won in the Olympics. But very great 400 hurdlers vary the tempo. World record holder* ***Ed Moses,*** *USA, often ran 15 strides to the 6th hurdle, ran 14 between the 7th and 8th barriers and 13 strides to the finish. Modern synthetic-surface tracks enable runners to lengthen their stride.* ***Alternating lead legs is tricky****—only the best can do it and not lose velocity.*

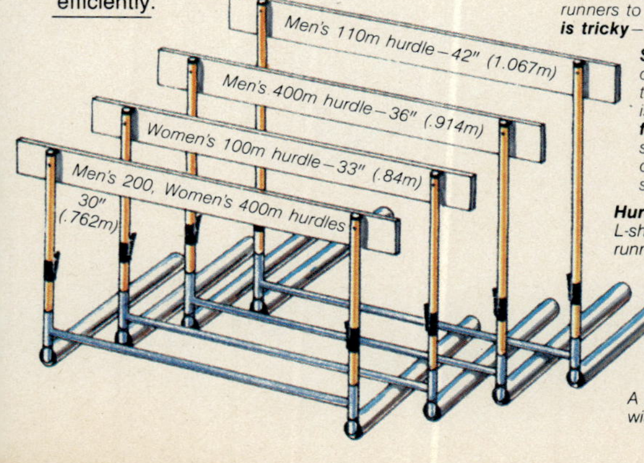

Strategy: *Loss of time around curves is countered by taking the hurdle to the inside of the lane with strong body lean. An even pace is a smart tactic. At 300m or more,* ***anaerobic fatigue*** *(exhaustion in absence of oxygen supply) sets in. Hurdlers at this extended distance save something for the final 40m spurt.*

Hurdles *are set in lanes and are engineered in an L-shape so that they swing down when hit by the runner, preventing injury.*

Each athlete must ***keep to his lane*** *throughout the race.*

An unlimited number of ***hurdles may be knocked down*** *without disqualification.*

A man who ***trails one leg alongside*** *any hurdle without truly clearing it is disqualified.*

Olympic Steeplechase Record
Men only: 8:08.02 (**Anders Garderud,** SWE, 1976)

One small slip in this distance race can mean disaster. In the 1976 Olympics, East Germany's **Frank Baumgartl** had pulled even with the leader on the next-to-last hurdle when his lead foot hit the obstacle's crossbar. Baumgartl went sprawling on the track. Rising shaken, he valiantly resumed running and finished 3rd—but the big medal was gone.

George Young, one of the very few Olympic steeplechasers from the USA, was closing on 1st place at the 1960 Rome Games with 330yds (302m) to go in a qualifying heat when he failed to clear the last hurdle. "I was badly torn up, a bloody mess, when I got up," Young remembers. His courageous sprint to the finish line just missed a placing position and Young was out of the Games.

Anything can happen in the ***steeple.*** It's just 240yds (219m) short of 2mi (3.22km). Only the most agile endurance runners need apply. The stride is interrupted by obstacles so many times that rhythm is easily lost.

Procedure: *The contest covers* ***7 laps*** *of the track. There are* ***28 hurdles,*** *each 3' (.914m) high, scattered around the course, plus* ***7 water jumps,*** *for a total of* ***35*** *obstacles. From the race's start at mid-straightaway to the beginning of the first lap, no hurdles are jumped. The hurdles are placed after the field has passed. Competitors bypass the water jump on this lap.*

At the 280m mark, the 1st hurdle is encountered. Successive hurdles are set 85yds (78m) apart. Following the 3rd hurdle comes the 1st water jump. The same water obstacle must be cleared on each lap (7 times). From the final hurdle to the finish line it's about a 75yd (69m) sprint.

Technique: *Steeplers divide the event into 3 phases:* ***hurdling, water negotiating*** *and* ***between-hurdle technique.***

Hurdling: *Except for the water jump, most use the same straight-over stride used in regular hurdling. They must be able to lead with either leg, for when weariness sets in after a mile or so, stride length tends to vary and perfect body mechanics become impossible.*

Water jump: *This is the 4th jump on each lap of the track. The water gradually slopes up to track level at the farthest end of the obstacle. The hazard has a concrete base, with a web matting surface, to enable feet to grip.*

Water negotiating: *This requires a technique very different than no-water hurdling and is the most crucial part of the race. Because the runner doesn't want to land in the deep end where the water is nearly hip-high, he needs to maintain his forward thrust above and beyond the hurdle guarding the water jump. These requirements are best met by making a gymnastic leap to land with the lead foot atop the bar. Several critical movements are:*

The lead (usually right) foot's instep comes down flatly on the bar. This is called the ***prop leg*** *and it provides balance and thrust.*

Landing is done from a ***bent-back position*** *with as little standing up on the rail as possible.*

As the prop leg straightens, the ***trailing leg*** *follows it, skimming close over the rail. As the trailer advances, the prop foot slips over the edge of the rail and pushes off with full force – launching the leap into the water.*

With ***arms widespread*** *for balance, the landing leg hits the drink fully extended. World-class steeplers are able to splash water 9-10' (2.7-3m) from the top bar takeoff in about 8" (20cm) of water. One stride takes the steepler out of the water and back into track-racing stride. The entire action is smoothly coordinated. To avoid slips, the hurdler focuses on the bar as he appoaches.*

A runner may clear any hurdle in any of 3 ways: ***jumping, hand vaulting over,*** *or* ***landing with a foot on the top bar and pushing off.*** *However, he must go over the barrier and over and through the water without stepping aside or trailing a leg alongside any hurdle.*

Dry Hurdles: *The 3' (.914m) barriers are a formidable challenge. They're solidly set on 4'7" (1.4m) bases and weigh 220½lbs (100kg). The black-and-white striped bar is 5" (13cm) square. Hit it hard and a runner can break a foot or leg.*

Vaulting *a hurdle is a desperation move.* **George Young** *(USA) once got into a pushing match with a Soviet runner, was knocked out of stride, had to hand-vault a hurdle and lost a fatal 10yds (9.2m).*

Shoes: *They get soaked, so the spiked footwear of steeplers features 1/8" (.32cm) perforations on both sides from toe to arch to provide water-drainage.*

Watch for changes in style as the race progresses and fatigue sets in.

RELAYS

Olympic 4×100-Meter Relay Record
Men: 38.19sec (USA, 1972)
Women: 41.60sec (GDR, 1980)

The main concern in relays is **not** dropping the baton. In a tragic bobble-and-drop at the 1968 Games, the USSR team eliminated itself. In 1960, the USA was disqualified for an illegal baton-pass.

Procedure: *In the 400m, each member of the national team runs roughly a quarter of the total distance. The race is run entirely in lanes from staggered starts.*

Order of runners: *National thinking varies, but in general:*

No. 1 *man is the team's* ***quickest starter*** *and a skilled curve-negotiator.*

No. 2 *is slick at baton-exchange and* ***fast down a straight.***

No. 3 *may be the slowest of the 4, but a* ***good curve runner.***

No. 4 *is the anchor and the team's* ***fastest member,*** *with a great winning* ***kick.***

Two passing techniques *are used – the* ***upward thrust*** *of the baton by No. 1 into No. 2's hand, which is held with palm inward and thumb separated from the fingers, or the* ***downward thrust,*** *where the palm is held upward and a thumb-fingers V formed. Exchanges are made at full extension of both runner's arms and at hip height.*

What to watch for: Watch the baton ***receivers*** as they time their starts to match velocity with incoming partners.

Relay zones: *In the baton exchange, the dream of every coach is that the incoming runner will arrive at top speed and the outgoing runner (receiver) will take off at the split second needed to match the speed of the former. Two all-important exchange zones are involved:*

–10m acceleration *zone in which the outgoing runner stands and begins his or her run. The baton may not be passed in this clearly marked area.*

–20m takeover (exchange) zone. *The outgoing runner sprints from the 10m zone into the 20m zone and within the latter the pass is made. Matched velocity of the 2 teammates is attained here.* ***Any pass beyond the 20m restraining line means disqualification.***

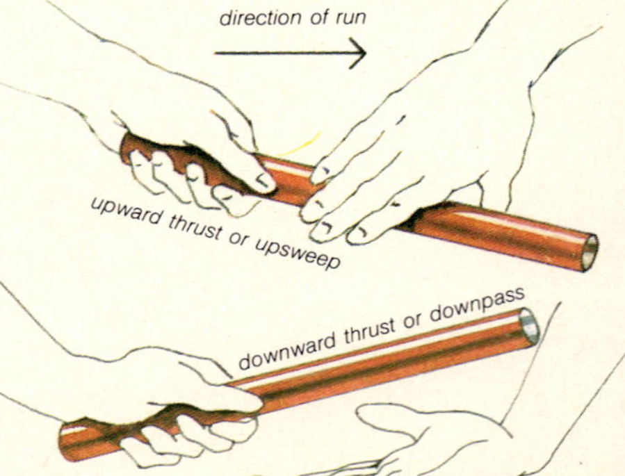

Baton: *11-11¾" (28-30cm) long and made of aluminum or alloy, it must be carried in one hand; if dropped, it must be recovered by the athlete who dropped it. Weight is 50oz (1.4kg). Batons are hollow and colored for visibility.*

Olympic 4×400 Relay Record
Men: 2:56.16 (USA, 1968)
Women: 3:19.23 (GDR, 1976)

The American men's relay team of **Vince Matthews, Ron Freeman, Larry James** and **Lee Evans,** which set the existing world record 15 years ago, may have been the greatest collection of quarter-milers ever assembled. They averaged about 400m per 44sec, or close to the world mark for 400m flat racing. The 4×400 relay askes each runner to cover one lap around the track, handing off the baton at each 400m mark. A 20m exchange zone is used.

Procedure: *Unlike the sprint relay previously described, this one is run in lanes, but only by the 1st runner, and by the 2nd runner only as far as his or her exit from the first curve. From there, runners are free to take any lane position available if they cause no obstruction.*

Because a 400m dash is so fatiguing, *the receiver of a baton after the no-lanes rule begins to operate must be especially alert. He or she must judge in which lane the incoming teammate will arrive, as well as the final speed. Runners come pouring in with much lane cross over and it's easy to commit a foul.*

Strategy: *Many teams pull a switch on 4x100-relay procedure by starting their fastest, strongest-bodied member first and not last. In this longer relay, in most cases, the No. 1 runner runs about 2m more than the No. 4 anchor. The idea is to build a lead and hold it.*

Rapport: *Forging a strong bond, the team shares the dream of an Olympic gold medal—and each winning team's member is awarded a gold at the victory ceremony.*

800-METER RUN

Olympic 800 Meter Record
Men: 1:43.50 (**Alberto Juantorena,** CUB, 1976)
Women: 1:53.43 (**Nadyezhda Olizaryenko,** USSR, 1980)

There's no better test of all-around running ability than the metric half-mile. It combines a 400m runner's speed with a miler's stamina, and it is too short to forgive mistakes. It can get pretty rough as a result. Unlike events contested in lanes, this is a free track battle. Elbow and hip jabs are exchanged while jostling for position, making the 800m a race for survival (and judges are reluctant to call fouls in the go-for-broke Olympics).

Olympic Firsts: 1928, Amsterdam *Women first allowed full competitive status in track & field events.*

Procedure: *The race is run for* ***2*** *laps around the track from staggered starts. Lanes are used only until the end of the 1st turn is reached. Then the runners break for the pole (inside lane), seeking the shortest route.*

Strategy: *Avoiding the lead is a primary rule. Pacesetters act as windbreaks for the others, and worse, can't see a rival spurting to pass. Other strategies include:*
Never passing on the turns*—going wide eats up energy. Mostly, passing is relegated to the straightaways.*
When following a strong leader, *never letting him get more than 10m ahead.*
Staying alert to being jumped *(suddenly passed).*
If jumping, *making the move quickly and stealthily, with quiet footsteps.*
If the other runners play rough *with elbows and body, trading blows with them—not being intimidated.*
Kick finish: *In the last 80-100m, great runners have enough energy left to stage a* ***kick****, or final sprint. Champions can flog themselves into covering the last 200m in 23sec or so—a feat unheard of in the 1970s.*

1500-METER RUN

Olympic 1500 Meter Record:
Men: 3:34.91 (**Kip Keino,** KEN, 1968)
Women: 3:56.58 (**Tatyana Kazankina,** USSR, 1980)

The metric mile is the classic Olympic duel. Legendary male milers include: **Paavo Nurmi** (FIN), **John Landy** (AUS), **Peter Snell** (NZL), **Jim Ryun** (USA), and **Kip Keino** (KEN). When Landy set a world mark of 3:41.3 just over 25 years ago, astounded fans thought the record would stand for a long time. But **Steve Ovett's** (GBR) current world record of 3:31.36 makes Landy's shining mark look dim by comparison.

White is boxed in—runners to the front, side and rear hamper maneuverability

What to watch for: Runners jockey for position in the 800- and 1500-meter runs. Getting boxed in during these events can cost precious seconds; watch runners maneuvering to avoid this trap.

Procedure: *The race consists of* ***4*** *laps around a 400m track. The* ***start*** *is at the head of the backstretch, down a straightaway. Finalists (usually 12 or so runners) begin from a* ***curl*** *or* ***waterfall*** *start setup, designed so that competitors on the inside have no great advantage over outside-laners. A sprint for inside position starts the 1500m, after which a single file emerges—until jockeying for an edge begins. The 1500m world record of 3:31.36 is about equivalent to a 3:49.90 mile, or average laps of about 57.5sec.*

The 1500 *has its own esoteric language:*
Positional Running *is staying behind the leader or leaders, finding an unimpeded route and gradually improving position as the race unfolds.*
Oxygen debt *refers to the ability of the heart and bloodstream to deliver enough oxygen to sustain the effort. World-class milers amaze doctors with tremendous* ***stroke volume*** *(amount of blood pumped per heartbeat) and pulse rates as low as 28 per minute.*
Shock treatment *means suddenly stepping up the race's pace while holding the lead or passing the field—a demoralizing maneuver for the other runners.*

There are golden rules in the 1500:

Have a stopwatch in your head and ***know your splits*** *(split times, or time each portion of the race has required) at 400, 800 and 1200m to the second.*

Lie slightly back off the pace and make your challenge of the frontrunners as ***late as possible,*** *leaving them too few meters in which to respond.*

Don't stay in a ***box*** *(surrounded)—sprint your way out.*

The ***finishing kick*** *comes sooner in the 1500m than in the 800m, sometimes with 300m or more to go. When passed, it's standard strategy to move out from the track's curb and take position on the right shoulder of the runner who went by, to prevent others from moving up and boxing you from the side and front.*

A runner must be ***2 full strides*** *ahead of a man he's passed before cutting back to the pole (inside) lane.*

Wild arm-swinging *is prohibited.*

Grabbing a vest or shirt, *even accidentally, can mean disqualification.*

In 1947 and 1948, ***Harrison Dillard*** *(USA) took 82 consecutive sprints and hurdle races.*

3-5-10,000-METER RUNS

Olympic 5000 Meter Record
Men only: 13:20.34 (**Brendan Foster**, GBR, 1976)

Olympic 10,000 Meter Record
Men only: 27:38.35 (**Lasse Viren**, FIN, 1972)

When you look upon these masters of stamina, you're seeing runners who—if their careers have lasted 10 years—have run twice the distance around the world or more in training. A conditioning routine of 100-200mi (161-322km) per week has forged them into Olympians.

Distance running is a battle against oxygen debt, a matter of having the heart and guts to overcome the main reason for fatigue—buildup of *lactic acid* in the body cells. This can be combated only by a fanatical desire to win, expressed in the toughest practice regimen in sports. Whereas one gulp of air will last a sprinter for 100m (about 110yds), at 5000m (3.1mi) it's 90% inhalation against 10% oxygen reserve.

The fatigue barrier runners must overcome is called the ***bear.*** After a few miles and enough gain in debilitating lactic acid, runners say, *"the bear jumped on my back."* This happens when the runner has called upon his **anaerobic** energy resources by traveling faster than his **aerobic** system can produce energy.

In 1984, a long distance run has been added to women's Olympic events: the 3,000m (1.86mi).

Procedure: *The 2 men's runs are so similar that Olympic runners often enter both. But only 7 men in history have won both the* **5** *and* **10** *in the Games, the last being* **Miruts Yifter** *of Ethiopia in 1980.* **Lasse Viren** *of Finland scored a* ***double*** *in both 1972 and 1976 – 4 gold medals! The 5000m run covers 12.5 laps of the 400m track; the 10,000m is 25 laps. The new women's 3000m is 7.5 times around the track.*

Strategy: *Most competitors have a predetermined race plan:*

Sprint for the lead at the start and seize it. *Advantages: less jostling; running the inside, shorter lane. Disadvantage: acting as a windbreak for those behind.*

Take a position in the middle of the field. *Advantages: a good view of what's going on ahead when the runner makes his move, and windsheltering. Disadvantages: getting jostled and boxed in.*

Run from the rear. *Advantages: energy-saving pace, opportunity to gradually pass others as the field strings out; good timing of the finishing* ***kick.*** *Disadvantage: Running in last place is a psychological minus.*

Today's trend is to race in the middle of the pack.

In the final straightaway, *a runner must stay in the same lane unless there is a runner directly in front, in which case he can go around the obstructor inside or outside; but* ***he must not interfere with any other contestant.***

The finish **kick** is the decisive factor in most races. Timing is vital. To sprint the final distance after going 3-6mi (4.82-9.66km) is an awesome feat—with the final lap of a 5000m race sometimes done in 55-60sec.

MARATHON

Olympic Marathon Record
Men: 2:09:55 (**Waldemar Cierpinski**, GDR, 1976)

This most grueling test of stamina has been won in the Olympics by an Argentinean newsboy who ran his paper route to develop his leg muscles, a Finnish sewing-machine salesman, a French auto mechanic, an Ethiopian army sergeant and a Czech freedom-fighter. It's been won by a Buenos Aires fireman, age 30, who trained by running to blazes behind his fire truck.

The 26-mile-plus run has more glamour attached to it than anything on the Olympics track & field program. It is the spectacle of supreme athletes pushing themselves to the absolute limit of physical endurance—what marathoners call ***red-lining.*** This race is over 4 times longer than the next most demanding Olympic run, the 10,000 meter, and it's run in the varied terrain of city streets. A Portuguese runner died after one Olympic marathon, and hundreds of others have collapsed in their tracks.

Women's Marathon

The IOC has added the women's marathon to the 1984 Olympics roster, but the first female marathoner ran, unofficially, in 1896 at Athens, turning in a time just under 4½hrs. Women runners have been exploding marathon time barriers ever since. In 1964 **Dale Grieg Ryde** (GBR) broke the 3½hr mark. Twenty years later a full hour has been whittled from the old records—watch for a 2:25:00 or better in the first Olympic running of the women's marathon.

Hazards: Dehydration *– loss of body fluid through perspiration and lung evaporation can amount to more than 10% of a 140lb (63.5kg) runner's body weight, or over 14lbs (6.35kg) in 26mi.*

Heat *– because of increased skin blood flow, runners can't lose heat efficiently. World-class marathoners can tolerate a body temperature up to 40°C (104°F). But above that comes heat stroke.*

Equipment: *Most go* ***bareheaded*** *to allow heat to escape from the head. Others wear* ***visors, hats*** *or* ***caps – popping ice cubes*** *under a cap and letting the melt drip down is a favored tactic.* ***Net vests,*** *or singlets, are highly perforated for ventilation. Nylon* ***shorts*** *are the briefest possible to prevent chafing. White is preferred because it reflects sunlight. Some runners have pockets sewn in their briefs for carrying spare shoelaces, candy, tissue paper, etc.*

Shoes *are the paramount item for marathoners. Special spikeless racing flats weighing 7.8-8.8oz (220-250g) and with heel cushions built up ¾" (1.9cm) are most widely used. A wide, stable heel prevents* ***rear shift*** *of the shoe. Some runners use soles with 75 or so* ***waffles*** *built in for traction. Top-drawer shoes run $40-$50.*

Marathon route elevations

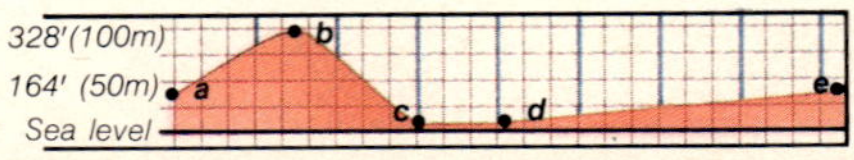

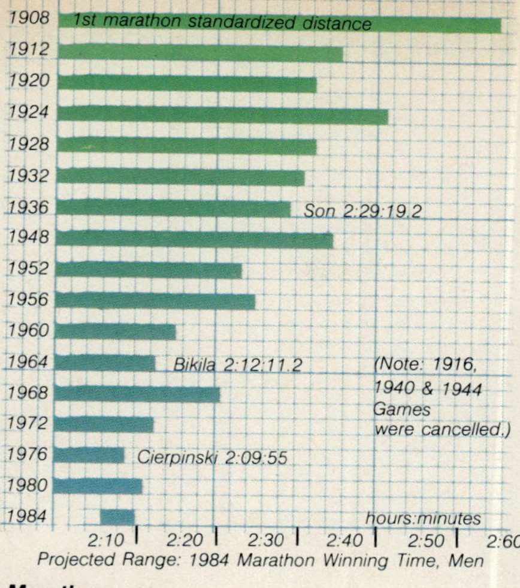

Projected Range: 1984 Marathon Winning Time, Men

Marathon
km mi

Start — Santa Monica College
1mi — 5:00 — 4:54
5km
The Bear
5mi — 25:00 — 24:15
10km
15km
10mi — 50:00
20km
15mi — 1:15
25km
30km
20mi — 1:40 — 1:37:29
35km
40km
25mi
Finish: Memorial Coliseum 26mi 285yds (42.195km)
2:11:06
2:08:13

Procedure: *This is a contest where the international TV audience sees all of the race and the live audience sees only the start and finish (other than on in-stadium screens). Seventy or more contestants usually start within the main stadium, make one lap of the track and head out a gate or tunnel into the adjacent city streets. At the 1984 Games, however, the field will take off at* ***Santa Monica College,*** *wend along the Pacific Ocean (to beat the expected hot weather), and loop eastward to finish at the L.A. Coliseum. Women will run on Sunday, August 5th; the men's marathon finish is part of the closing ceremonies on the following Sunday, August 12.*

Strategy, technique: *Individualism prevails—each runner adheres to a pre-set plan as to speed and placement in the pack. Some strive for an early lead to avoid bumping; others hang well back. Normally, a* ***lead pack*** *of 15-20 favorites forms at 4-5mi (6-8km) out. By 10mi (16km), the pacesetting group may have 10-12 runners. Thereafter, the frontrunners diminish in number as the field strings out over many city blocks and some runners drop out.*

Pace: *The main component of strategy, pace (speed of progress) is often determined by a runner who picks a realistic time goal and sets as even a pace over each section as possible to keep on schedule for that goal. In the last 25% of the marathon, the runner begins to* ***pick up*** *(pass) opponents as his pace increases. If he can step up the pace and hold it, he might come in first.*

What constitutes a winning pace? Some guidelines:

For the world-record pace, ***2:08:13,*** *set by* ***Alberto Salazar*** *(USA) in 1981, the average per mile must be* ***4min 54sec.*** *Some of Salazar's record run splits are shown left (red dots). Splits for a steady pace of* ***5min*** *per mile are also shown (green dots). A* ***2:11:06*** *would be the finish time at the 5min/mile pace—just about equal to the winning Olympic time in 1980 (2:11:03, Cierpinski).*

Crowd control: *More than a million people are expected to line the marathon route at the Games. Crowd control will be tight, with streets blocked off, motorcycle patrols preceding runners and TV trucks and the whole course secured for maximum protection from interference.*

What to watch for: The average per-mile pace to render a 2:10:00 marathon is 4:57. And a 2:10 could come close to winning the 1984 Olympic gold medal.

20 & 50-KILOMETER WALKS

Olympic 20-Kilometer Walk Record
Men only: 1:23:35.5 (**Maurizio Damilano,** ITA, 1980)

Olympic 50-Kilometer Walk Record
Men only: 3:49:24 (**Hartwig Gauder,** GDR, 1980)

Race walkers—the grimmest bunch of pedestrians on earth—are the curiosity item of Games athletics. Newcomers to watching the 2 long-distance walks are at first inclined to laugh. Never have they seen such leg-snapping, pelvis-swaying, arm-pumping action by a human biped. How can you describe it?

In his day, the late IOC president **Avery Brundage** was national champion at race-walking, then called ***heel-and-toe.*** Said Brundage, seriously, "It's a torturous event. This is the closest man can come to the pains of childbirth."

After closer inspection of athletics walking, not running, more than 12mi in the 20km contest and more than 31mi in the 50km match, the viewer has to agree that this *is* agonizingly hard work. The 50km is the longest competition on the Games schedule—almost 5mi (8km) farther than the marathoners' race.

Basic rule: Athletes are prohibited from taking any step or steps that simulate a run. A walker must have ***a part of 1 foot in contact with the track or pavement at all times.*** Rule 191 of the IAAF/Olympics reads: "At each step the advancing foot of the walker must make contact with the ground before the rear foot leaves the ground. During the period of each step in which a foot is on the ground, the leg must be straightened (not bent at the knee) for at least one moment; and, in particular, the supporting leg must be straight in a vertically upright position."

This makes the walks the most difficult of events to judge. Officials spotted along the route squat down and sometimes almost press their noses into the track to detect a violation. Did he break into a run for a few seconds? It's a marginal difference between what's legal and what's not. And controversy has flared in this Olympic event time and again.

The procedure: *The field of super-pedestrians takes off within the stadium, covers 1 lap of the track and then heads for the road circuit. Traffic is blocked. And, as in the marathon, refreshment stations are available at every 5km (3.1mi). Sponging stations are also set up. These are closely monitored by 2 or more officials at each station. "A competitor taking refreshments at a place other than the (official) stations is liable to disqualification," reads the rule.*

Watch for an official carrying a **white flag,** which is a caution or warning device. It tells the walker he's suspected of running. A **red flag** informs the walker he's disqualified.

Judges: *If 3 or more judges agree that "the mode of progression" is illegal, the culprit is disqualified.*

Technique: *A top-flight walker goes at a lively 9mph (15km/hr) clip, taking up to 4 strides per second. He strives for* ***good overlap*** *(both feet on the ground for a tiny moment) and a precise* ***locking*** *of the legs, or straightening of the legs as they approach the ground or leave it.* ***Toes*** *are pointed straight ahead and there's little or no* ***hip sway.*** *Walkers who crouch a bit are called* ***Groucho Marxes*** *or* ***creepers.***

The winners: *Great Britain's athletes won 3 gold medals up to 1960; since then East and West Germany, Italy and Mexico have produced the most champion heel-and-toers.*

sector lines extend 311'6" (94.95m)

30°

foul board

(A)

check mark area

Javelin runway

114'7" (34.9m)

check mark area

13'1½" (4m)

Javelin: *The modern version of this aerodynamic weapon credited to USA champion* **Bud Held**, *came along in the 1960s to change the event dramatically. Held increased the surface area by 26-27%, giving the spear greater sailing capability. At once, the Olympic Record went from 260 to over 270' (79 to 82m), then to 296' (90m) in the 1970s and surpassing 310' (94.5m) at the Montreal Games of '76.*

Olympic Javelin Record
Men: 310'4" (94.58m) (**Miklos Nemeth,** HUN, 1976)
Women: 224'5" (68.4m) (**Maria Colon,** CUB, 1980)

Spear slinging dates to primitive man and was incorporated into the Games in 1908. This is the most complex of the throwing contests because of the aerodynamic factors involved. The javelin is by far the lightest and *flightiest* of implements used in the weight events, and it travels 90-odd feet (27m plus) farther than the discus and 50-odd feet (15m) farther than the hammer.

As they soar in great, graceful arcs, *javs* are sensitive to lift/drag effects. The optimum angle of release in most breeze conditions is well known and exploited to best effect by the Hungarians, Finns, Norwegians, Soviets and Germans.

Measurement *is made from the mark made by the tip of the javelin to center of sector point (**A**).*

Rules of the IAAF:

Only pre-weighed *and calipered spears supplied by the IAAF may be used.*

No mobile parts *are allowed.*

The spear must be thrown ***over the shoulder or upper part of the throwing arm and not slung or hurled*** *(i.e., sidearm).*

Three qualifying trials and ***6 final tries*** *are allowed.*

The metal tip must strike the ground *before any other javelin part or the throw is not valid. If the javelin breaks at any time, it does not count as a try.*

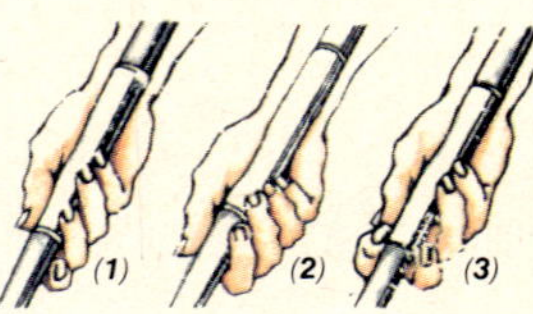

Grips *vary, but the 2 most-used grips are (**1**) held on palm with index finger and thumb behind the cord grip, or (**2**) on palm between the index and second finger. Also popular is the (**3**) Finnish style grip, with the index finger on the same side as the thumb.*

As it leaves the thrower's grip, the spear is often traveling at a terrific ***100'****/sec (30.5m/sec).*

Tips *are metal alloy.*

Shafts *are metal alloy or wood.* ***Grips*** *are wound cotton cord.*

Weight: 1lb,12.2oz (800g) ***Tapering,*** *midpoint to tips: not more than 90% of maximum diameter of shaft.*

Men's javelin: *length 8'10¼" (2.7m)*

Weight: 1lb,5.16oz (600g)

Women's javelin: *length 7'6½" (2.3m)*

Wind pressure *turns jav up so that point goes down—angle of attack remains similar throughout throw.*

Throw: *A* ***run-up*** *of 120' (36.5m) or so begins the action. The aim is to achieve maximum momentum and maintain it until the last moment. In a little-wind situation, at a release angle of 20-30°, it has been established that approximately* ***25%*** *of the velocity of the javelin is gained from run-up momentum,* ***75%*** *from plain old hurling power.*

*(**1**)*

Carry: *3 methods of carrying the jav are employed: above shoulder with point down (Finnish style); closer to shoulder level, point just above the horizontal (used by many North Americans); and arm down and extended far back (used variously).*

Acceleration: *It is gradual, reaching full speed at the final check mark and for 1 or 2 strides beyond.*

Approach and braking: *Charging into the throw-ready zone, spearmen use any of 3 types of footwork—the hop-step style, rear cross-step, front cross-step or a combination of the hop and front cross—to begin the braking action. The spear starts back and the posture is still erect. At a crucial moment, brakes are applied hard to stop the forward momentum of the lower body while transferring power to the throwing arm and hand. In the front-cross style, (**1**) the right foot crosses over the left and digs in while hips rotate and the head is pulled aside (**2**).*

*(**2**)*

angle of attack

angle of release

spin

Throwing: *This is done from a wide-legged stance, body angled back to form a C-curve (**3**) of the spine. There's an explosive thrust of the left foot which forms a fulcrum (**4**). The spear is whipped forward with rear leg powering the effort. Two angles come into play: the* ***angle of release,*** *which is the angle between the flight path of the jav and the ground; and the* ***angle of attack,*** *the angle between the flight path and the relative wind. Back muscles, arm muscles and hand grip flow together in a smooth launching, with a final flip or twist of the wrist (**5**) called a* ***whipcrack***.

Reverse: *Often, lacking enough brakes, javelinists go sprawling over the foul line, nullifying their throw. Bringing the back leg around and shifting body weight to it, in an instant, avoids the foul.*

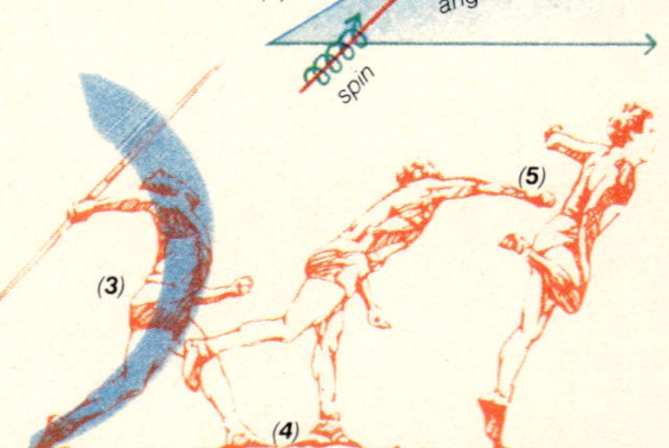

What to watch for: Note footwork as athletes near the throw line, and smoothness of javelin in flight—wavering may indicate a faulty or inefficient release.

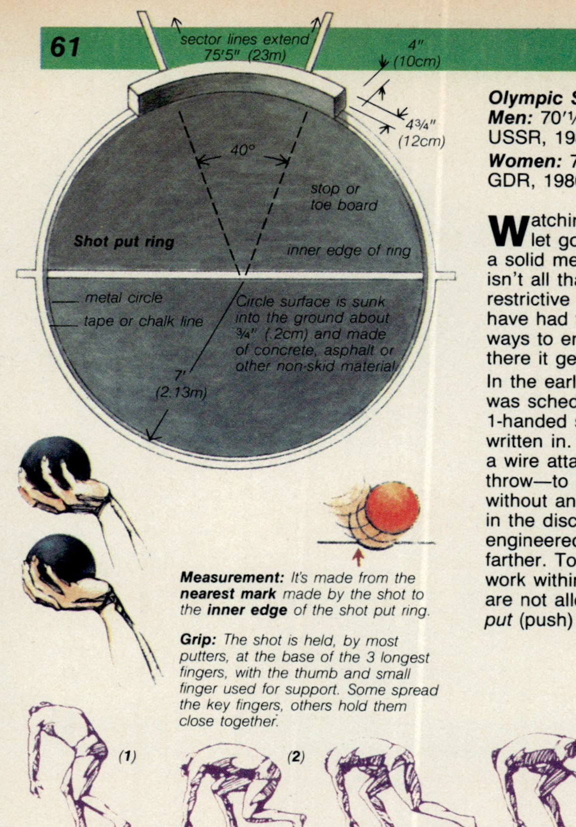

Measurement: *It's made from the* ***nearest mark*** *made by the shot to the* ***inner edge*** *of the shot put ring.*

Grip: *The shot is held, by most putters, at the base of the 3 longest fingers, with the thumb and small finger used for support. Some spread the key fingers, others hold them close together.*

Olympic Shot Put Record

Men: 70′½″ (21.35m) (**Vladimir Kiselyov**, USSR, 1980)

Women: 73′6¼″ (22.41m) (**Ilona Slupianek**, GDR, 1980)

Watching kingsize individuals groan and let go with explosive cries while lofting a solid metal ball, you'd think the shot put isn't all that complicated. Wrong. It is so restrictive in its rules that mighty athletes have had to cudgel their brains to find better ways to employ their muscle groups—and there it gets complicated.

In the early Olympics, a 2-handed shot put was scheduled. That was dropped for the 1-handed style, with a lot of restrictions written in. To begin with, the shot is without a wire attachment—as in the hammer throw—to increase centrifugal force. It is without any flat surface to give it air-lift, as in the discus throw. And the shot can't be engineered, as has the javelin, to sail farther. To make it tougher, putters must work within a skimpy 7′ (2.13m) circle. They are not allowed to throw the ball, but must *put* (push) it from above the shoulder.

Procedure: *Putter takes his or her stance at the rear of the circle with the shot tucked under the neck, below the jawbone. The athlete is flexed (bent down) over the right leg* ***with his or her back to the direction of the put (1)****. Until* **Parry O'Brien** *of the USA turned his back, putters faced forward at the outset. In the 1950s, the* **O'Brien Shift** *vastly changed the event and gave O'Brien 2 Olympic gold medals.*

Putter goes into the **glide (2)**. *This begins with a deep crouch and a mighty drive forward off the right leg. The putter travels* **backward** *to the flight line until his or her weight shifts to the left leg and hips. On the turn to face forward, the gliding action results in the right foot landing near the center of the circle and the left (launch) leg slamming against the toe board at the front of the circle.*

Coming erect and leaning back, the putter's center of gravity shifts from the right leg to the left. He or she **drives** *upward with leg, trunk, back, shoulder and arm muscles, with the right elbow positioned behind the weight* **(3)**.

The very fast (under 3sec) overall action is completed with the **delivery (4)**, *wherein the shot is let go at a 40-43° angle and well above the head off a fully extended right hand* **(5)**. *To check momentum, a* **reverse** *is performed, with the right foot whipping around to replace the left in a balancing act.*

Technique: *The* **O'Brien Shift** *and modifications thereof remained the basic method of shot putting for many years, but in 1972 the* **discus** *or* **rotational technique** *was introduced. This method of putting from a 540° spin adds a claimed 3′ (.91m) to the amount of travel across the circle.* **Barisnikov** *of the USSR set a (then) world record of 72′2¼″ (22m) with the rotational technique in the early 1970s, and the winner at the '84 Games will probably use this style. Watch for the Soviets and Europeans to use the spin; in the USA it is still an experimental throwing technique.*

It's a foul if *any part of* ***the body touches*** *the earth* ***outside the circle.***

Supportive ***leather belts are allowed,*** *but no gloves or spray substances may be used on shoes or the circle surface.*

Three qualifying and ***6 final puts*** *are permitted.*

Shot: *solid iron, brass, or metal not softer than brass. Baseball shown for scale.*

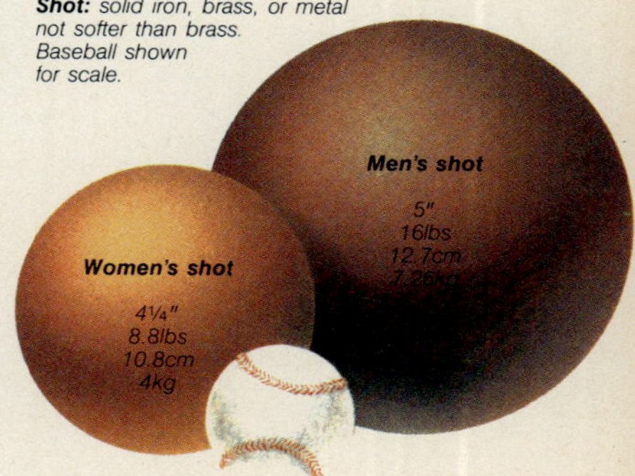

What to watch for: keep an eye on the **path** of the shot **while** it's being thrown. An erratic, jerky put wastes energy. And note the follow-throughs; everyone has his or her own style when it comes to slamming on the brakes.

Mental-emotional factor: *Because of the penned-up throwing area and other restrictions, shot putters rate the* **psychological factor** *as 10-15% of a throw. They go into trances before stepping into the ring, which can involve total silence or snarling at everyone.*

DISCUS THROW

Discus aerodynamics are such that a 16′ (5m)/sec ***headwind*** *can* ***increase*** *throwing distances up to* ***10%.***

Olympic Discus Throw Record
Men: 224′ (68.28m) (**Mac Wilkins**, USA, 1976)
Women: 229′6″ (69.96m) (**Evelin Jahl**, GDR, 1980)

Discus-slingers operate from within a net-enclosed cage which insiders call the ***beast's lair.*** It's too bad the fans can't get closer or see better through the net, because this is a marvelously explosive exhibition of balance, footwork and controlled momentum.

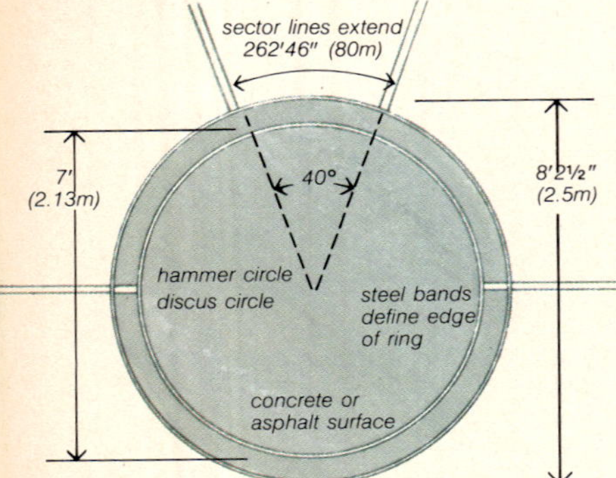

*The Throw: (**a**) The thrower stands at the **rear** of an 8′2½″ (2.5m) diameter circle, facing **away** from the line of throw and with feet 12-18″ (30-46cm) apart.*

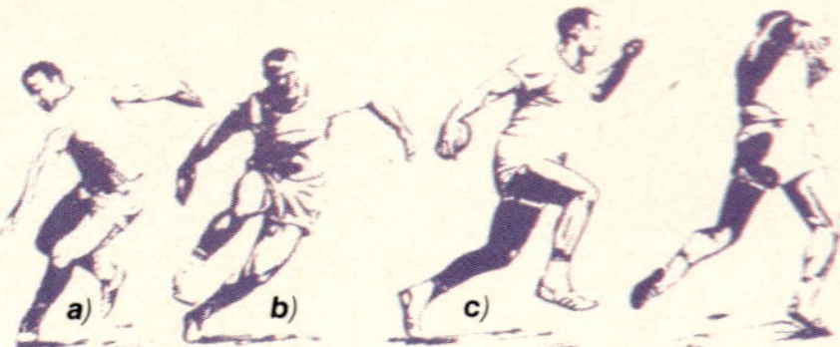

*(**b**) A full 540° turn begins with the **running rotation,** a counterclockwise movement. A righthanded thrower shifts weight from the right foot to the left; the right foot leaves the ground to come over and around the pivotal left foot. The discus is extended well back of the whirling body.*

Strategy: Discus throwers con the pants off each other. It's one big psyche job, with favorites strutting about like lords, using magic talismans and diverse methods of psychological intimidation. The basic strategy is to **make the first throw a good one** in case of later fouls. Knowing the aerodynamic effect of **wind** is vital. A headwind up to 8mph (12.9km/hr) helps elevate the disc and carry it farther; a brisk following wind can reduce the flight by up to 8%.

HAMMER THROW

Olympic Hammer Throw Record
Men only: 268′4″ (81.8m) (**Yuriy Syedikh**, USSR, 1980)

In some fans' opinions, this ball-and-chain whirligig is more fun to watch than the discus or javelin tosses. Bulky guys with terrific footwork spin like mad to hurl a 16lb (7.26kg) ball, attached to a spring-steel wire, out of the stadium. The world record is now less than 25′ (7.6m) short of an American football field's length—and a 300′ (91.44m) hammer throw is forecast by the year 1995.

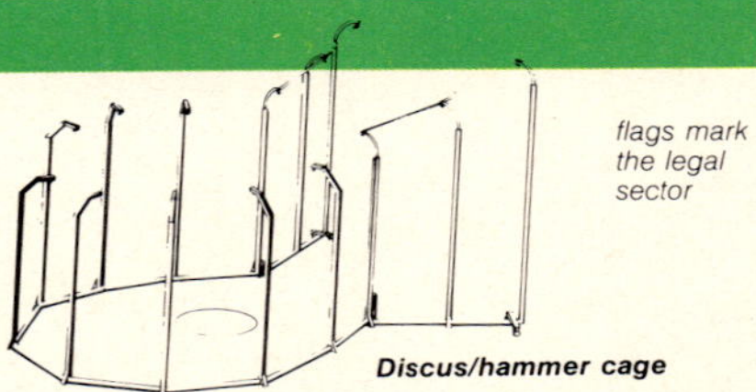

Discus/hammer cage

Cage: *Designed to stop errant disci or hammers moving at 8 1/5-9′/sec (2.45-2.75m/sec), the U-shaped cage is composed of 6 or more panels of synthetic cord fiber netting or of steel wire. Throwers work from within the cage, hurling through an opening into a **legal-throw sector** of 40°, marked by 50mm chalklines. Flags mark the legal sector.*

Procedure: *(**a**) Slinger stands at the rear of a 7′ (2.13m) circle, gripping the handle in 2 hands. His back is turned to the throwing line.*

*(**b**) A series of **preliminary swings** begins from a bent-kneed stance.*

*(**c**) The **1st turn** begins when the hammer's head is at its lowest point–6″-12″ (15-30cm) above the ground–and it's done with a 180° pivot off the heel of the left foot. At first the hammer is ahead of the body, but that changes during the initial turn. Legs and hip torque move the body ahead.*

*(**e**) The complete 2nd turn is followed by a full **3rd turn**–and now the thrower is a blur of frantic action. His arms merely hang onto the spinning weight, while passing on power through hip-shoulder torsion.*

*(**f**) As the final turn ends, both feet are solidly planted, the head is lifted back and, with it, the torso. At peak momentum, the hammer literally is torn from the*

(**c**) ***Torque*** *is created by the wide sweep of the* ***crossing-over*** *(right)* ***foot.*** *Torque (twisting force) is increased as horizontal speed builds up. Finishing the full turn with the right foot back on the ground, thrower goes into the* ***delivery*** *or* ***release*** *of disc.*

(**e**) *The* ***release*** *is made with a wrist snap; the best angle of release depends upon wind direction and velocity, but 30-35° is an optimal angle against little or no wind.*

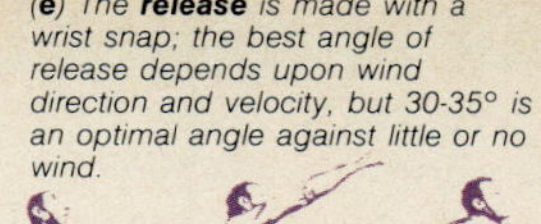

(**d**) *With feet now about 36" (90-92cm) apart, thrower initiates the* ***drive*** *by making another 1/2 to 3/4 turn. The left leg lands near the front of the circle, powerfully extended. Shoulders rotate and the throwing arm follows in a whipping motion.*

Disci: *Made of hardwood or fiberglass with smooth metal rims, and metal weights buried in the centerparts.*

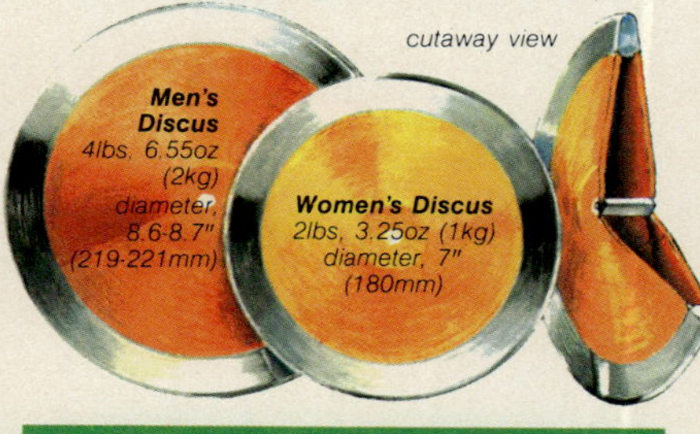

Flag reference: *On TV screens, you'll see rectangular* ***flags*** *or* ***discs*** *set out along the throwing sector. These indicate the current Olympic and World records and will tell you how this Olympiad's crop of saucer-launchers is doing. (This also applies to other throwing events.)*

Referee's tape measure

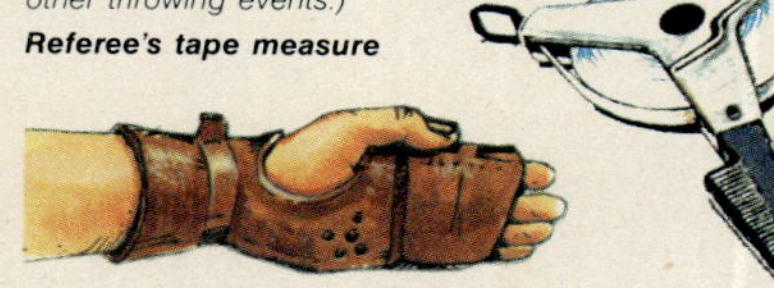

Hammer glove: *leather with reinforced palm. Fingers must be exposed.*

The ***reverse*** *ends the act. It is done to maintain balance and prevent* ***fouling*** *(going out of ring) by shifting the left foot forward and reversing the right—a very nimble act. Fouling is common and the most dreaded element in the discus world. The trick is for a massive, fast-accelerating athlete to check himself or herself instantly to a dead stop.*

Measurement *is from the nearest mark made by the discus to the inner edge of the discus ring. Distances in both Discus and Hammer are measured to the nearest inch* ***below*** *the distance thrown.*

For both ***Hammer*** *and* ***Discus, only implements supplied by the IAAF may be used.*** *(They're weighed and measured beforehand with precision caliper-scale devices costing $5000 or more.)*

Order of throwing *is determined by drawing lots.*

Three qualifying trials, and ***6 final tries*** *are allowed.*

A ***foul*** *occurs when any part of the thrower's body touches to the top of the circular perimeter or beyond. Foul throws are* ***lost tries*** *and do not count.*

Fingers may not be taped *together.*

No ***spray-type substance*** *may be used on shoes or the throwing surface. But* ***resin*** *or other stickum may be used on hands.* ***Leather belts*** *to protect the spine are permissable.*

Hammer: *It is 3-parted, with a* ***head*** *of solid iron or a shell filled with lead; a* ***wire*** *just under 4' in length (1.2m), of non-stretchable steel, connected to the head with a ball-bearing swivel; a* ***grip*** *of single or double-loop construction.*

Referee's ***hammer test device*** *(tests for regulation length)*

The ball circles the thrower's head in the widest possible arc, picking up speed with each revolution.

These ***wind-ups*** *set up the 1st turn.*

(**d**) *The* ***2nd turn*** *is executed faster than the 1st, building velocity. Balance of the rotating 200-250lb (91-113kg) body is maintained at all times over the left foot, which never loses contact with the ground.*

At the same release velocity, a difference of 4° in the release angle can mean a difference of as much as 14' (4.25m) in measured distance.

thrower's grip—and away it flies at about a 45° angle to the ground. In this ***delivery*** *phase, a last, split-second whip or flick of the forearms is applied.*

Note: *A few exceptionally fast spinners make 4 or more* ***turns*** *of the throwing circle instead of 3.*

(**g**) *A fast* ***reverse*** *is made by swinging the rear leg back to the circle's center; this prevents going out of the ring and fouling.*

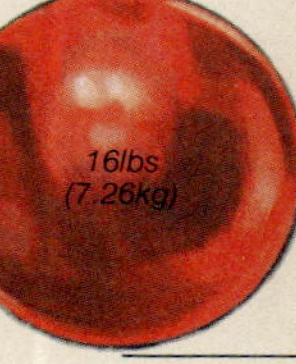

HIGH JUMP

16′4″
(5m)

13′3″
(4m)

82′ (25m)

***Runway area:** the fan-shaped runway enables jumpers to approach the bar from the side and at varying angles.*

Olympic High Jump Record
Men: 7′8¾″ (2.36m) (**Gerd Wessig,** GDR, 1980)
Women: 6′5½″ (1.97m) (**Sara Simeoni,** ITA, 1980)

Outdoors, the high jump bar doesn't seem so impressively high, because it's overshadowed by the giant arena and the sky. But the height, more than the top of an average door frame, is an incredible mark. **Charlie Dumas,** USA, was the first man to reach 7′ (2.14m), at the Los Angeles Coliseum in 1956. Dumas used the ***straddle*** style of leap. Twelve years later, the backward ***flop*** method was developed, helping push the record nearly 9″ (22.9cm) over Dumas'. Perhaps the most incredible competitor was **Franklin Jacobs,** USA. Standing 5′8″ (1.73m), Jacobs used the flop to clear 7′7¼″ (2.32m), almost 2′ (61cm) higher than his head.

***The takeoff must be from one foot** on a level runway.*

*A jump is a failure **if the bar is knocked off its supports,** or **if the jumper touches any part of the landing area** or ground around it with any body part **without first clearing the bar.***

*Jumpers may commence competing at **any height above the prescribed minimum** and jump **at his or her discretion**—foregoing trials at a particular height—and elect to jump at a subsequent height. **Three consecutive failures mean elimination.***

***Height measurement** is made from takeoff level to the lowest portion of the upper side of the bar (where sag is greatest).*

***Strategy:** Jumpers sometimes pass up certain heights to **psyche** opponents. They try to find a takeoff area where the ground has been the least disturbed, and to go over the bar at its point of deepest sag.*

***Procedure:** The event's 3 phases are: **1) runup** or approach, **2) takeoff**, and **3) clearance** of bar.*

*In the total motion, the jumper goes upward vertically, parallel to the bar, and then downward vertically. The jump's most important element is **leg-spring,** which rates 85-90% of the event.*

***Runup:** This depends upon which of the various leap-styles is used. Using the **straddle,** many jumpers start 50′ (15.2m) from the bar and take 7 strides before takeoff. Angle of approach varies from 30-45°. In the **flop** style, a faster runup along a curved path from 55-70′ (16.7-21.3m) away is favored.*

***Takeoff:** A straddler's takeoff foot leads him over the bar. The lead leg swings high and the torso moves to a parallel position along the bar, face down, with the body skimming over the bar. In the flop, the outside foot is lifted to the chest, lifting the body upward. The head leads the rest of the body over the bar, face to sky. A double armlift provides further thrust as back then hips and finally legs clear the bar.*

***Clearance:** As the straddle jumper clears the bar, the body is inclined backward. At the apogee of the jump, the jumper quickly brings the head and shoulders across the bar and moves hips and legs up. Clearing the trailing leg is the trickiest part. If the trail-leg toes point skyward, it helps raise the limb. A flopper tucks heels under buttocks, arches the back and drops the head. In all methods, relaxation—for a limp, flexible body—is an absolute requirement.*

Watch for the differences between the straddle and flop styles.

***Standards** (uprights) are 13′3″ (4m) apart and made of rigid material such as anodized aluminum. Steel tubing **riser** mechanism allows the **crossbar** to be raised to 8′4″ (2.54m).*

***Crossbar and Supports:** The bar is delicately set on supports 1½″ (40mm) wide by 2⅓″(60mm) long with a space of at least ⅓″ (10mm) between the bar's ends and the inner plane of the uprights. The bar is set so that it can easily fall either forward or backward. The bar weighs 2kg (just over 4lbs).*

***Shoes:** Hot controversy has surrounded footwear in World/Olympic competition. In the late 1950s, the USSR came up with the **inclined plane** jumping shoe with a beveled sole up to ¾″ (1.9cm) thickness. This enabled the Soviets to get better lift-up off a fast approach to the bar. In 1958 the shoe was banned. Soles were limited to ½″ (1.27cm) thickness. Today the limitation continues. However, special high-jump shoes have been created with the shoe sole of the takeoff foot built up to ½″ (1.27cm) for better leverage. A 6-spike sole and, infrequently, a 2-spike heel is used.*

***The flop was invented by** **Dick Fosbury,** USA, the 1968 Olympic champion. Today, variations on Fosbury's revolutionary style include the **power flop** (accent on leg-strength training) and the **speed flop** (accent on greater run-up velocity). The **dive-straddle** is yet another technique, usually with takeoff farther from the bar.*

Pole vault runway

4.4lb (2.0kg)

Olympic Pole Vault Record

Men only: 18′11½″ (5.78m) (**Wladyslaw Kozakiewicz,** POL, 1980)

Pole vaulting can be traced to 16th-century Europe. By the 1800s, the British were using long, wooden poles to vault stone walls—and thus keep up with their hunting dogs on the scent of wild game. Before long that practical usage evolved into an athletic contest.

The basic aim of vaulting is to convert linear movement into upward movement by building and storing kinetic energy in the pole. Here, timing is everything.

Procedure: run-up: *The grip is with the hands, from 18-30″ (46-76cm) apart, and with an average* ***grip height*** *of 15′6″-15′8″ (4.7-4.8m). Grip height is the distance from the upper hand to the pole's tip. A fast-accelerating sprint of 130-150′ (39.6-45.7m) is made down a synthetic-surface pathway. One or 2 checkmarks beside the path are used, the first at the start, the others at various distances along the way. These assure vaulters of reaching the planting box with their takeoff foot.*

Pole plant and takeoff: *At 3 to 4 strides from the sunken planting box, full speed is attained. Then comes the crucial lifting of a pole carried at waist height to directly above the head. The slanted-down pole is jammed into the box. Here body momentum has built up kinetic energy, which is tranferred from man to pole. The pre-bend of the pole begins.*

Swing and rock-back: *The aim here is to ascend by increasing the pole's bend to more than 90°. The lead knee is lifted up toward the chest, with hips following. The legs come together in the swing-up's first phase. In the 2nd phase, the vaulter rocks back and his legs shoot up in the beginning of a headstand in the air.*

Pull: *Now the pole is a bent-back catapult as the vaulter* ***muscles*** *(pulls) his way up (arm triceps dominating). It's an explosive action ending with a full handstand and a turning of the body toward the crossbar.*

vault box *(side view)*

(top view)

Strategy: *Competitors may commence vaulting* ***at any height*** *(above the minimum) that they select and continue to accept successive heights at their discretion. That is, a man can forego a particular height and still jump at a subsequent height.* ***Three*** *successive failures at a given height mean elimination. Sophisticated* ***strategy*** *is involved here; skipping some heights can save vital energy. In the 1968 Games,* ***Bob Seagren*** *(USA) gambled and passed up heights up to 17′6¾″ (5.35m), saved his energy and won the gold medal at 17′8½″ (5.4m).*

Under Olympic rules, the man with the ***lowest number of jumps*** *at which a tie occurs is awarded the superior medal.*

A vault fails if a contestant ***knocks the bar off its supports;*** *leaves the ground and* ***doesn't finish the vault;*** *places his* ***lower hand above his upper hand*** *along the pole while in the air.*

If a pole breaks, *it doesn't count as a failure.*

Competitors may use their own poles, *which can have 2 layers of tape in the gripping area and taped tips; adhesive substances are allowed on the hands.*

Pole: *Originally vaulters used poles of hickory or ash. Bamboo was introduced in the mid-1800s and gained popularity, after great controversy, when its superiority was demonstrated at the 1900 Paris Games. By the 1940s, steel poles, with a more consistent and safer action, had replaced bamboo. After World War II, fiberglass had revolutionized vaulting, adding 1′6″ (46cm) to the old record, and was the pole of choice. Perfected in the 1960s, the spun glass tissue bonded with synthetic resins called fiberglass have lifted the vault from a 16′ (4.88m) ceiling to past 19′ (5.79m) in 1983. Advantages of the space-age poles are multiple: the tremendous bend* ***flips*** *the body over, but more importantly, fiberglass poles allow for a* ***higher hand grip****, by as much as a 1′ (30cm), adding to the final height. These advantages have a major drawback: fiberglass' spring gives the vaulter a faster vertical lift. He must compensate with a backward thrust to gain fractions of a second to prepare his body position when he reaches the bar.*

Pole vault

Pushoff and clearance: *Now comes the moment of truth—will he make it over the crossbar or send the bar spinning? Turning belly-down to the bar, the vaulter gets legs over first, then hips and torso. Both arms are used to push the pole away and himself, back arched, over the bar.*

Landing *is a gymnastic feat in which the vaulter lifts arms high to clear, pikes backward and lands in a super-soft pit on his upper back.*

Landing pit: *Originally sawdust and wood shavings, now the cushion for the long fall is* ***foam rubber.***

Transporting the 15-16′ *(4.6-4.9m) implements can cause chaos. Former world record-holder* ***John Pennel*** *(USA) once checked his precious poles at an airline ticket counter and arrived at a track meet to find they'd been sawed into 4′ (1.22m) lengths—to fit into the baggage compartment.*

Standards *(uprights) are aluminum and 14′-14′3″ (4.3-4.37m) apart. The circular metal crossbar is 14′8″ (4.5m) long, without rubber tips or any other hold-in-place material.*

Peg supports *for the 14′8″ (4.5m) bar can be only ½″ (13mm) in diameter "and the crossbar shall rest on them so that if touched by the contestant or his pole it will fall easily to the ground."*

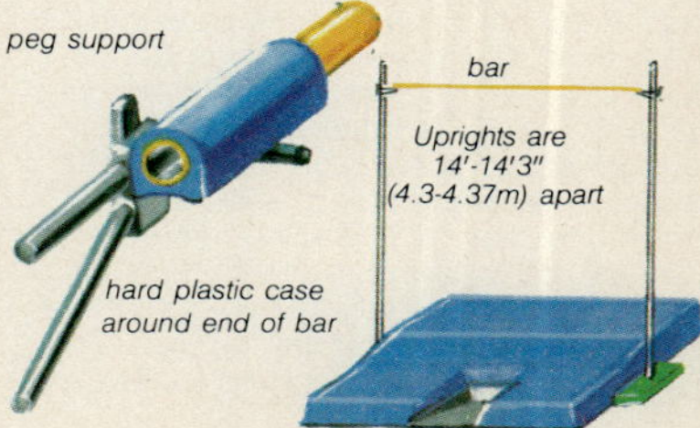

LONG JUMP/TRIPLE JUMP

Olympic Long Jump Record
Men: 29′2½″ (8.9m) (**Bob Beamon,** USA, 1968)

Women: 23′2″ (7.06m) (**Tatyana Kolpakova,** USSR, 1980)

Olympic Triple Jump Record
Men only: 57′¾″ (17.39m) (**Viktor Saneyev,** USSR, 1968)

Worldwide, the ***triple jump*** is the more popular of the Olympics' 2 distance jumping competitions. Countries which consistently produce ace ***triplers*** include the USSR, Brazil, East Germany, Romania and Czechoslovakia. But the USA's **Bob Beamon** and his 1968 record (above) gave the ***long jump*** sudden and continuing fame. In one of the greatest sports feats of modern history, Beamon added an incredible 1′9¾″ (55.24cm) to the record. The thin air at Mexico City's 7349′ (2240m) altitude is sometimes mentioned as a contributing factor, but generally Beamon's perfect form and fabulous effort are given full credit for the magnificent performance. Twelve years later the 28′ (8.53m) mark was finally broken by **Lutz Dombrowski** (GDR); a handful of other world-class jumpers have also passed 28′. But Beamon alone has crossed the 29′ (8.83m) line.

Procedure: The aim is to convert horizontal velocity into an upward leap; body action is used to increase distance before landing in a sandpit. The 4 phases involved are ***run-up, takeoff, flight and landing.***

Run-up: *It starts from a bent, relaxed stance and turns into a dead sprint down a synthetic-surface path to the* ***takeoff board.*** *Body control—so that a foul doesn't occur by overstepping the board—is of key importance.*

Takeoff: *In the last 3-4 strides, the jumper leaves the leaning position, rises almost erect and lowers the gravity center by shortening the last stride—from about 7′6″ (2.28m) to 6′10″(2.08m). The takeoff foot hits the foul board heel first, then flattens. Contact with the board is as little as 5/26sec. The opposite or* ***free*** *leg swings through and the jumper is launched. Takeoff angle is about 25°.*

Flight: *Viewers will note various mid-air styles. These are* ***sailing*** *(legs together in sitting position),* ***hanging*** *(a pronounced lead-leg sweeping action) and the* ***hitch-kick*** *technique. The latter is most used and with it the leaper is* ***running in the air.***

Landing: *Legs are extended, arms thrown forward, buttocks arched to get every possible fraction of an inch (gold medals have been won by a ½″ margin). Some jumpers use a sideways flip out of the sand, others the swift* ***bounce-out.***

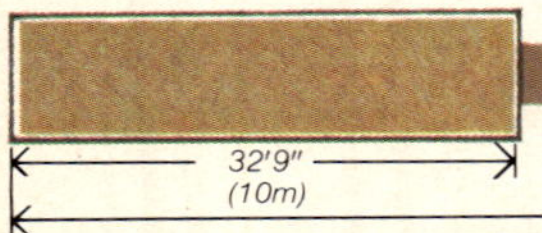

The combined long jump/triple jump runway has a pit at either end so that competitors may jump in either direction according to wind conditions.

DECATHLON/HEPTATHLON

Olympic Decathlon Record
Men only: 8617pts (**Bruce Jenner,** USA, 1976)

If an Olympic Oscar were awarded, it probably would go to the decathlon. The dramatic ***all-around*** fascinates mankind; its winner earns the title "greatest athlete in the world" for the next 4 years.

It's difficult to quarrel with that label. Each contestant is required to show his world-class skill in ***10*** very different disciplines. The 10 tests are the most technically difficult athletic events in Games athletics. The tests not only vary, but often are directly contradictory in their demands. For example, a heavily muscled shot putter-discus type is asked to pole vault, run hurdles and long jump. A speed merchant who shines in the sprints must cover 1500 meters. Or a natural leaper is faced with hurling the javelin. A decathlete must be a very fine ***dashman, middle-distance runner, thrower of weights, vaulter, long*** and ***high jumper*** and ***distance galloper***—all in a single body.

To handle the 3 weight contests, decathletes must be hefty men. For this reason, most of them find the ***pole vault*** to be the most difficult single event. Some 200lb (91kg) entrants rate the ***400-meter run,*** which must be done under 48sec in the Olympics to score high points, as the hardest. A ***javelin*** throw of well over 200′ (61m)—one near 225′ (68.6m) has been achieved in the Games—comes hard for muscular types. All decathletes agree that the ***1500 meter,*** coming last on the program when extreme exhaustion has set in, is the most fatiguing. Collapses at the tape are frequent.

Just as tough, the 2-day spread of the decathlon—5 events on each day—means that the competitors are at work for up to 30 hours. Maintaining concentration and strength over that grind requires extraordinary skill.

The number of entrants drags out the battle interminably. When **Bob Mathias** (USA) won the Olympic title in 1948, he was on the field from 10:30AM of the second day until darkness set in 13 hours later. At the 1960 Rome Games, victor **Rafer Johnson** (USA) was in action for 14 straight hours. At the Montreal Olympics of '76, **Bruce Jenner** (USA) didn't finish his chores until 7:15PM under stadium lights. "I'll never do this again," groaned Jenner—who retired on the spot, with the current Games record of 8617pts.

Heptathlon

Russian superwoman **Nadyezhda Tkachenko's pentathlon** Olympic record of 1980 will now stand forever; at Los Angeles, the women's combined event will become the 7-sport heptathlon for the first time. All-around female athletes will compete in the 100m hurdles, 800m run, long jump, high jump, shot put, and, added in 1984, the javelin and 200m dash. In the 1930s, the **triathlon** became the first combined athletics event for women. The pentathlon survived from the 1964 Tokyo Games until 1980. That same year, the heptathlon was introduced to international competitions, and world record marks have surpassed 6700pts.

Triple jump procedure: *Action consists of 3 synchronized, rhythmic actions: 1) the* ***hop,*** *2) the* ***step,*** *and 3) the* ***jump.*** *These are not separate jumps, but a continuous flow from the takeoff board to the landing pit. For a 58′ (17.68m) total distance,* ***triplers*** *will soar about 20′ (6m) on the hop, 17′ (5.2m) or more on the step and 21′ (6.4m) on the jump.* ***Speed*** *to the takeoff point is rated 60% of the total effort.*

Basic rule: *In hop-step-jumping, the man must land on the same leg employed for the takeoff in phase 1 (the hop), land on the leg opposite the takeoff leg in phase 2 (step), and land on both legs in the final, third phase.*

Three qualifying jumps and ***6 final trials*** *are allowed. A foul is called when a man* ***touches the indicator board,*** *takes off* ***beyond the ends*** *of the takeoff board,* ***somersaults*** *or uses any* ***weight in his hand.***

Long jump/triple jump measure device

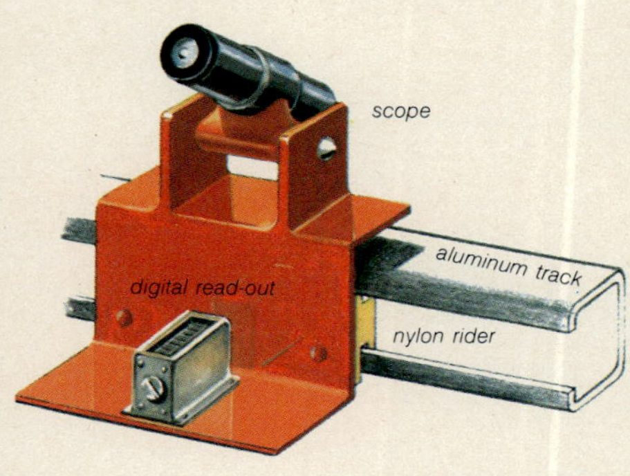

Run-up: *It's a bit shorter than in the long jump – 120-145′ (36.6-44.2m). Checkmarks placed along the 4′ (1.2m) runway aid in correct stride placement to the takeoff board.*

Hop: *Initiating the phases, it's done with a mighty push off either foot; the landing is on the same foot used in this takeoff. A lower body trajectory is wanted here than in the long jump.*

Step: *When the hopping leg hits the ground, the trailing leg is whipped forward and the landing is on the opposite foot. Knee and arm action helps maintain velocity.*

Jump: *In the concluding phase, the jumper takes off on his right foot and executes a long jump, using that event's techniques. At the conclusion, he's touched the ground 3 times.*

Landing pit: *Made of moistened sand. A special sweep instrument keeps the pit level with the takeoff board. Pit is 9′ (2.74m) wide and 30′ (9.14m) long.*

Takeoff board: *Sunk flush with the runway, it is 4′ (1.22m) long, 7¾″ (20cm) wide and painted white.*

Indicator board: *Set flush against the takeoff board on the pit side, it is a 4′ long plasticine sheet used to detect spike marks which mean the jumper has* ***fouled*** *by overstepping the board.*

Plasticine indicator board

Takeoff board

7¾″ (20cm)

(shows spike marks if there is a foul)

direction of jump

Triple jump takeoff

Long jump takeoff

32′9″ (10m)

Digital devices are used to measure wind speeds. Record long jumps are designated wind-assisted if the wind speed is more than 2m/sec.

Scoring table: Some critics argue that each of the 10 events should carry the same point value. They do not. More value is given to speed and leaping ability than to power or endurance.

Most decathletes don't strive for a balanced performance; they concentrate on gaining as ***many points as possible in their strongest events.***

Rest period: 30 minutes between events

Added time factor: Groups in running event heats are drawn by lot; thus a man who is *last* to high jump may be the *first* to compete in the exhausting 400m sprint. He may be the last in the discus throw, then first-called to make a pole vault.

Chart below compares Bruce Jenner's record-setting 1976 performance with marks needed in each event for scores of 800 and for scores of 1000.

Chart below shows marks in each event needed for scores of 800 and 1000 in the new women's 7-event heptathlon.

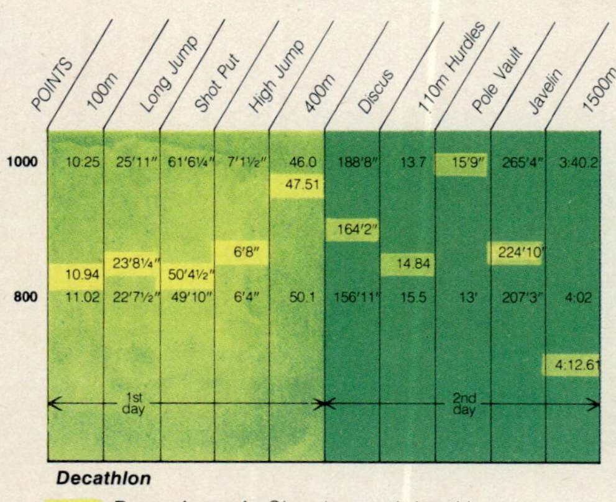

Decathlon

Bruce Jenner's *Olympic record decathlon performances, 1976. Total points,* ***8617***

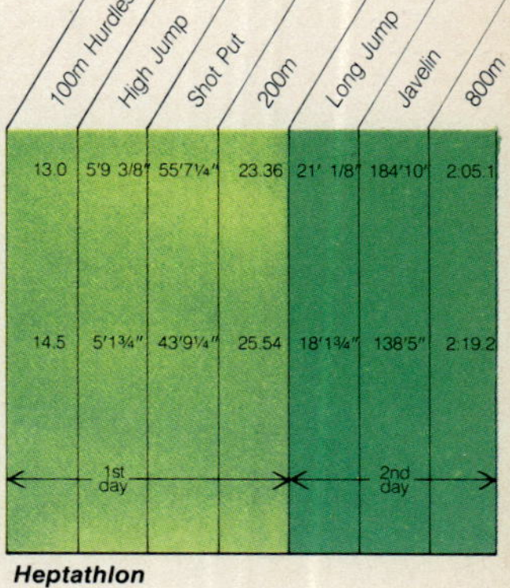

Heptathlon

1980 Olympic Volleyball Champions
Men: USSR **Women: USSR**

Court: *It's 59' (18m) × 29'6" (9m) and covered with Teraflex, a synthetic rubberite laid over concrete. Attack lines 2" (5.08cm) wide are laid 9'9" (3m) to either side of the center line and parallel to the net. The area formed between the attack line and the net is called the* ***attack zone.*** *Back row players may not touch the ball above the height of the net within this zone.*

Net: *For men, the height is 7'11 5/8" (2.42m); for women the net is 7'4 1/8" (2.24m). Rising 2'8" (81m) above the height of the net on either side are fiberglass foul poles designating each sideline. Balls passing outside of these poles are considered out of bounds.*

net antenna
white tape
mesh net 4" (10cm)
centerline
9'9" (3m)
3'3" (1m)
attack line (extends indefinitely to the sides)
9'10" (3m)
service area
backline
29'6" (9m)
Women: 7'4-1/8" (2.24m)
Men: 7'11-5/8" (2.42m)
backline
59' (18m)
2'8" (81cm)
service area

Volleyball court

Some volleyball internationalists say that their sport's most thrilling moment didn't come on any court, but in an IOC hall in Sofia, Bulgaria in 1957.

The USA-invented game had long sought to be accepted into Olympicdom. After much stalling, the IOC overlords agreed to watch an exhibition.

"A brilliant game was played, with spikes, volleys and blocks all over the place," wrote an eyewitness. "But Games chiefs sat stony-faced and reacted not at all to the crowd's roar. We thought we had just received the kiss of death.

"Next day, the IOC voted unanimously to make volleyball an Olympic event at Tokyo in 1964. We were flabbergasted."

This diving, leaping, net-and-ball team contest caught on around the world after World War II, with an estimated 50 million participants and crowds of 60,000 watching matches. It was inevitable that policymakers should include it in the Big Show.

For 1984, 10 men's teams and 8 women's teams which survive worldwide regional qualifying rounds will meet in the Long Beach Arena. More than 200 players will take on opponents in a series of round-robin matches producing men's and women's finalists.

Procedure (Team selection): *The Olympic women's field is named from winners of zonal tournaments in Europe, Asia, South America, Africa and North America, plus a team from the host nation, the defending Olympic champion (USSR), and the World Champion (China). The men's field will come from the same zonal playoffs, plus the host, defending champion (USSR), World Cup champion (Cuba), World Champion (Brazil) and 2 other qualifiers.*

For the Games, entries will be divided into pool-groups, with men playing 4 round-robin matches and women playing 3 matches before advancing to other pairings leading to the semi-finals and finals.

Officials: *Volleyball is officiated by 2 referees. The* ***first referee*** *is positioned at one end of the net on a stand tall enough that his head is at least 19.7" (50cm) above the height of the net. This official is in full control of the match, but is assisted by the* ***second referee,*** *who stands opposite and facing the first referee. Duties of the second referee include signaling net, center and attack line violations, time keeping during time-outs, and supervision of the serving order and positions of the receiving team at the time of service. Referees may be assisted by 2 or 4 linesmen. The first referee may overrule any of the other officials.*

Point — Time-out — End of game or match — Substitution — Ball violation inbounds or line

The game: The purpose in volleyball is to hit the ball over the net in such a manner that the opposing side is unable to return it within 3 contacts. Only the serving team can score points. If the serving team fails to score, a ***side out*** is awarded and the service changes to the opposing team. Games begin with a coin toss. The winner of the toss has a choice of 1) first serve, or 2) choice of side for the first game. The loser of the toss has the remaining option.

Teams: Each team consists of 12 players—6 starters and 6 reserves. As the ball is served, the 6 players are arranged according to serving order in positions designated right, center and left back; left, center and right front. These positions are rotated in a clockwise direction by the serving team with each change of service. After the serve, players may move from their respective positions. Teams are allowed 6 substitutions per game.

Matches: The winner of a volleyball game is the first team to score at least ***15pts*** with a 2pt advantage over the opponent. If the score is tied at 14-14, play continues until one team lead by 2pts (e.g. 16-14, 17-15, etc.) There is no time limit. A match consists of the best 3 out of 5 games.

Serve: *The ball is put into play in the back position serving from an area behind the rear boundary line 9.84' (3m) wide. Most teams employ the* ***floater*** *serve. Having no top spin, this serve follows an unpredictable flight path due to wind resistance on the surface of the ball, making it difficult to receive. Two common variations are:*

American style

a) ***The overhand floater serve*** *(used by most American teams), in which the ball is hit with an open hand above the head and slightly in front of the player in an action similar to throwing a football or softball.*

Roundhouse

b) ***The roundhouse serve*** *(Japanese style), in which the ball is again contacted with an open hand above the head, but without elbow flexion and with the player facing sideways to the net. This serve may follow a dropping side-to-side flight pattern.*

VOLLEYBALL

Santa Barbara
5
405
San Gabriel Mountains
Hollywood
Coliseum
Santa Monica Beaches
11
7
5
Long Beach Arena
405
San Diego
Distance from Coliseum: 23mi (37km)

Offense: After receiving the serve, a team attempts to control the ball in such a manner that it may be set to any of its front row spikers. In the ***set*** or ***set pass,*** one player hits the ball to send it high in the air in position for a teammate to spike. ***Spiking*** is the game's most dramatic offensive maneuver, in which the ball is hit forcefully downward from above the net with an open hand. A spiked ball may travel at speeds in excess of 100mph (160.9km/hr). A ***typical play sequence*** consists of these players: ***a)*** ***service receiver,*** who generally uses a forearm or ***bump*** pass; ***b)*** a ***setter*** who, using an overhead volley, employs one of a variety of sets to place the ball in the air; ***c)*** a ***spiker.***

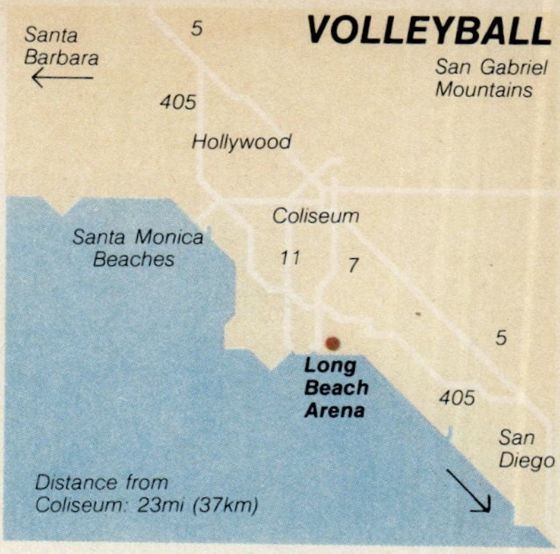

Spike

c

a

Dig

b

Volley (Set)

Playing the ball: The ball may be legally contacted with any part of the body above the waist, but must be hit in such a manner that it rebounds cleanly after contact with a player. Scooping, lifting, pushing or throwing the ball all constitute ***holding***—a ball handling fault.

Defense: The first line of defense is to attempt to stop the spike using the ***block.*** This may involve 1, 2, or 3 front row players who, with arms and hands extended overhead, create a wall in front of the spiker, causing the spike to be deflected back over the net. Defensive players not involved in blocking are responsible for playing balls which are hit around, over or through the block. Specific areas of defensive court coverage are assigned, and the defense may be seen to shift according to the position of the spiker.

__Ball:__ Made of white, laceless leather, it has a 26"-27" (66cm-68.6cm) circumference and weighs 9-10oz. (255g-284g). The Japanese-made Mikasa __World Class__ ball will be used in the Olympics.

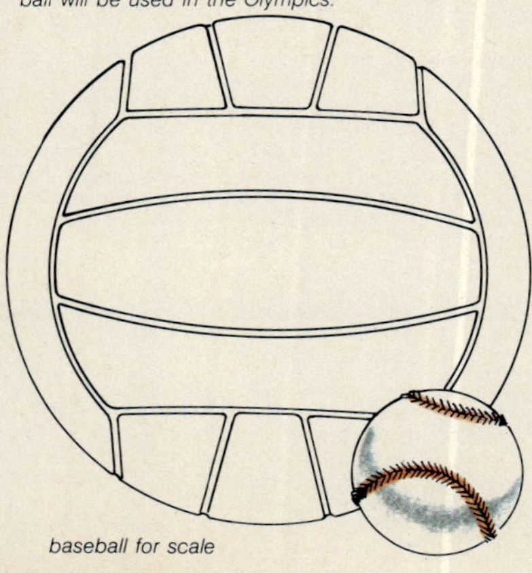

baseball for scale

Spike defense

Players on both teams must line up according to serving order as the ball is put into play. These positions may be switched as soon as the ball is served to gain offensive or defensive advantage. The offensive team may bring a setter up from the back row; front row players may switch with one another to assigned positions designated ***middle blocker, strong-side (power) hitter,*** and ***weak-side hitter.***

What to watch for: Identify the **setter** on each team. This is the playmaker of the offense. In the split second that it takes to receive the first pass, this player must read both offense and defense in making the decision of which spiker (and which set) to use for each offensive play.

__Uniforms:__ Low-cut flexible shoes with synthetic rubber treads are worn. Synthetic knit jerseys and shorts carry player numbers from 1 to 15. __Team captains__ have a bar under their number to indicate rank (only captains may address the referees). In the Japanese system, players are awarded numbers according to merit—the lowest numbers are worn by the strongest players. Thus, #1 would be worn by the strongest player, #15 by the weakest, etc.

Heavyweight and superheavyweight division lifters, in all their sweaty straining, seem like incarnations of fabled Atlas and Hercules. At the 1964 Games, the 360lb Russian giant **Leonid Zhabotinsky** set a combined 3-lift record of 1262lbs (572.5kg). It was thought this mark would last awhile, but in '72 **Vasily Alexeev,** USSR, hoisted 1411lbs (640kg).

Now that the Olympics feature a 2-lift program instead of the old 3 lifts, those amazing marks will stand forever. And even though today's 2-lift totals seem deceptively low in comparison, per-lift records are being broken in major competitions every year.

By no means should the smaller weightlifters be overlooked. The combined weight of 2 lifts by these muscular men is equal to lifting and suspending 5 times their body weights. The 1968 Games sight of **Mohammed Nassiri** of Iran, weighing only 123lbs (55.8kg) but putting up 330½lbs (150kg) in the clean and jerk event could only be described as incredible.

At Moscow, these world records were broken by less-than-middleweight lifters, and all have been broken since:

In the 123½lb (56kg) class, Cuba's **Daniel Nunez** had a 2-lift total of 606lbs (275kg). In the 132lb (60kg) class, Russia's **Viktor Mazin** lifted 639lbs (290kg). In the 149lb (67.5kg) division, Bulgaria's **Yanko Rusev** lifted 755lbs (342.5kg)

At the 1980 Games, a total of 9 Olympic and 5 world records were set, one of the most extraordinary international competitions of all time.

Watch weightlifters **prepare** to lift. Concentration, breathing and attitude must work together for record lifts. The psychological factor here is significant.

Olympic lifts: *3 lifts were contested until 1972, when the controversial* ***press*** *was abolished as too difficult to adjudicate. Two remain: the snatch and clean-and-jerk.*

2-hands snatch: *With the bar placed horizontally on the platform in front of the lifter's legs, the bar is gripped palms down. It must be pulled from the platform in a single, continuous motion to the full extent of both arms above the head. There must be no break in the action. Other than not pausing during any part of the snatch, the lifter cannot:*
a) ***turn his wrists over*** *until the bar has passed over the top-plane of his head;*
b) ***extend his arms unevenly*** *or not completely.*

Snatch technique: *Many lifters use the* ***squat*** *as they draw the bar above waist level, raising the weight over the head in a single motion.*

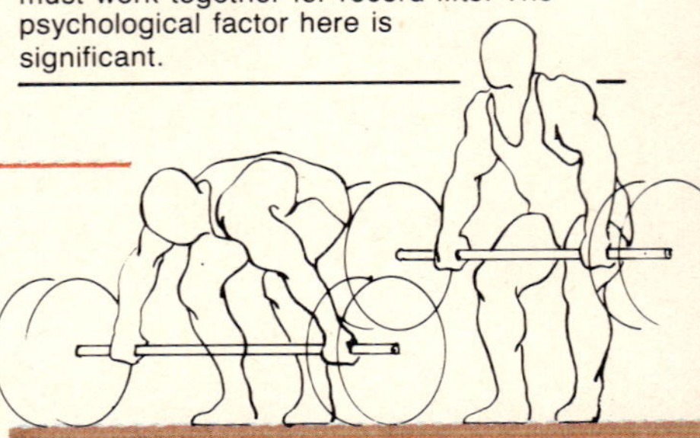

Others prefer the ***split*** *technique, with 1 leg thrust forward and the other thrust backward. From either stance, the feet must wind up on the same line.*

Rules and scoring: Each nation may enter 10 men, one in each weight class, or a nation may ***double up***—if they are unrepresented in one class, they may enter 2 (but no more) in another class. Winners are those who lift the most ***total weight*** (sum of the snatch and clean-and-jerk). The 3 referees each control a red light and a white light. White indicates a valid lift, red an illegal lift. Majority rules when the officials disagree. All referees must be of different nationalities.

Each lifter has ***3 chances at each lift. If a man fails a lift, he can go to a higher lift.*** *Order of lifting is determined by the weight on the bar. Each lifter performs when the weight he wants is loaded on the bar.*

2-handed clean-and-jerk: *This feat of speed and power is composed of 2 distinct movements. The clean-and-jerk asks that:*
a) the barbell be hoisted from the platform to a temporary position at the shoulders while an erect stance is achieved. (That's the ***clean*** *portion of the lift); b) The bar be thrust in one continuous motion from the shoulders to an overhead hold with outstretched arms. (This is the* ***jerk*** *part.)*

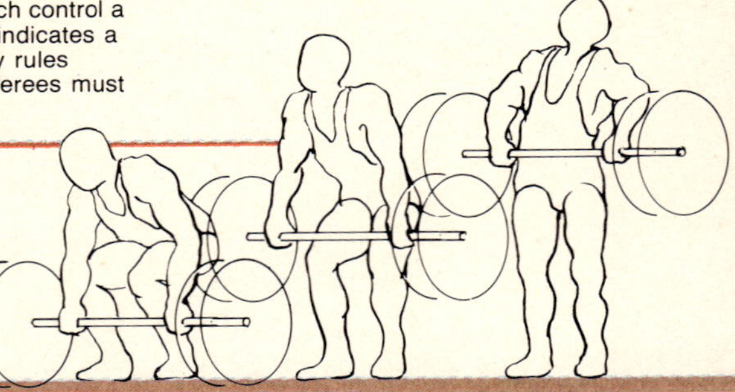

First, the bar is raised to hip level with leg-and-buttocks drive.

Clean-and-jerk technique: *This is a complex set of acts requiring fine coordination. A* ***hook*** *grip (thumbs placed around the bar and underneath the index and second fingers) is often used.*

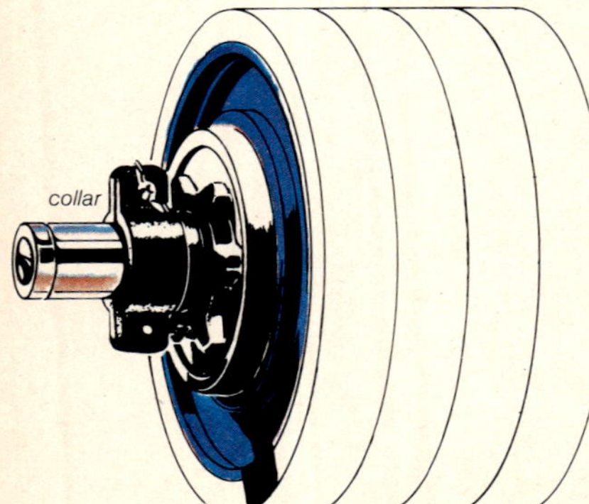

Barbells and weights: *The bar is 7' (2.13m) long, 1.1" (2.8cm) thick and made of machine-tooled chrome vanadium. The ends are covered by revolving sleeves where the weight-plates are attached. Weights range from small 1.25lb (2.76kg) disks to large disks (****bumper plates****) going up to 99.2lbs (45kg). Diameter of the largest bumper plate is 17.7" (45cm). Discs and plates are identified by the colors green, red, blue, yellow, white, and black.*

Equipment: *Low or high-topped leather or suede* ***shoes*** *(cost: $110) are used; soles are usually of rubber. A broad, 4½" wide (12cm)* ***lifting belt*** *of leather ($25) is allowed to protect the back and midsection. Gauze wrist (3" or 7.62cm wide) and knee (1½" or 3.81cm wide)* ***bandages*** *are the legal limit. All the* ***chalk*** *wanted may be applied to the hands and* ***talc*** *may be used on the thighs to facilitate bar-sliding.*

Bodyweight classes: *Until the 1984 Games, names were used to designate competing weight classes—* **flyweight** *through* **superheavyweight.** *This has been dropped for '84 and the 10 weight divisions are:*

(**1**) Up to 114.50lbs (52kg)
(**2**) Up to 123.50lbs (56kg)
(**3**) Up to 132lbs (60kg)
(**4**) Up to 149lbs (67.5kg)
(**5**) Up to 165.25lbs (75kg)
(**6**) Up to 182lbs (82.5kg)
(**7**) Up to 198.25lbs (90kg)
(**8**) Up to 220.50lbs (100kg)
(**9**) Up to 242lbs (110kg)
(**10**) Over 242lbs (over 110kg)

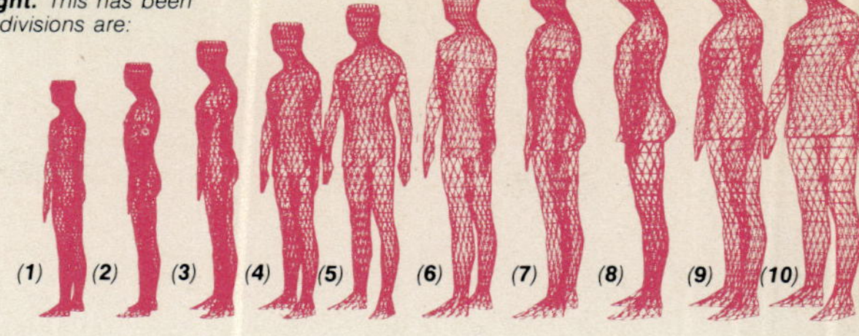

Of all weightlifting movements, the snatch is rated the most difficult because it's done in a 1-piece, continuous action.

Under the great pressure of hoisting 360lbs (163kg) or more, the lifter is given an unlimited time in which to adjust and recover his position.

Upon completing the lift, the position must be motionless (showing control), with both feet on the same line.

In the clean-and-jerk, far more weight can be raised and held than in the snatch event.

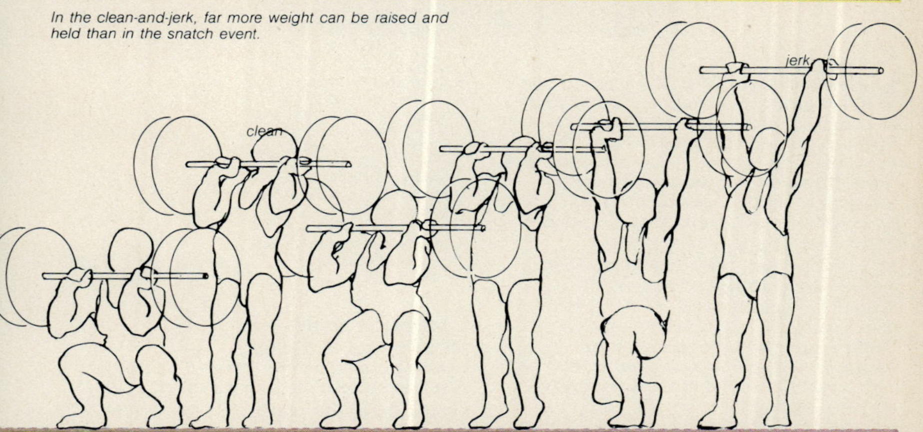

Then it **flows** *up to rest on the clavicle or shoulder girdle. Now, from an erect position, the lifter bends knees slightly.*

He rises on his toes in an upward spring. Rapidly, the legs are split while arms and shoulders push the weight up. Finally, the legs are brought together with small, alternating steps, into a fully erect stance.

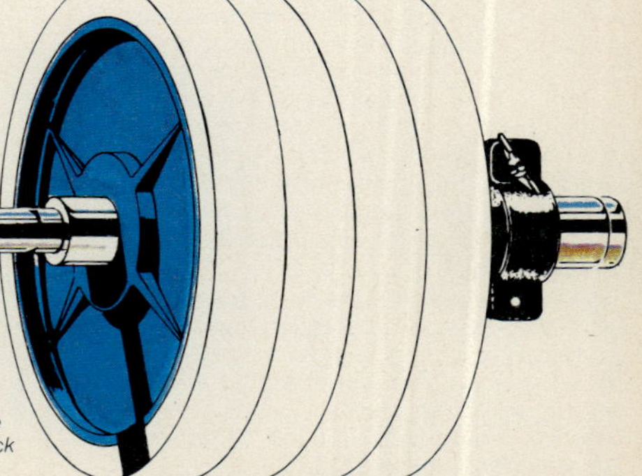

Hold time: *In both Olympic lifts, the bar must be maintained overhead until the chief referee's command of* **down.** *This usually comes in about 2sec by sounding a horn.*

45kg (99.2lbs)-green
25kg (55.11lbs)-red
20kg (44.09lbs)-blue
15kg (33.07lbs)-yellow
5 & 10kg (11.02 & 22.04lbs)-white
1.25 & 2.5kg (2.76 & 5.51lbs)-black

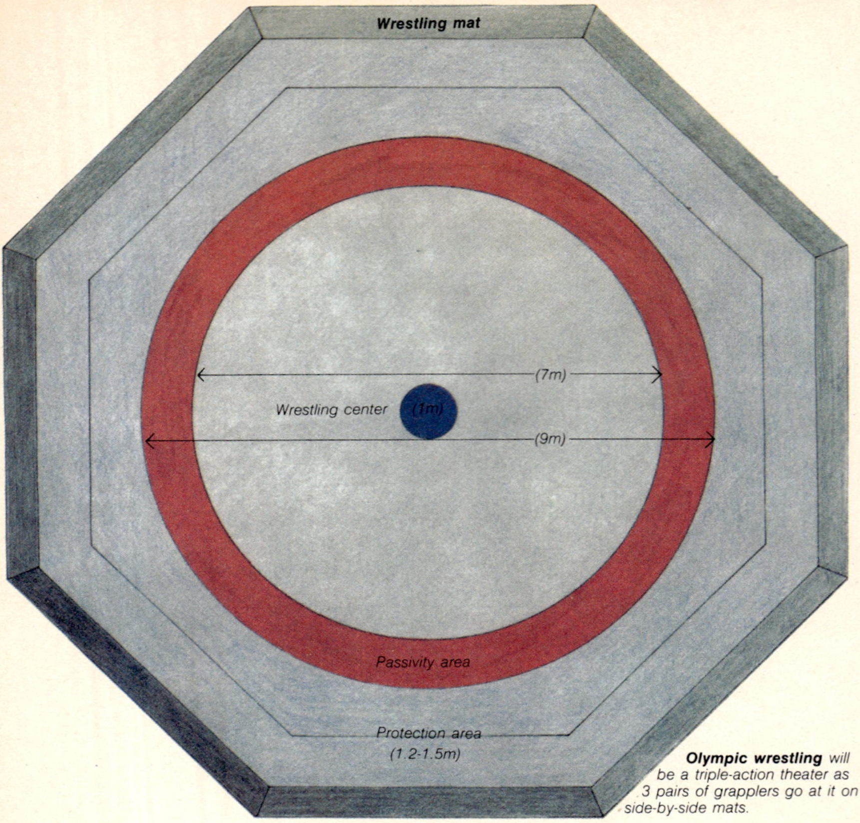

Wrestling mat

(7m)

Wrestling center (1m)

(9m)

Passivity area

Protection area (1.2-1.5m)

Olympic wrestling *will be a triple-action theater as 3 pairs of grapplers go at it on side-by-side mats.*

Wrestlers of the 23rd Olympiad are the end product of more than 5000 years of grappling, dating at least to ancient Egyptian athletic contests. In later times, many countries created their own distinctive wrestling styles: **schwingen** (Swiss), **Lancashire** (Scots), **glima** (Iceland), **Cornwall** (Britain), **pankration** (Greece), **catch-as-catch-can** (early U.S.).

The Olympic **bad mark** or penalty scoring system is a complicated method of rewarding aggressiveness; it penalizes **safe** defensive wrestling. If there's anything the **Federation Internationale de Lutte Amateur,** the sport's worldwide governing body, wants to stamp out it is **passivity** in the ring. Among the more than 500 contestants expected at Los Angeles, watch for the Soviets, Bulgarians and Hungarians, who grab off most of the medallions.

Procedure: There are 2 styles of Olympic wrestling, with 10 weight divisions in each. A nation may enter 1 contestant per weight division, or a total of 20.

1 Greco-Roman: This is the purest form of wrestling, a legacy of the Greek Olympics. No holds below the waist are allowed and contestants may not use their legs (head scissors, leg scissors, etc.). From a standing position at the outset, using the arms only, opponents try to take each other down for a **fall** or **pin.** Only 1-arm head-holds are permitted. In a takedown, the attacker's body must touch the mat before his foe's upper body touches down.

2 Freestyle: Far more wide-open than Greco-Roman, this style allows for most standard wrestling tactics. A bout can be won by pinning an opponent's back or shoulders to the mat for ½sec. Or it can be won by accumulating points by gaining advantages over the opponent.

If one wrestler goes out-of-bounds on his back, the opponents return to the ring center; the man who went out assumes a kneeling position and action resumes with the other placing his thumbs on the former's backbone. If a man goes out of bounds ***not*** *on his back, the rivals return to the center in a standing position.*

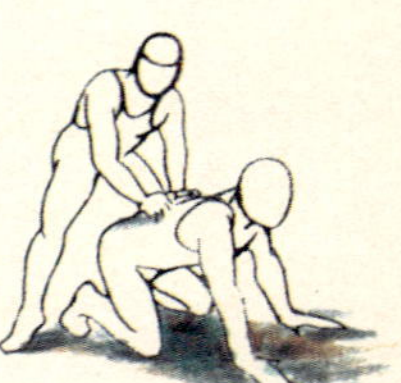

Scoring of bouts:

1 point is awarded for:
taking a man to the mat and momentarily ***holding him there*** under control;

moving from an underneath position to an ***uppermost*** position and applying control (a reverse).

2 points are awarded:
when a wrestler puts his foe ***in danger*** (holds shoulders at less than a 90° angle to the mat);

for execution of a spectacular ***lift and throw*** for a near fall.

3 points are awarded:
for any hold in which an opponent is taken immediately to his back.

4 points are awarded:
for a ***grand amplitude*** in which an opponent is sent with feet flying onto his back. In this classic technique, no pin of the shoulders is needed.

Attire *is a 1-piece, close-fitting garment in red or blue. Light knee wraps are allowed. Mat shoes must be soft with no nailed soles or buckles. They come heavily laced. Beards are allowed only if they are "not stiff and several months old."*

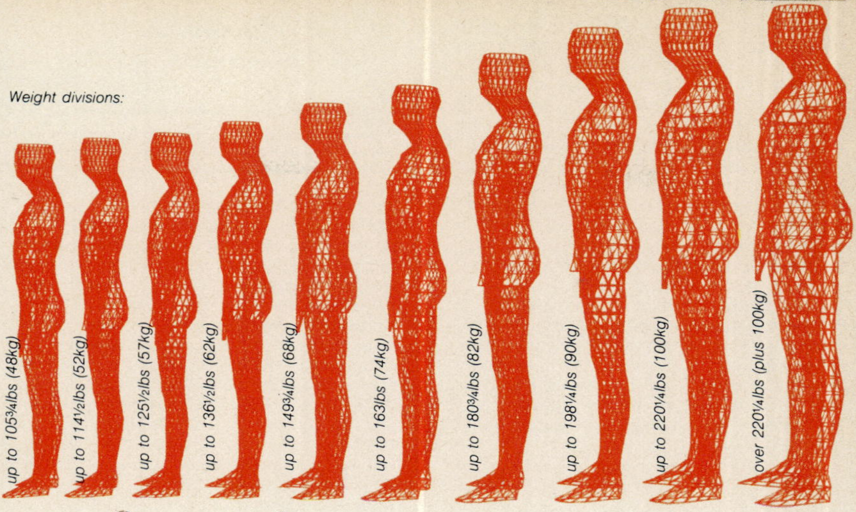

Weight divisions:
up to 105¾lbs (48kg)
up to 114½lbs (52kg)
up to 125½lbs (57kg)
up to 136½lbs (62kg)
up to 149¾lbs (68kg)
up to 163lbs (74kg)
up to 180¾lbs (82kg)
up to 198¼lbs (90kg)
up to 220¼lbs (100kg)
over 220¼lbs (plus 100kg)

Computer Graphics by William Fetter

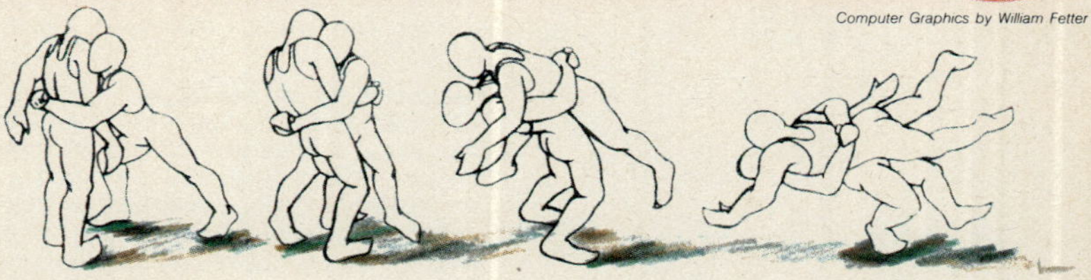

Grand amplitude throw

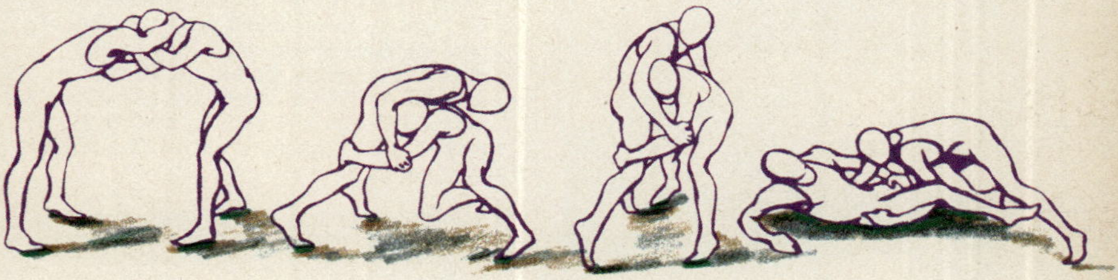

Takedown

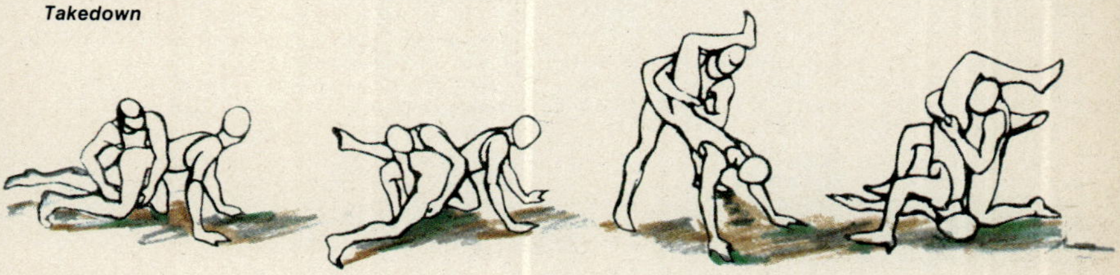

Crotch lift

Rounds are 3min in duration for each of 2 rounds, with 1min between rounds. Elapsed time of a round is announced by the timekeeper at 1min intervals. The average time of an Olympic bout is between 7-8min.

Olympic kingpins: Soviet domination in the last 3 Games has run to 33 medals in freestyle and Greco-Roman. Bulgaria's 6 medals and 4 each by Japan and the USA put the only real dent in that remarkable record.

Santa Barbara
San Gabriel Mountains
405
10
Anaheim Convention Center
5
Distance from Coliseum: 24 miles (39km)

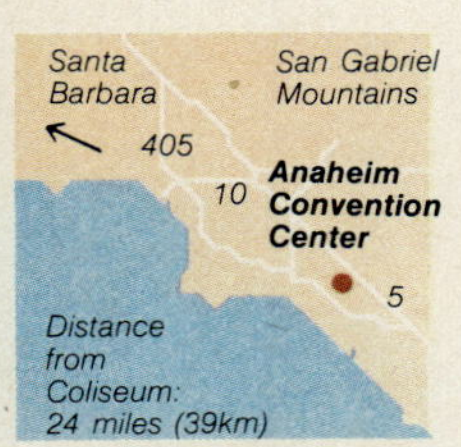

Super-sized ***Chris Taylor*** *(USA), bronze medal wrestler at the 1972 Munich Games, tipped the scales at 420lbs (190.5kg). The all-time Olympic behemoth was as strong as* ***3*** *average men.*

Winner: A match may be terminated and winner named when one wrestler piles up 12 or more points over his opponent. Otherwise, the wrestler with the highest accumulated point total wins. Ties are broken on the basis of the wrestler with the most 2pt, 3pt and 4pt scores in the match.

Judges include a 3-member international jury, 3 judges per match and a referee.

What to watch for: Wrestlers with the advantage of being on top relax or float, using their body weight and a little leverage to maintain a position which forces the underneath man to work twice as hard to escape.

Egyptian wall paintings date the sport of wrestling to 2350 BC, but until the 20th century, no weight classifications were used to equalize matches. Japanese sumo wrestling dates from the 3rd century BC. Modern Greco-Roman style, a French refinement of ancient Greek and Roman rules, was organized in the 1860s.

Carl Westergren *and* **Ivar Johansson** (SWE) and **Aleksandr Medved** *(USSR) all captured 3 Olympic wrestling golds.*

YACHTING

Racing sailors know that if you want ideal wind and water conditions for small yachts, you come to California's San Pedro Bay south of Los Angeles. "Skill and not luck determines winners there," say Olympic veterans.

Unpredictable wind conditions have raised havoc with past Olympic Games yachting, such as in 1968 in Acapulco. Skippers came to Mexico from across the world with light-weather boats rigged and tuned for expected light zephyrs. They got a Pacific storm with capsizing swells and hot winds, which upset all planned tactics.

But San Pedro Bay has a consistent yet demanding quality. Winds are usually west-southwesterly at a steady 10-15 knots, with an increase to 18-22 knots in the afternoon. The bay's current is a regular north-to-south. Fog is rare, so are the storms. Temperature in July-August averages about 70°F (21°C).

*Of interest to Olympic sailors is the **Catalina Eddy**. This low pressure area is centered near Catalina Island, 35mi (56km) to the southwest. It spins the air and can cause tough wind conditions, up to 25 knots on occasion.*

Olympic sailing events in 1984 will number 7, plus a demonstration sport. Racing will be offered for keel, centerboard and catamaran boats of from about 14' (4.2m) to over 26' (7.9m). In addition, 2 sailboard events will be featured: Windgliding, the newest of the Games sailing events; and Windsurfing, the demonstration event.

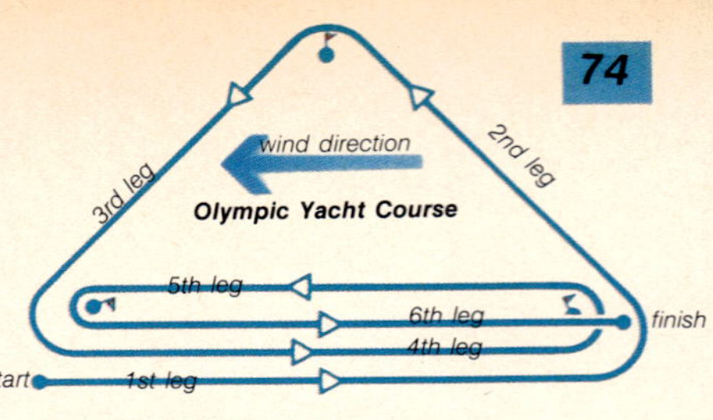

Course and Procedure

The winner is the yacht which legally crosses the starting line, traverses a set number of buoys in official order and is first across the finish line. Olympic courses are a combination of triangles and windward/leeward legs (see diagram above). Yacht classes are assigned to different sailing areas designated ***Alpha*** (windglider), ***Bravo,*** (470/Finn), ***Charlie*** (Soling/Star) and ***Delta*** (Tornado/Flying Dutchman). Upwind legs are sailed with much ***tacking*** (zigzag action) into the wind at about a 45° angle. Downwind legs are sailed straight with the wind directly behind (pushing) the boat. Boats sail toward bright-colored inflated buoys. The average distance will be 12mi (19.3km).

Windsurfing will premiere in 1984 as an Olympic demonstration sport. Like the newest of the Games' official yachting events, Windgliding, this is a sailboard event; the 2 types, or classes, of sailboard differ in size and shape and sail dimension. While Windgliders will be limited to the triangular race course of other yachting events, board surfers in the Windsurfer class will try to establish the versatility of these *surfboards with sails* in 3 events: long-distance race, slalom and freestyle. Men and women will compete separately for medals in these contests as well as for medals to be presented to the all-around high scorers.

Trapeze: *Racers have marked physical agility. Those bodies you see leaning far out over the water are held in a harnesslike* ***trapeze*** *clipped to a securing wire. The principle is to get some of the crew's weight further outboard, thus increasing the boat's total righting moment under stronger sail or wind conditions.*

Start of race: *While skippers maneuver in various ways to be in position to hit the starting line promptly, the order of signals given at 5min intervals is:*

Warning signal: *hoisting of the* ***Class flag***

Preparatory signal: *code flag* ***P*** *hoisted*

Starting signal: *both the 2 above flags are lowered and a gun or* ***hooter*** *is sounded.*

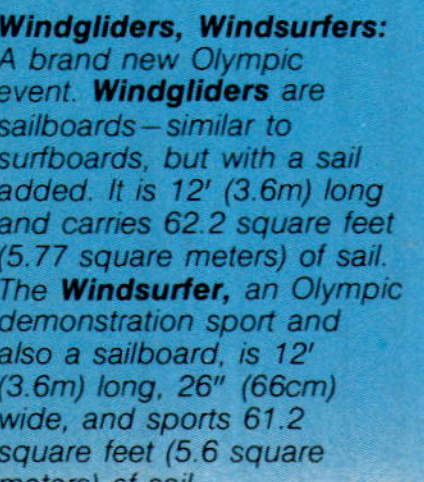

Windgliders, Windsurfers: *A brand new Olympic event.* ***Windgliders*** *are sailboards – similar to surfboards, but with a sail added. It is 12' (3.6m) long and carries 62.2 square feet (5.77 square meters) of sail. The* ***Windsurfer,*** *an Olympic demonstration sport and also a sailboard, is 12' (3.6m) long, 26" (66cm) wide, and sports 61.2 square feet (5.6 square meters) of sail.*

Finn: *It's one of the smallest boats raced, at 14'9" (4.50m), beam of 4'11" (1.51m), and 107 square feet (9.91 square meters) of sail area. These centerboard dinghies are sailed by a single crewman.*

470: *A 15'4¾" (4.70m)-long centerboard dinghy, the 470 has a 27'7¾" (8.43m) beam and sail area of 145 square feet (13.48 square meters). It carries* ***spinnaker*** *and crew of 2.*

Flying Dutchman: *A centerboard boat of 19'10" (6.04m) and 202 square feet (18.76 square meters) of sail, the Dutchman has a 2-man crew. It carries a* ***spinnaker,*** *a billowing, parachute-like sail that pulls a boat downwind. It's the most picturesque of all sails.*

Point scoring: Olympic yachting employs a low-scoring system whereby the 1st place boat receives no points, as:

Place	Points
1st	0
2nd	3
3rd	5.7
4th	8
5th	10
6th	11.7
7th	13
8th	place + 6

Prohibitions:
Banned actions include releasing into the water any substance which reduces hull friction, ***pumping*** *(frequent, rapid trimming of sails in a bird-wing effect),* ***ooching*** *(crew lunging forward or aft suddenly) and repeated forceful movement of the helm, called* ***sculling.***

Sailing Terms
Windward *– direction from which wind is blowing*
Leeward *– direction to which wind is blowing*
Tacking *– to change from port to starboard, or vice versa, turning bow of boat into wind. Command is* ***hard alee.***
Jibing *– to change from port to starboard tack, or vice-versa, turning bow of boat away from the wind*
Beating *– sailing to windward*
Closehauled *– about 45° from direction of the wind*
Veering *– change in wind direction clockwise in relation to the compass*
Slot effect *– funneling of air behind the mainsail through slot formed between the main and the jib*
Heeling *– when boat leans over*
Luffing *– shaking of sails when boat is headed too much into wind or sails are improperly trimmed*

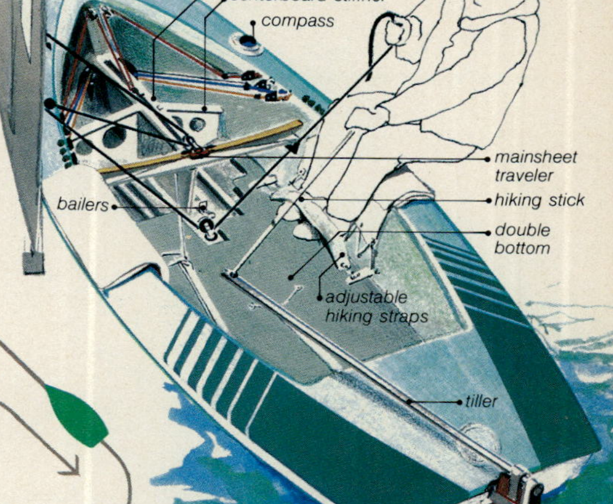

wind direction

A

B

C

Green has right-of-way

Rules/Right of Way:
A yacht ***passing*** *a mark on the wrong side must return by that side and pass correctly.*
When yachts are on the ***same tack,*** *the windward yacht must keep clear (**A**).*
When yachts are on ***opposite tacks,*** *the port tack yacht must keep clear (**B**).*
At a time when both yachts are ***changing tack,*** *the yacht on the opponent's port side keeps clear (**C**).*

Watch the boat on the left-hand side, or inside, along the triangular-shaped Olympic courses. With a westerly wind, the advantage is to the insider. When 2 boats are sailing up to catch a westerly, the yacht on the left catches the wind first and turns in front of the boat on the outside.

Tornado: *This is a 2-hulled catamaran, just 20′ (6m) long, beam of 10′ (3.05m) and sail area of 235 square feet (21.83 square meters). It has a crew of 2. Very fast craft.*

Star: *One of the most popular boats among racers, the Star is 22′8½″ (6.91m) with a keel and crew of 2.*

Soling: *This is the largest Olympic yacht class. Keeled boats are 26′9″ (8.16m) long, with a beam of 6′4″ (1.91m) 250 square feet (23.22 square meters) of sail and a crew of 3.*

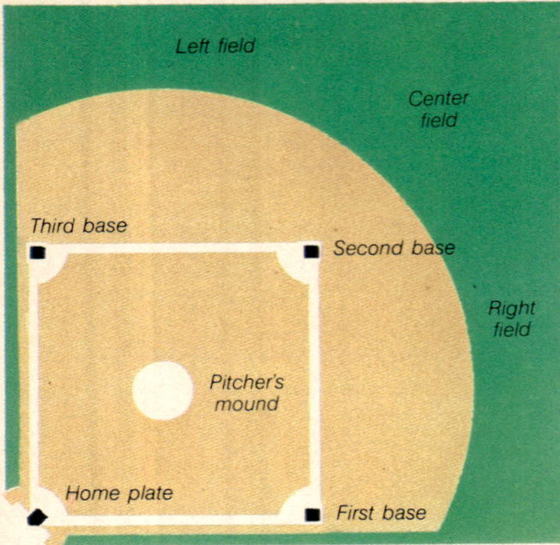

Pitcher: *This is the showman of the game. All eyes focus on the pitcher as he uses subtle variations of ball-throwing to cause the batter to* ***strike out.***

Fielding team positions: *catcher, pitcher, 1st baseman, 2nd baseman, shortstop, 3rd baseman, right fielder, center fielder, left fielder.*

Outs: *While the batting team is trying to advance men around the bases, the fielding team is trying to get 3 opponents out. They can do this by a) catching a batted ball before it touches the ground, called a* ***fly ball,*** *b)* ***tagging*** *(touching) a runner with the ball, or c) tagging the base to which a runner is running if the base he left becomes occupied (called a* ***force out****).*

Double play: *2 outs on one batted ball;* ***triple play*** *is 3 outs.*

Officials: *They include a* ***chief umpire*** *standing behind the catcher and umpires for 1st, 2nd and 3rd bases.*

Home run: *occurs when a batter hits the ball far enough away or the fielding team fumbles the ball long enough (an* ***error****) for the batter to completely circle all 4 bases. When a home run is batted with a man on each base, 4 runs are scored (one for the batter and one for men on 1st, 2nd and 3rd bases). This is called a* ***grand slam.***

Home plate: *the base from which the batter bats and to which he must return to score.*

Wind-up: *the series of motions a pitcher goes through before he releases the ball. These motions compress the energy of the pitcher's body into the ball's momentum. Body energy moves from the legs and hips to the shoulder, then the arm, then to the final flick of the wrist and into the hurling baseball. A strong pitcher can throw a baseball up to 98mph (157km).*

Different ***grips*** *vary the ball's flight pattern in hopes of tricking the batter into making a strike.*

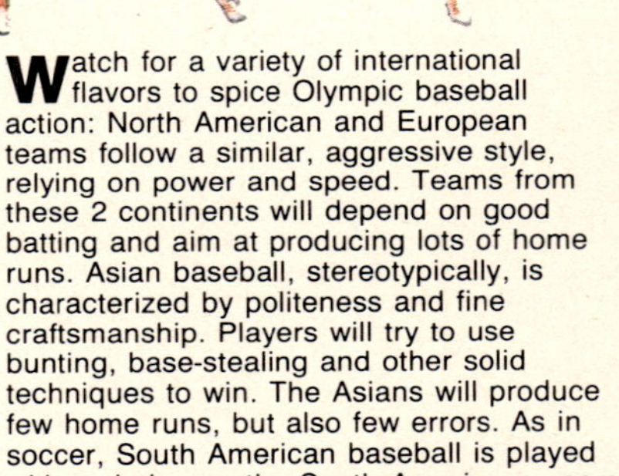

Baseball is rapidly becoming a true international sport. Of the 77 countries where 9-inning baseball is played today, 47 are members of the ***International Association of Amateur Baseball*** (AINBA). Six times, enthusiasts have demonstrated the game at the Olympics, but 1984 will be the first time a full tournament will be played.

A baseball team consists of 9 men, plus a designated hitter—a tenth man who doesn't play defensively but only bats for the pitcher.

Scoring ***runs*** are achieved by batting the ball and attempting to progress once around the 4 bases (corners) of the diamond-shaped playing field. The ***batting*** (offensive) team continues until the ***fielding*** (defensive) team has gotten 3 opponents out (see ***outs***). At this time the teams switch places, the fielders getting their turn at bat and the batters positioning themselves in the field.

Special medals will be awarded at the Los Angeles demo of baseball, and competition is expected to be intense. Six countries will reach the finals after a round-robin. Teams expected to dominate play include Cuba, Japan, the Dominican Republic, Venezuela, Holland, Korea, Italy and the USA.

Watch for a variety of international flavors to spice Olympic baseball action: North American and European teams follow a similar, aggressive style, relying on power and speed. Teams from these 2 continents will depend on good batting and aim at producing lots of home runs. Asian baseball, stereotypically, is characterized by politeness and fine craftsmanship. Players will try to use bunting, base-stealing and other solid techniques to win. The Asians will produce few home runs, but also few errors. As in soccer, South American baseball is played with melodrama; the South Americans seem to have a special, highly emotional attachment to their sports. So expect lots of volatile reactions, arguments and intensity from these teams.

Innings: *Designates that each team has both fielded and had 3* ***at bats.*** *A game has 9 innings; in case of rain, a game is considered finished after 5½ innings, or 4½ if the home team is winning.*

Ball: *pitch not swung at by the batter that is outside the* ***strike zone.*** *Four balls allow the batter to advance to first base, called a* ***walk.*** *If a batter is hit by a pitched ball, provided he tries to avoid being hit, he automatically walks.*

Steal: *when a runner progresses to the next base by stealth, not by being advanced by the next batter's hit, walk or error.*

Strike: *when the batter attempts to hit a pitched ball but misses; or, when the batter fails to hit a ball that is pitched within the strike zone. Three strikes by a single batter counts as an out against the team and is called a* ***strike out.***

Foul ball: *ball batted into the foul zone. The first 2 foul balls each count as a strike, the 3rd and subsequent fouls do not count towards an out.*

Catcher's equipment

Baseball bat: *Made of hickory, hardwoods or aluminum, bats come in various sizes and weights. Aluminum bats will probably be the choice of Olympic batters. Tape may be used to improve grip, but only along the lower ⅓ of the bat.*

Ball: *The raised stitching which holds the leather cover of a baseball together gives the ball unusual air resistance characteristics. Pitchers know these characteristics and use them to advantage in trying to create strikes. Inside the cover is wound thread over a hard rubber core.*

TENNIS (DEMONSTRATION)

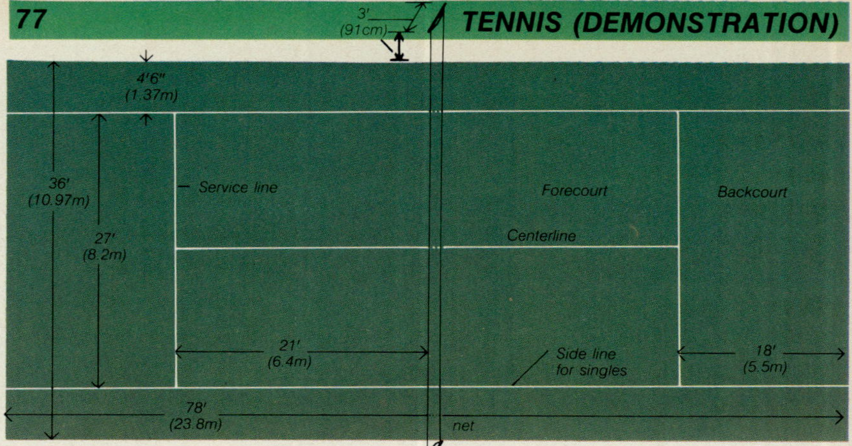

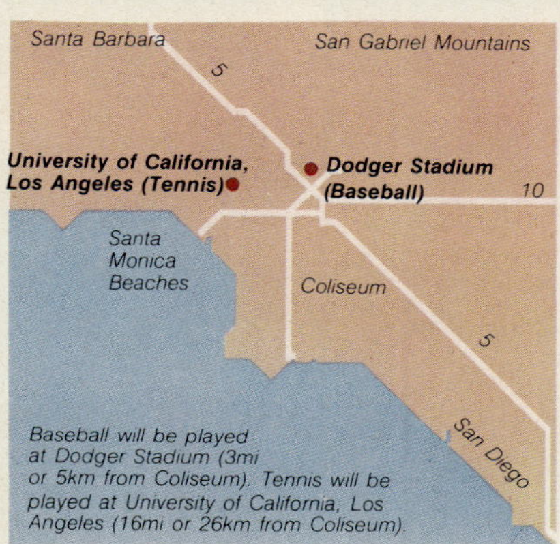

This veteran sport was last played, as a demonstration, at Mexico City in 1968. But it was in 1900 that lawn tennis gave Charlotte Cooper (GBR) the first women's Olympic gold medal.

The Los Angeles demo of tennis will follow most traditional tournament rules. One major exception involves amateur athletes. This will be an ***open competition;*** both amateur and professional players will be allowed to compete. The only limit is one of age—contestants must be 20 years of age or younger.

Nations around the world will send a total of 32 men and 32 women to compete in singles (one against one) matches. The USA, as host country, will enter 4 men and 4 women players. Other nations will be limited to 2 each.

Olympic tennis will also employ tie-breaker games.

Racquet: *The frame may be wood, metal or a composite material such as graphite. Usual tournament weight is between 13-14½oz (369-411g). String tension, along with frame material, is a major variable. The nylon, gut or hybrid (nylon and gut) strings are tightened or loosened according to a player's preference. Tighter strings give more rebound to the ball.*

Scoring: *This is perhaps the most confusing part of the game.*

Zero points *is called* ***love,*** *from the French* ***l'oeuf*** *(egg) for zero.*

Deuce, *also from the French, means the player must win 2 consecutive points.*

1pt *is called* ***15.***

2pts *is called* ***30.***

3pts *is called* ***40.***

The ***4th point*** *is* ***game,*** *unless there is a* ***deuce*** *(see below).*

A ***point*** *is lost by a player if he:*

hits the ball into the ***net***

hits the ball ***outside*** *the court*

fails *to hit the ball*

lets it ***bounce twice*** *before hitting it*

Service: *A player serves the ball for a full game, then service passes to his opponent for the next game. The person serving is generally considered to have an advantage in scoring.*

A ***line ball*** *– one landing on a boundary line – is considered hit within the court.*

To win a game, *a player must score 4pts, unless the score is 3 each (**deuce**). Then, a 2pt lead must be taken. Because of this rule the deuce situation, where no player has a 2pt lead, can continue indefinitely.*

A ***set*** *is won with 6 games, unless contestants tie at 5 games each (5-all), then play continues until one wins by a 2-game margin. Women must win 2 of 3 sets to win a* ***match;*** *men must win 3 of 5 sets. When games stand at a 6-all tie, a tie-breaker game is played. Rules of a tie-breaker differ from a regular game.*

Gear: *Traditionally white to reflect the sun, shirts and shorts, or tennis dresses, are comfortable, non-binding and sweat-absorbant. Tennis shoes are traditional athletic shoes but with a thicker sole and canvas, and stronger seams.*

Tennis ball: *2 rubber half spheres fused together, with a Dacron and wool cover, it measures 2½-2 5/8" (6.35-6.66cm) at the diameter and weighs 2-2½oz (56.7-70.8g). Air pressure varies; the greater the pressure, the* ***faster*** *the ball.*

OLYMPIC & WORLD RECORDS

100 Meters

Men
Olympic Record: 9.95
Jim Hines, USA, 1968
World Record: 9.93
Calvin Smith, USA, 1983

Women
Olympic Record: 11.01
Annegret Richter, FRG, 1976
World Record: 10.79
Evelyn Ashford, USA, 1983

one length = 100m

200 Meters

Men
Olympic Record: 19.83
Tommie Smith, USA, 1968
World Record: 19.72
Pietro Mennea, ITA, 1979

Women
Olympic Record: 22.03
Barbel Wockel, GDR, 1980
World Record: 21.71
Marita Koch, GDR, 1979

one length = 100m

100 Meter Hurdles

Women
Olympic Record: 12.56
Vera Komisova, USSR, 1980
World Record: 12.36
Grazyna Rabsztyn, POL, 1980

one length = 100m

110 Meter Hurdles

Men
Olympic Record: 13.24
Rod Milburn, USA, 1972
World Record: 12.93
Renaldo Nehemiah, USA, 1981

one length = 100m

1500 Meters

Men
Olympic Record: 3:34.91
Kipchoge Keino, KEN, 1968
World Record: 3:31.24
Sydney Maree, USA, 1983

Women
Olympic Record; 3:56.58
Tatyana Kazankina
USSR, 1980
World Record: 3:52.47
Tatyana Kazankina
USSR, 1980

one length = 1,000m (one kilometer)

4 × 400 Meter Relay

Men
Olympic/World Record: 2:56.16
USA, 1968

Women
Olympic Record: 3:19.23
GDR, 1976
World Record: 3:19.04
GDR, 1982

one length = 1,000m (one kilometer)

10,000 Meters

Men
Olympic Record: 27:38.35
Lasse Viren, FIN, 1972
World Record: 27:22.4
Henry Rono, KEN, 1978

one length = 10,000m (ten kilometers)

Marathon

Men
Olympic Record: 2:09.55
Waldemar Cierpinski
GDR, 1976
World Record: 2:03.18
Alberto Salazar
USA, 1981

one length = 10,000m (ten kilometers)

Errata: Salazar's Marathon World Record should read 2:08:13.

400 Meters

Men
Olympic/World Record: 43.86
Lee Evans, USA, 1968

Women
Olympic Record: 48.88
Marita Koch, GDR, 1980
World Record: 47.99
Jarmila Kratochvilova
TCH, 1983

one length = 100m

800 Meters

Men
Olympic Record: 1:43.50
Alberto Juantorena
CUB, 1976
World Record: 1:41.73
Sebastian Coe
GBR, 1981

Women
Olympic Record: 1:53.43
Nadyezhda Olizaryenko
USSR, 1980
World Record: 1:53.28
Jarmila Kratochvilova
TCH, 1983

one length = 100m

400 Meter Hurdles

Men
Olympic Record: 47.64
Edwin Moses, USA, 1976
World Record: 47.13
Edwin Moses, USA, 1980

one length = 100m

4 × 100 Meter Relay

Men
Olympic Record: 38.19
USA, 1972
World Record: 37.86
USA, 1983

Women
Olympic/World Record: 41.60
GDR, 1980

one length = 100m

3000 Meter Steeplechase

Men
Olympic Record: 8:08.02
Anders Garderud, SWE, 1976
World Record: 8:05.40
Henry Rono, KEN, 1978

one length = 1,000m (one kilometer)

5000 Meters

Men
Olympic Record: 13:20.34
Brendan Foster, GBR, 1976
World Record: 13:00.42
David Moorcroft, GBR, 1982

one length = 1,000m (one kilometer)

20 Kilometer Walk

Men
Olympic Record: 1:23:35.5
Maurizio Damilano, ITA, 1980
World Record: 1:20:06.8
Daniel Bautista, MEX, 1979

one length = 10,000m (ten kilometers)

50 Kilometer Walk

Men
Olympic Record: 3:49:24
Hartwig Gauder
GDR, 1980
World Record: 3:41:39
Raul Gonzales
MEX, 1979

one length = 10,000m (ten kilometers)

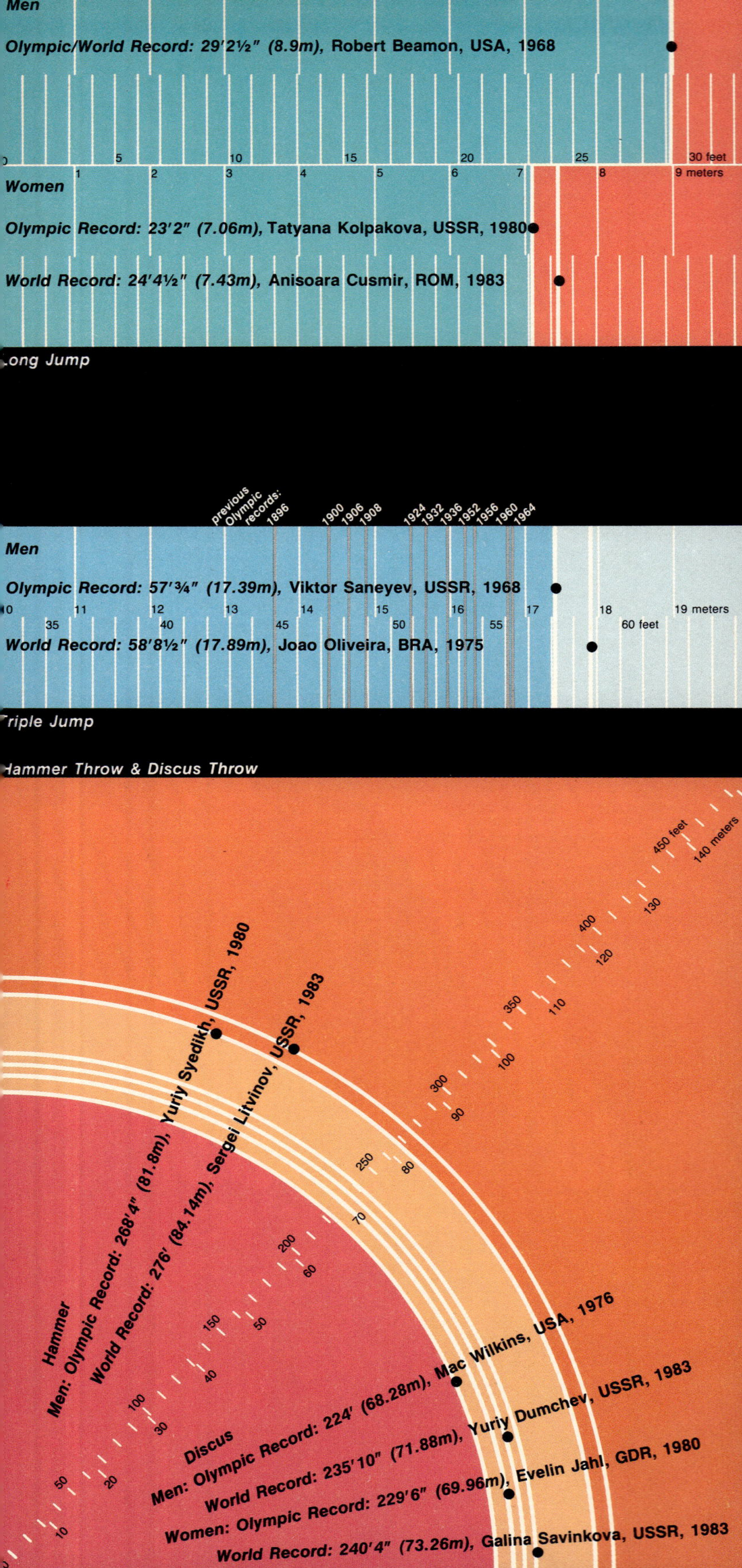
Men
Olympic/World Record: 29′2½″ (8.9m), Robert Beamon, USA, 1968
5
10
15
20
25
30 feet
1
2
3
4
5
6
7
8
9 meters
Women
Olympic Record: 23′2″ (7.06m), Tatyana Kolpakova, USSR, 1980
World Record: 24′4½″ (7.43m), Anisoara Cusmir, ROM, 1983
ong Jump
previous Olympic records:
1896
1900
1906
1908
1924
1932
1936
1952
1956
1960
1964
Men
Olympic Record: 57′¾″ (17.39m), Viktor Saneyev, USSR, 1968
10
11
12
13
14
15
16
17
18
19 meters
35
40
45
50
55
60 feet
World Record: 58′8½″ (17.89m), Joao Oliveira, BRA, 1975
riple Jump
ammer Throw & Discus Throw
Hammer
Men: Olympic Record: 268′4″ (81.8m), Yuriy Syedikh, USSR, 1980
World Record: 276′ (84.14m), Sergei Litvinov, USSR, 1983
Discus
Men: Olympic Record: 224′ (68.28m), Mac Wilkins, USA, 1976
World Record: 235′10″ (71.88m), Yuriy Dumchev, USSR, 1983
Women: Olympic Record: 229′6″ (69.96m), Evelin Jahl, GDR, 1980
World Record: 240′4″ (73.26m), Galina Savinkova, USSR, 1983
10
20
30
40
50
60
70
80
90
100
110
120
130
140 meters
50
100
150
200
250
300
350
400
450 feet

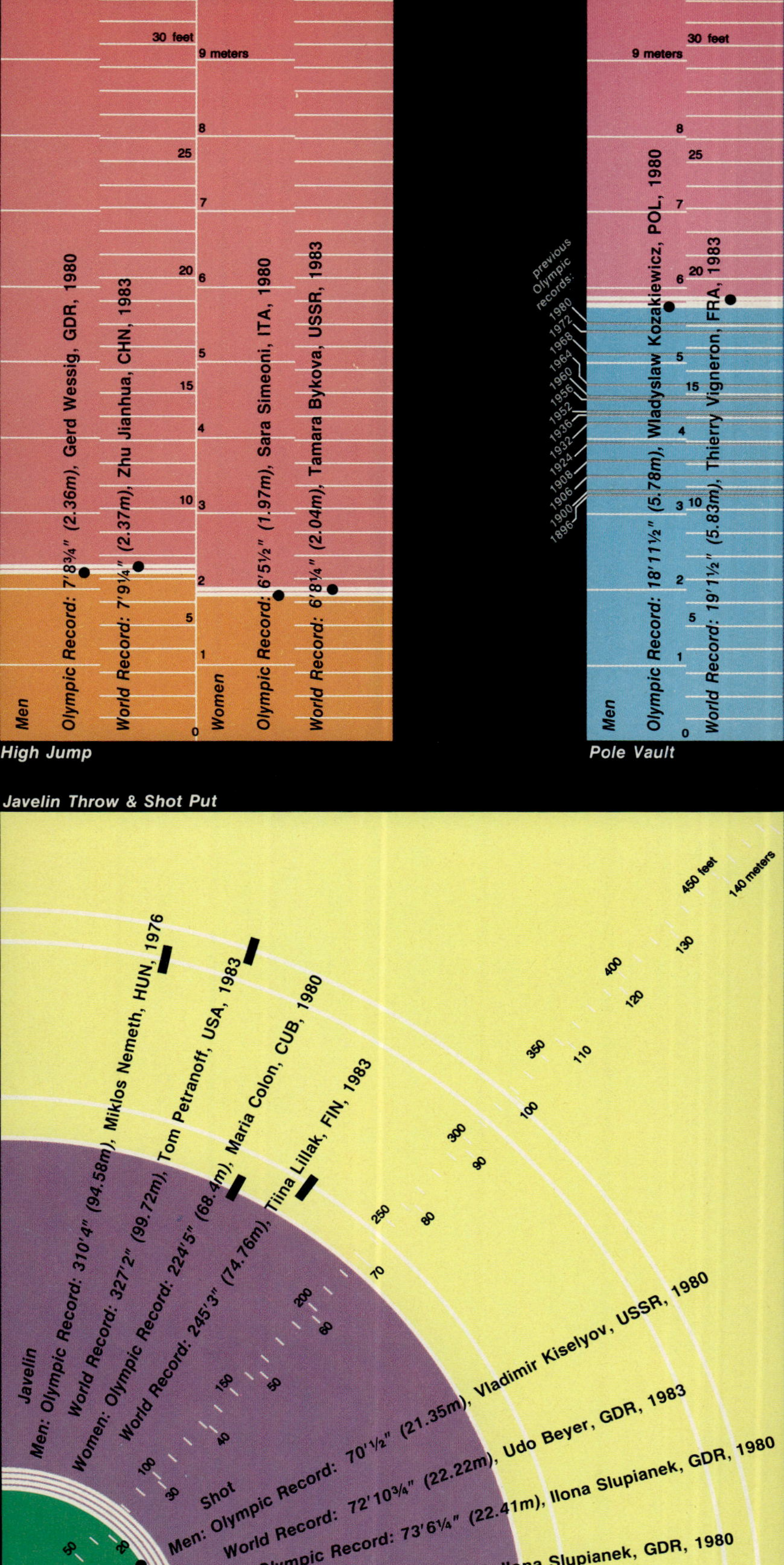
High Jump
Men
Olympic Record: 7'8¾" (2.36m), Gerd Wessig, GDR, 1980
World Record: 7'9¼" (2.37m), Zhu Jianhua, CHN, 1983
Women
Olympic Record: 6'5½" (1.97m), Sara Simeoni, ITA, 1980
World Record: 6'8¼" (2.04m), Tamara Bykova, USSR, 1983
30 feet
9 meters
Pole Vault
Men
Olympic Record: 18'11½" (5.78m), Wladyslaw Kozakiewicz, POL, 1980
World Record: 19'1½" (5.83m), Thierry Vigneron, FRA, 1983
previous Olympic records:
1980
1972
1968
1964
1960
1956
1952
1936
1932
1924
1908
1906
1900
1896
Javelin Throw & Shot Put
Javelin
Men: Olympic Record: 310'4" (94.58m), Miklos Nemeth, HUN, 1976
World Record: 327'2" (99.72m), Tom Petranoff, USA, 1983
Women: Olympic Record: 224'5" (68.4m), Maria Colon, CUB, 1980
World Record: 245'3" (74.76m), Tiina Lillak, FIN, 1983
Shot
Men: Olympic Record: 70'½" (21.35m), Vladimir Kiselyov, USSR, 1980
World Record: 72'10¾" (22.22m), Udo Beyer, GDR, 1983
Women: Olympic Record: 73'6¼" (22.41m), Ilona Slupianek, GDR, 1980
World Record: 73'8" (22.45m), Ilona Slupianek, GDR, 1980
450 feet
140 meters

100 Meters	Event	Record
Men	Freestyle	*Olympic Record: 49.99* Jim Montgomery, USA, 1976 *World Record: 49.36* Ambrose Gaines, USA, 1981
	Backstroke	*Olympic Record: 55.49* John Naber, USA, 1976 *World Record: 55.19* Rick Carey, USA, 1983
	Breaststroke	*Olympic Record: 1:03.11* John Hencken, USA, 1976 *World Record: 1:02.28* Steve Lundquist, USA, 1983
	Butterfly	*Olympic Record: 54.27* Mark Spitz, USA, 1972 *World Record: 53.44* Matt Gribble, USA, 1983
Women	Freestyle	*Olympic/World Record: 54.79* Barbara Krause, GDR, 1980
	Backstroke	*Olympic/World Record: 1:00.86* Rica Reinisch, GDR, 1980
	Breaststroke	*Olympic Record: 1:08.51* Ute Geweniger, GDR, 1980 *World Record: 1:08.60* Ute Geweniger, GDR, 1981
	Butterfly	*Olympic Record: 1:00.13* Kornelia Ender, GDR, 1976 *World Record: 57.93* Mary T. Meagher, USA, 1982

400 Meters	Event	Record
Men	Freestyle	*Olympic Record: 3:51.31* Vladimir Salnikov USSR,1980 *World Record: 3:48.32* Vladimir Salnikov USSR, 1983
	Individual Medley	*Olympic Record: 4:22.89* Aleksandr Sidorenko USSR, 1980 *World Record: 4:19.78* Ricardo Prado, BRA, 1982
	Medley Relay	*Olympic Record: 3:42.22* USA, 1976 *World Record: 3:40.42* USA, 1983
	Freestyle Relay	*Olympic Record: 3:26.42* USA, 1972 *World Record: 3:19.26* USA, 1982
Women	Freestyle	*Olympic Record: 4:08.76* Ines Diers, GDR, 1980 *World Record: 4:06.28* Tracey Wickham, AUS, 1978
	Individual Medley	*Olympic Record: 4:36.29* Petra Schneider, GDR, 1980 *World Record: 4:36.10* Petra Schneider, GDR, 1982
	Medley Relay	*Olympic Record: 4:06.67* GDR, 1980 *World Record: 4:05.79* GDR, 1983
	Freestyle Relay	*Olympic/World Record: 3:42.71* GDR, 1980

Olympic Record: 1:49.81
Sergei Kopliakov, USSR, 1980
World Record: 1:47.87
Michael Gross, FRG, 1983

Olympic Record: 1:59.19
John Naber, USA, 1976
World Record: 1:58.93
Rick Carey, USA, 1983

Olympic Record: 2:15.11
David Wilkie, GBR, 1976
World Record: 2:14.77
Victor Davis, CAN, 1982

Olympic Record: 1:59.23
Michael Bruner, USA, 1976
World Record: 1:57.05
Michael Gross, FRG, 1983

Olympic Record: 2:07.17
Gunnar Larsson, SWE, 1972
World Record: 2:02.25
Alex Baumann, CAN, 1982

Olympic Record: 1:58.33
Barbara Krause, GDR, 1980
World Record: 1:58.23
Cynthia Woodhead, USA, 1979

Olympic Record: 2:11.77
Rica Reinisch, GDR, 1980
World Record: 2:09.91
Cornelia Sirch, GDR, 1982

Olympic Record: 2:29.54
Lina Kachyusite, USSR, 1980
World Record: 2:28.36
Lina Kachyusite, USSR, 1979

Olympic Record: 2:10.44
Ines Geissler, GDR, 1980
World Record: 2:05.96
Mary T. Meagher, USA, 1982

Olympic Record: 2:23.07
Shane Gould, AUS, 1972
World Record: 2:11.73
Ute Geweniger, GDR, 1981

800 Meters
Men Freestyle Relay

Women Freestyle

1,500 Meters
Men
Freestyle

Weight class	Olympic Record (combined score, snatch and jerk)	World Record (combined score, snatch and jerk)
242lbs/110kg (over)	970lbs/440kg Sultan Rakhmanov, USSR, 1980	1,014lbs/460kg Alexander Kurlovich, USSR, 1983
242lbs/110kg	931lbs/422.5kg Leonid Taranenko, USSR, 1980	959lbs/435kg Leonid Taranenko, USSR, 1982
220½lbs/100kg	871lbs/395kg Ota Zaremba, TCH, 1980	970lbs/440kg Yuri Zakhavevich, USSR, 1983
198¼lbs/90kg	843lbs/382.5kg David Rigert, USSR, 1976	931lbs/422.5kg Blagoi Blagoyev, BUL, 1983
182lbs/82.5kg	882lbs/400kg Yurik Vardanyan, USSR, 1980	882lbs/400kg Yurik Vardanyan, USSR, 1980
165¼lbs/75kg	794lbs/360kg Assen Zlatev, BUL, 1980	806lbs/365.5kg Yanko Rusev, USSR, 1982
149lbs/67.5kg	755lbs/342.5kg Yanko Rusev, BUL, 1980	761lbs/345kg Joachim Kunz, GDR, 1981
132lbs/60kg	639lbs/290kg Viktor Mazin, USSR, 1980	667lbs/302.5kg Beloslav Manolov, BUL, 1983
123.5lbs/56kg	606lbs/275kg Daniel Nunez, CUB, 1980	634 lbs/287.5 kg O. Mirzoyan, USSR, 1983
114.5lbs/52kg	540lbs/245kg Kanybek Osmanoliev, USSR, 1980	566lbs/257kg Neno Terviiski, BUL, 1983

1 Takashi Ono, JPN This master gymnast won golds in the horizontal bars in 1956-60, long horse vault in 1960, team combined exercises in '60 and '64.

2 Gary L. Anderson, USA An unusual left-handed shooter, he scored 11 individual and 10 team international gold medals during the 1960s. His pair of Olympic golds were won in '64 and '68.

3 Teofilo Stevenson, CUB He swept the heavyweight boxing matches in 3 consecutive Games, 1972-80.

4 Robert Beamon, USA He astounded the world when he bettered the long jump mark by 21½" at Mexico City with a 29'2½" leap.

5 Kornelia Ender, GDR Perhaps the greatest female swimmer of all time, her 4 golds and 1 silver at Montreal set 3 world records.

6 Sergio Bianchetto, ITA A world leader in cycling events, he was top medalist in the 2000m tandem in '60 and '64, an individual 1000m sprint silver in '64.

7 Abebe Bikila, ETH The Olympics' first two-time marathon winner (1960, 1964) and black Africa's first gold medalist.

8 Francina Blankers-Koen, HOL In 1948, she collected 4 track & field golds: 100m, 200m, 80m hurdles, and as a 4×100m relay team member.

9 Lasse Viren, FIN A *double-double* in the long runs: he captured both the 5000m and 10,000m golds in '72 and '76.

10 Capt. Dhyan Chand, IND When India led the world in hockey, this army officer led India's team, playing center forward in 3 straight Olympic wins (1928-36).

11 Larisa Latynina, USSR Her 9 Olympic golds tie Nurmi and Spitz for 2nd place in total titles (Ewry has 10). Competing from 1956-64, the technically splendid gymnast also won 9 silver and bronze medals.

12 Daniel Morelon, FRA The Olympics' all-time cycling champ won the 1000m individual sprint in 1968-72 and the 2000m tandem in '68, setting new speed records.

13 Shirley Strickland De La Hunty, AUS One of the all-time great hurdlers, she set numerous world marks and received gold medals in '52 and '56.

Sidelines: *Careers of Olympic athletes have included:* **Dorando Pietri,** *Italian marathoner, a candy maker;* **Lasse Viren,** *Finnish runner, a village policeman;* **Micheline Ostermeyer,** *French weightlifter, a concert pianist;* **Horace Ashenfelter,** *steeplechaser from the USA, an FBI agent;* **Abebe Bikila,** *Ethiopian marathon runner, a palace guard;* **Duke Kahanamoku,** *USA's famed Hawaiian swimmer, a sheriff;* **Ferenc Torok,** *Hungarian horseman, a medical doctor;* **Chris Finnigan,** *British boxer, a bricklayer;* **Chuck Walker,** *USA boxer, a professional tap dancer;* **Yan Krummish,** *USSR basketball player, a woodchopper.*

14 Mildred *"Babe"* Didrikson, USA The Olympics' first female star took the 80m hurdles and javelin titles, the silver in the high jump in 1932.

15 Ilona Elek, HUN One of the greatest foil-style fencers of the century, she collected golds in '36 and '48, the silver in '52.

16 Jack Beresford, GBR The top oarsman and sculler in Olympic history, he earned golds in 3 Games, silvers in 2 others (1920-36).

17 Deborah Meyer, USA Winning golds in the 200m, 400m and 800m freestyle swimming races in 1968, she became the first person to win 3 individual gold medals at a single Olympics.

18 Dawn Fraser, AUS She won golds in the 400m freestyle swim in 3 straight Games, 1956-64, a first-ever feat, and 8 medals overall.

19 Willem Ruska, HOL World champion judokan, he took the heavyweight and open judo titles in 1972.

20 Kipchoge *"Kip"* Keino, KEN Africa's amazing runner won the 1500m in '68, the 3000m steeplechase 4 years later.

21 Lars Hall, SWE He won successive individual gold medals in the modern pentathlon in '52 and '56, the only man to achieve the feat.

22 Alberto Juantorena, CUB Accomplishing a first in Games history, he took the 400m and 800m footraces in a single meet, 1976.

23 Duke Paoa Kahanamoku, USA Famed Hawaiian swimmer scored 3 golds in freestyle events, plus 2 silvers, 1912-24.

24 Shane Gould, AUS She set world records in 3 swimming events in a single Games (1972) and took 3 golds, a silver and a bronze.

25 Olga Korbut, USSR Princess of Olympic gymnasts, at age 17 she won 3 golds (1972 team combined exercises, beam and floor exercises), another gold 4 years later (1976 team combined exercises), and 2 individual silver medals.

26 Nadia Comaneci, ROM At age 14 she became the first gymnast to score a perfect 10pts in the Montreal Olympic competition, taking home 3 gold, a silver and a bronze from Montreal; in 1980 she again scored 2 golds.

27 Johnny Weissmuller, USA Often cited as the greatest swimmer of the first half of this century, he won 5 golds in 1924-28. Many of his 28 career world records stood for decades. He became famous as Tarzan in the movies.

Oldest Olympic medalist **Oscar G. Swahn** *(SWE) was 65 years old when he competed on a 1912 gold medal shooting team.* **Marjorie Gestring,** *(USA), age 13, won a gold medal in the 1936 diving competition.*

28 **Iain Murray Rose, AUS** Perhaps Australia's greatest swimmer, he captured the 400m, 1500m and 4×200m freestyle golds in 1956 and the 400m freestyle 4 years later.

29 **Wilma Rudolph, USA** Number 17 of 19 children, she overcame childhood paralysis to win golds in the 100m, 200m and 4×100m team relay in 1960.

30 **Gert Fredriksson, SWE** King of Olympic canoeing, he scored 6 gold, a silver and a bronze from 1948-60.

31 **Viktor Saneyev, USSR** At Mexico City he won the triple jump with a record-setting mark. He also earned the next 2 Olympic triple jump golds for 3 consecutive titles.

32 **Peter Snell, NZL** The Olympics' only 3-time mid-distance gold medalist, he won the 800m in 1960, the 1500m in 1960-64.

33 **Mark Spitz, USA** In a single Olympiad (1972), he collected 7 individual and team gold medals in swimming, more than ever had been won before: 100m, 200m freestyles; 100m, 200m butterfly; 100m freestyle relay; 4×200m freestyle relay; 4×100m medley relay. He also took relay golds in '68, for a total of 9.

34 **Nikolai Andrianov, USSR** After scoring a gold at Munich when only 19, he went on to dominate male gymnastics.

35 **Karoly Takacs, HUN** He began competition as a right-handed shooter but, when he lost that hand in a hand-grenade explosion, taught himself to shoot left-handed. He scored rapid-fire pistol gold medals in '48 and '52.

36 **Jim Thorpe, USA** Legendary American Indian athlete held the Olympic decathlon record for 15 years; he won both decathlon and pentathlon in 1912, but his medals were withdrawn when his amateur status was questioned (he had played baseball for a small salary). In 1982, 20 years after Thorpe's death, his medals were returned to his family and his marks reinstated.

37 **Vera Caslavska, TCH** This glamorous gymnast amassed 11 Olympic medals, 1960-68, 7 of them gold.

38 **Patricia *"Pat"* (Keller) McCormick, USA** She twice scored a double, taking both diving contests in consecutive Games—the only Olympic athlete to accomplish the sweep. She won in the '52 and '56 springboard and highboard events.

39 **Emil Zatopek, TCH** One of the stars at Helsinki's 1952 Games, he took the 5000m, 10,000m and marathon races. Four years earlier he had won the 10,000m gold and 5000m silver.

40 **Edoardo Mangiarotti, ITA** This left-handed championship fencer's wins include the épée individual in '52; épée team in '36, '52, '56 and '60 (Olympic wins spanning 24 years); and a foil team gold in '56. He also had 7 silver and bronze wins.

41 **Robert B. Mathias, USA** At age 17, he won the Olympic decathlon, amazing his competitors. Then he returned in 1952 to defend his title successfully, the first and only 2-time decathlon winner.

42 **Ray C. Ewry, USA** Ten gold medals! He took the now defunct standing high, standing long and standing triple jumps from 1900-08, the top Olympic medalist of all time.

43 **Betty Cuthbert, AUS** A superstar at both Melbourne and Tokyo, she won 3 women's sprint golds in '56, sat out the '60 Games with an injury and returned in '64 for another gold at 400m.

44 **Charles F. Pahud de Mortanges, HOL** One of the Olympics' most charismatic equestrian champions, he and his beautiful mount, **Marcroix,** won the individual 3-day event gold in 1928 and 1932, team golds in '24 and '28.

45 **Nedo Nadi, ITA** Master fencer and international celebrity, he took the 1912 foil without defeat and, in the 1920 Olympics, won 5 fencing golds.

46 **Akinori Nakayama, JPN** Illustrative of Japan's great male gymnasts, in the 1968 and 1972 Games he amassed 6 gold medals: rings (both Games), parallel bars ('68), horizontal bars ('68) and team combined exercises (both Games).

47 **Paavo J. Nurmi, FIN** All-time great in mid- and long-distance races, he set 22 world records and won 9 gold (including 2 team) and 3 silver Olympic medals.

48 **Alfred A. Oerter, USA** Four consecutive Olympics, 4 consecutive discus gold medals—no one has matched the win record he set from 1956-68.

49 **Vasily Alexeev, USSR** Outstanding weightlifter of the decade, he won the superheavyweight gold medals in 1972 and 1976.

50 **James C. *"Jesse"* Owens, USA** A tremendous track & field athlete, he met the racism of Hitler's '36 Games head on, winning 3 individual and a team gold. He set 9 world records in his career.

51 **Shirley Babashoff, USA** An outstanding freestyle swimmer, she was on the winning 4×100m relay teams in 1972 and 1976. She also collected 1 team and 5 individual silver freestyle medals.

52 **Volmari Iso-Hollo, FIN** The Games' only 2-time steeplechase winner ('32 and '36).

53 **Johannes *"Hannes"* Petteri Kolehmainen, FIN** Pacesetting long distance runner took the 10,000m, 5000m and 8000m cross-country individual in 1912, the marathon in 1920, and helped win the 8000m cross-country team silver in 1912.

54 **Harrison W. Dillard, USA** Inspired by Jesse Owens, he scored golds in the 100m and 4×100m relay in '48, the 4×100m relay and the 110m hurdles in '52.

55 **Vladimir Kuts, USSR** As the star of long distance running at Melbourne in 1956, he won the 5000m and 10,000m golds.

56 **Roland Matthes, GDR** For 8 years he was never beaten in a backstroke swim race, earning both the 100m and 200m golds in '68 and '72, as well as 4 other medals.

57 **Valeri Borzov, USSR** One of Europe's all-time great sprinters, he took the 100m and 200m golds in 1972.

58 **Irena Kirszenstein Szewinska, POL** The first woman runner to beat the 50sec mark at 400m, she was on the winning 4×100m relay team in '64. She won the 200m in '68, the 400m in '76.

59 **Andre Jousseaume, FRA** A military horseman, he won dressage team golds in 1932 and 1948, 5 Olympic equestrian medals in all.

60 **Alvin Kraenzlein, USA** In 1900 he collected 4 golds: long jump, 60m, 110m and 200m hurdles.

61 **Viktor Chukarin, USSR** A great parallel bar gymnast, he won 7 golds in the '52 and '56 Games, including pommelled horse, rings and floor exercise.

62 **Wyomia Tyus, USA** The Olympics' only 2-time sprint winner, she took the 100m gold in 1964 and 1968. In '68 she was also a member of the winning 4×100m relay team.

63 **Maj. Henri St. Cyr, SWE** Riding **Master Rufus** in '52 and **Juli** in '56, he became the only winner of 2 individual dressage golds.

64 **Glenn A. Davis, USA** In '56 and '60, he won consecutive 400m hurdles, setting 2 Olympic records.

65 **Vyacheslav Ivanov, USSR** Three-time single sculls rowing champion: '56, '60 and '64.

66 **Aleksandr Medved, USSR** This great heavyweight wrestler collected gold medals in 3 consecutive Olympics starting in 1964.

67 **Lucien Gaudin, FRA** Great European fencer was several times World and European champion, but didn't win his first individual gold of 4 Olympic golds until age 42.

68 **Herb Elliott, AUS** Never beaten in his favorite 1500m or 1mi races. His 1500m gold-medal win at Rome in 1960 set a world record.

69 **Laszlo Papp, HUN** Middleweight champ of the '48 Games, light middleweight crown winner in '52 and '56.

70 **Hans G. Winkler, FRG** All-time show jumping titleholder, he captured the individual gold in 1956, 4 team golds from '56-'76, a silver and a bronze.

71 **Donald A. Schollander, USA** With this champion swimmer's sophisticated front crawl, he and his relay team won 5 gold medals in '64 and '68.

72 **Rudolf Karpati, HUN** Great saber fencing champ won 2 straight individual golds, and helped win 4 team golds.

73 **Bobby Morrow, USA** Winning the 100m and 200m dashes and a member of the 4×100m relay team (Melbourne, 1956), he was one of the finest Olympic sprinters.

74 **Tamara Press, USSR** Top world strongwoman, she won shot Olympic title in '60 and '64 and discus gold in 1964.

75 **Alfred G. A. Swahn, SWE** Gold, silver and bronze medals—3 of each—in shooting contests. His father was Oscar (see #83 below).

76 **Klaus Dibiasi, ITA** At age 17 he won the silver medal in highboard diving and went on to take 3 straight golds in that event.

77 **John B. Kelly, USA** Olympic sculler extraordinaire, he took an individual gold in '20, double sculls golds in '20 and '24. His son, Jack, Jr., took the sculling bronze in '56.

78 **Ivar Johansson, SWE** Top Swedish athlete garnered 3 wrestling gold medals, 1932-36.

79 **Georges Miez, SUI** One of Switzerland's greatest sportsmen, he devoted his life to gymnastics, winning golds in '28 and '36.

80 **John J. Flanagan, USA** Pioneer hammer throwing champion won 3 times from 1900 to 1908.

81 **Boris Lagutin, USSR** The Olympic middleweight boxing champ throughout the 1960s, and winner of 2 golds and 1 bronze.

82 **Boris Shakhlin, USSR** From 1956 to 1964 he amassed 7 gymnastics gold medals.

83 **Oscar G. Swahn, SWE** A legend to fans of target shooting, he competed for 65 years, winning 3 gold medals, 1908-12.

84 **Sawao Kato, JPN** Winner of gymnastics combined exercises in '68 and '72, as well as gold and silver in team and individual contests.

ANCIENT HISTORY

Nearly 3000 years ago, a dozen or more footrace finalists lined up at the start of the ***dromos,*** a 200yd (183m) track. The title of fastest man in the known world was at stake.

Sprints covered one ***stade*** of 200-210yds (183-192m), or the length of the stadium. A 2-stade race—down the course, around stone pillars and back again—was called the ***diaulus.*** The distance run was the ***dolichus,*** 7 times 24 stades, or up to 3mi (4.8km). These footraces, along with the pentathlon of 5 skills—running, leaping, ***diskos*** (discus), javelin throwing, and wrestling—were the featured events of the original Olympics.

Perhaps the most amazing spectacle was the victory ceremony. As trumpets blared, winners were ushered before the **Hellenodikai** tribunal. There they were crowned with wreaths of wild olive from the sacred grove of Zeus. No higher honor could come to any son of Hellas than to wear the wreath. A winner feasted gratis for months, his statue was erected, he became a lifetime hero and was exempt from taxation forever.

The early Olympic Games were held to celebrate **The Festival of Heracles** (the god who raised the infant Zeus) and had a semi-religious tone which endured for more than 10 centuries. Celebrated every 4 years, the festival was held at holy Olympia, in an idyllic valley near the Altis, the forested shrine of Zeus. As many as 40,000 spectators came from throughout the Panhellenic world—from the Greek colonies in Ionia, Egypt and Asia Minor, from Africa, Italy and all corners of the Mediterranean. Rich and poor were equal. The multitude slept on the ground, worshipped, feasted, drank wine and cheered.

The stadium, only 35yds (32m) wide and about 200yds (183m) long, was a narrow rectangle without seats. Fans sat on the sloping hills of Mt. Cronus, or on temple steps. Close by was an 800yd-long (732m) equestrian hippodrome.

Superstars included repeat triple-winner **Leonidas of Rhodes; Chiones of Sparta,** who won the stade, diaulus and dolichus races in one Games; ***pankration*** (boxing & wrestling) champion **Cleitomachus of Thebes;** and giant wrestler **Milo of Croton,** who reputedly ate 7lbs of meat at a sitting and could carry a grown bull on his back.

Wars continually raging with invaders and between states and factions in the Athenian-Spartan-Macedonian world couldn't stop the Olympics; they endured through 320 stagings spread over nearly 1200 years, from the first recorded gathering in 776 BC to AD 394. No institution created by man has lasted so long.

Disintegration began when the high moral nature of the Games was destroyed by the rise of a class of professional athletes. Cash prizes were offered and ***stables*** of top performers were collected by wealthy sponsors. Bribery and other scandals followed. Wrote the tragic poet and ex-athlete **Euripides,** "Out of the tens of thousands of ills in Greece, none is worse than the tribe of professional athletes."

The warlike Macedonians swarmed over central Greece and captured the area around Mt. Olympus, interrupting the Games. Years of economic strangulation followed. The Roman conquerors ended Greek freedom in 146 BC, and converted the Games into a carnival of slaughter, featuring slaves as performers. In AD 394, **Emperor Theodosius the Great,** a Christian who considered the Olympics a pagan rite, abolished them. Fire, flood and earthquake obliterated Olympia in following centuries. Today—after extensive excavation by the French and Germans—only fascinating ruins remain. Yet the flaming Olympic spirit has survived.

MODERN HISTORY

1636—Cotswold Olympic Games
Englishman **Robert Dover** creates games which draw contestants from throughout rural Great Britain. Events include weight-throwing, swordplay, acrobatics and jumping. The annual event continues for 2 centuries.

1760—Englishman **Richard Chandler** discovers ruins of the original Olympic Games site in Greece.

1800s—Highland Games
Scotsmen test strength, speed and agility with contests that include the broad jump, hop-step-jump (now called triple jump), shot put and hammer throw.

1880s—Baron Pierre de Coubertin, father of the Modern Olympic Games, begins to lobby for a world sporting festival modeled after the ancient contests of Greece.

1890s—With support growing, including backing by the **King of Belgium, Prince of Wales, Crown Prince of Sweden** and **Crown Prince of Greece,** de Coubertin visits Greek tycoon **George Averoff** with his plans for a modern Olympics to be held at Athens. Averoff contributes funds for the renovation of the ancient Panathenaic Stadium at Athens (circa 33 BC) and sparks interest in the Games.

1896—Nearly 300 athletes from 13 nations meet at Athens for the first modern Olympic Games. The King of Greece presents winners with a gold medal and an olive branch—it is the first time Olympic olive branches have been awarded in 14 centuries.

1900—Despite Greek protests, the Second Olympiad is held in Paris. Ill-prepared sites and poor publicity mar the Games. In a modest step towards equality, **Charlotte Cooper** (GBR) becomes the first female Olympic medalist after winning lawn tennis competitions.

1904—Presented as an adjunct to the St. Louis World's Fair, this Olympics is even worse than Paris. The event drags out for 6 months; unsavory elements inject a sideshow atmosphere to draw new customers.

1906—The Olympics returns to Athens only 2 years after St. Louis. This is a better show, reviving hopes for the event's integrity. Still, the awards ceremony is misbalanced: the USA and Great Britain dominate track & field events.

1908—Bad weather and bad blood between the British and American teams mar the London competition. The Finns and Russians also nearly come to blows. At the dismal end, various countries claim, on a per-capita basis, to be the Olympic champion. Women take part in archery competitions and a gymnastic exhibition. Ice skating, a winter sport, is added.

1912—The V Games, held at Stockholm, rescue the foundering festival, seemingly doomed by the poor planning and poor sportsmanship of earlier meetings. In Sweden, 28 nations and 2541 athletes compete in a magnificent new stadium.

American Indian **Jim Thorpe,** USA, wins the pentathlon and decathlon and becomes the first Olympics superhero. "You, sir," **King Gustav V** of Sweden tells Thorpe at the awards ceremony, "are the greatest athlete on earth." "Thanks, King," is Thorpe's nonchalant reply. Later Thorpe's awards are taken away due to questions concerning his amateur status; they will be returned posthumously.

For the first of many Olympics, women's gymnastics and swimming prove to be favorite events.

Colorful Hawaiian swimmer **Duke Kahanamoku,** USA, wins the 100m freestyle gold and sets the world record.

1916—With World War I raging and the military conscripting many of the Western world's young athletes, the Games are cancelled. Many predict the end of this peaceful world contest.

Record of Olympic Participation

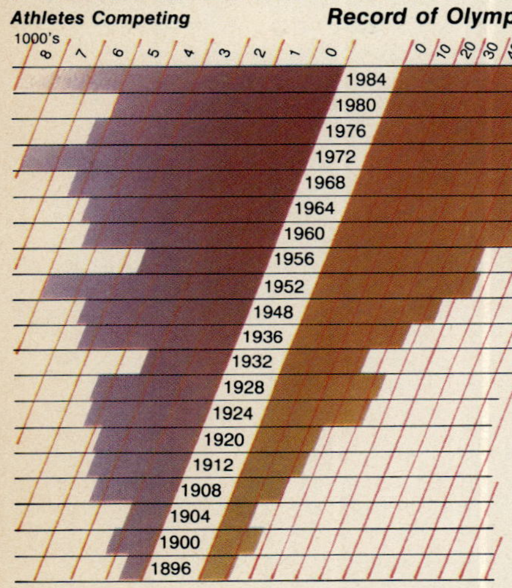

1920—Shell-shattered Belgium (Antwerp) volunteers to host the wound-healing post-war Olympics in a small (30,000 seat) school stadium. But only 29 nations and less than 3000 athletes show up; the war's toll is sadly reflected in the poor performances.

1924—Despite the world's larger conflicts, the Games refuse to die. Paris again is the host, and, in swimming and track & field alone, 8 world and 21 Olympic marks are bettered. **Paavo Nurmi** of Finland wins the 1500m, 5000m and 10,000m cross-country races—an incredible performance. Scotsman **Eric Liddell** sets a new 400m record while fellow Briton **Harold Abrahams** scores a huge upset in the 100m (their story will become the 1981 Academy Award-winning movie, **Chariots of Fire**).

1928—A record 46 nations and more than 3000 athletes meet in Amsterdam, Holland where, despite a war-torn geography and economy, a glorious contest establishes the secure future of the Olympic Games. Women's track & field events are brought into the Olympic mainstream for the first time.

El Ouafi of France knocks 9min off the marathon record; **Sabin Carr,** USA, ups the pole vault mark by 10″; **Johnny Weissmuller,** USA, swims the 100m freestyle in a record 58.6sec. **Mikio Oda** takes the triple jump to become Japan's first Olympic gold medalist. Several poorly trained runners collapse during the women's 800m race.

Slow-motion film techniques aid judges on close decisions. A balanced winner's roster begins to develop as more nations take home gold medals.

1931—The IOC awards the 1936 Olympic site to Germany's Weimar Republic; the contest will be held in Berlin. It is an act of faith aimed at further healing the wounds of WWI, but by the time the festival is held, **Hitler** has risen to power.

1932—The IOC agrees to let the Olympics be staged outside Europe for the first time (not including the pseudo-Olympics held at St. Louis in 1904). But, with the world in deep economic depression, many nations protest the expense of traveling to Los Angeles, California, USA. Just 6 months before the Games, no nation is firmly committed to the contest.

The IOC and its secretary, **Zack Farmer,** hit upon the idea that will miraculously save the Games—an Olympic Village where athletes can be housed and fed for only $2 a day. Steamship companies agree to cut rates for national teams.

The opening day sees 105,000 packing the Memorial Coliseum in Los Angeles; daily attendance at the Coliseum and Rose Bowl averages 65,000; more than a million watch the marathoners run through the city streets. Gate receipts bring in a substantial surplus.

In 1932, 16 world records are shattered and 2 tied, and 33 new Olympic records are set. There are many heroes, from Italy's **Luigi Beccali** in the metric mile to Japan's gold medal-reaping swimmers. **Mildred *Babe* Didrikson** wins 2 gold medals in women's athletics and becomes a world heroine. Sweden stands out in wrestling with 6 golds.

1936—Worldwide controversy rages as many nations question the wisdom of competing in the Nazi homeland. The American team, including its Jewish athletes, joins 50 other nations at Berlin. In flamboyant Nazi style, swastikas are draped everywhere; marching Storm Troopers add to the oppressive atmosphere. Racial hostility is blatant on the part of the Nazis, with Propaganda Minister **Goebbels** labeling the USA's black athletes its "African Auxiliary." But **Hitler** and Goebbels are in the 100,000-person crowd as black athletes, led by **Jesse Owens,** triumph in contest after contest. Owens wins the 100m and 200m sprints and long jump, all in either Olympic or world record time. The USA men's team, starring 6 black athletes, captures 12 gold medals; Germany's *Aryan* team captures only 4.

The Berlin Olympics are the first major sports event to be televised (locally).

A skinny redheaded New Zealander, **Jack Lovelock,** sprints the final 400m of the metric mile (1500m) in just 57.8sec. He wins the contest and betters the Olympic record by more than 3sec.

1939-1947—Tokyo, which had been awarded the 1940 Games, withdraws. Helsinki, Finland, the second site of choice, is invaded by Russia in 1939; shelling damages, among other things, the intended Olympic stadium. WWII cancels further games. In 1942 IOC president Count Baillet-Latour dies after hearing of his son's war death. This is the bleakest period of Olympic history.

1948—Still reeling from bombings and under food rationing, the British gallantly fight to make the most of the XIV Games in London. A record 59 national teams and 4689 competitors attend; crowds top 80,000 despite typically wet weather. Sweden wins 5 men's track & field golds; Czechs, Hungarians, Finns and Belgians each take one; the USA wins 11. For the first time, the Olympics' standout athlete is a woman: **Fanny Blankers-Koen** of the Netherlands takes 4 gold medals, bettering Babe Didrikson's 1932 performance.

The marathon run produces a dramatic spectacle when Belgium's **Etienne Gailly** enters the stadium a *human wreck* but in the lead after covering 26mi. Before a frantic crowd, Argentina's **Delfo Cabrera** passes the tottering Belgian war veteran to win the race. Finn movie actor **Kaj Rautavaara** wins the javelin competition, adding more drama to the festival. **Bob Mathias** of the USA, only 17 years old, takes an upset victory in the decathlon with 7139pts.

1952—At last the Finns are able to host the games, and 67 nations are on hand at Helsinki to make it a spectacular superfest. The gaiety is marred, however, by the USSR, which, after ignoring the contest for 40 years, shows up with a massive team, establishes separate living quarters away from the communal Olympic Village, and sets up a scoring table to show its lead in winning medal-points. But when the USA wins 14 men's track & field medals and Czechoslovakia's **Emil Zatopek** wins 3—to the USSR's nil—the Soviet boasting backfires.

Zatopek wins the 5000m and 10,000m runs and the marathon, overshadowing new records set by Brazilian **Adhemar da Silva** in the triple jump, the USA's **Bob Mathias** in the decathlon and Jamaica's stunning 1600m relay team.

The Soviet-initiated point contest erupts into a USSR-USA controversy, with both sides claiming victory. The bickering will continue at future Olympics.

1956—With all but one Olympiad held in Europe, the IOC awards these Games to Australia, with Melbourne as host city. Despite the USSR's invasion of Hungary and the Suez Canal crisis, the Olympics are the news item of the day, thanks to superb Aussie planning.

Australian **Betty Cuthbert** becomes the *Queen of the Games,* winning the 100m and 200m golds. The USA's **Charlie Dumas** is tops at 6′11½″ in the high jump and **Parry O'Brien** breaks the 60′ barrier in the shot put. Soviet ace **Vladimir Kuts** gives the USSR its first win in athletics when he takes the 5000m and 10,000m races. **Patricia McCormick,** USA, becomes the first person to win both the highboard and springboard diving championships in consecutive Olympics. In all, 36 Olympic and 11 world records fall. Australian swimmers capture 14 medals of all types.

For the first time the Closing Ceremony features athletes of all entrant nations running, arms linked, around the Olympic track.

1960—The Olympics becomes the most widely televised, costliest of international affairs. The Italians spend more than $30 million for the Rome Olympics, renovating ancient ruins for the event. Churches of ancient Rome ring their bells in unison to celebrate the event; the marathon runners follow the ancient Appian Way, finishing at the Arch of Constantine. Victories come out nicely balanced: Italians win in boxing and cycling; the Japanese in gymnastics; Hungary in fencing and the pentathlon; Turkey in wrestling; New Zealand in distance running. **Rafer Johnson,** USA, scores 8392pts to win the decathlon.

1964—Less than 20 years after a devastating war, Japan is able to spend more than $2 billion to ready Tokyo for the Games. Again a record 94 nations attend and, despite the number, no incidents mar the *Happy Games.*

Australia's **Dawn Fraser** wins the 100m women's swim race for the 3rd straight Olympic, **Al Oerter** of the USA does the same in the discus. **Peter Snell** of New Zealand becomes the first person to sweep the 800m and 1500m since 1952. **Joe Frazier,** USA, wins the gold in heavyweight boxing.

At the Closing Ceremony, hundreds of Japanese schoolchildren encircle the darkened stadium floor. On signal, each lights a torch, one of the most spectacular of all Olympic sights, as the lighted scoreboard flashes one word: *Sayonara.*

1968—A fabulous Mexico City fiesta is plagued with troubles. For the first time, more than 100 countries are present (actually 113) and an unprecedented 6123 contestants are entered. **Enrequita Basilo** is the first woman to light the Olympic flame.

Politics spoils the event when the IOC is forced to bar the South African team after a boycott is threatened to protest that country's policy of apartheid. Black athletes from the USA add to the uneasiness by raising the black-gloved fist of *black power* on the victory stand.

Outside the stadium, a demonstration by Mexican students breaks into a riot. More than 260 students are killed by police, more than 1000 are wounded. The tragedy takes place in the Plaza de las Tres Culturas, in the shadow of the Olympic Torch.

At the Games, coaches and athletes worry about the negative effects of Mexico City's 7350′ altitude, but worries prove groundless. **Bob Beamon,** USA, stuns audiences when he melds talent and training for a record 29′2½″ (8.9m)—a record that will stand for at least 15 years. And **Al Oerter** wins his 4th straight discus gold medal.

1972—The sensational sport action at Munich, West Germany, is totally eclipsed by the Arab terrorist kidnapping of 11 Israeli athletes. Televiewers watch the drama unfold, terrorists invade an Olympic village dormitory. After an anguished stand-off, both terrorists and hostages die in a shootout at a Munich military airport. The Games go into mourning, but they continue. Says IOC President **Avery Brundage,** "We have only the strength of a great ideal, and it cannot be stopped by anyone."

At the Games, tiny 17-year-old Soviet gymnast **Olga Korbut** becomes an international sweetheart, and interest in gymnastics skyrockets. **Mark Spitz** of the USA wins 7 gold medals and sets 4 world records in swimming. The first 1500m run for women is held; Russia's **Ludmila Bragina** wins in an incredible 4:01.4. Despite falling in the middle of the race, Finn **Lasse Viren** picks himself up to win the 10,000m run, then takes the 5000m. Munich-born **Frank Shorter** of the USA returns to the city of his birth and wins the marathon. Russian **Valeri Borzov** cops 100m and 200m medals. The USSR wins a controversial basketball game, ending the USA's domination of the sport. An estimated 1 billion TV viewers around the globe watch the mixture of international triumph and tragedy.

1976—With more than 700 entries in 23 events (the 50K walk was not held), there were many surprises at Montreal.

Trinidad, Jamaica and Cuba, a small trio of tropical countries, sweep the men's 100m, 200m, 400m and 800m contests. Cuban **Alberto Juantorena** sets a world record in the 800m run.

In another surprise, the Soviet Union manages only 2 gold medals in men's track & field. The USA wins 6, and Finland, East Germany and Poland each win 2. Hungarian **Miklos Nemeth** breaks the 300′ javelin barrier with a 310′4″ (94.58m) world mark. The USA's **Edwin Moses** sets a 47.64 world record in the 400m hurdles, and **Bruce Jenner,** also of the USA, takes the decathlon with a world record-setting 8617pts. Other Olympic stars include **Nadia Comaneci** of Romania, 14-year-old gymnastics sensation, and **Sugar Ray Leonard** of the USA, light welterweight champion.

Avery Brundage retires as IOC chief and Irishman **Lord Michael Killanin** takes over the Olympic helm.

1980—Despite a 64-nation boycott, a reported 700 contestants vie for 24 track & field prizes. Without tough Western competition, the USSR and East Germany take 14 gold (51% of all medals, 62% of all golds in the overall Games). But there are plenty of upsets and shocks:

Miruts Yifter of Ethiopia runs off with both 5000m and 10,000m races.

Allan Wells of Britain becomes the first Briton to outsprint the world at 100m since **Harold Abrahams'** 1924 win. Britain also wins an 800m-1500m double with its famed team of **Steve Ovett** and **Sebastian Coe** and, with huge **Daley Thompson,** adds the decathlon.

Seven Olympic men's track & field marks are broken, among them 3 world records. Outstanding efforts include Poland's **Wladyslaw Kozakiewicz's** setting of the Olympic's first world record pole vault at 18′11½″ (5.78m); Cuban **Teofilo Stevenson's** 3rd straight heavyweight boxing victory; Italian **Pietro Mennea's** victory in the 200-meter sprint run; France's fencing victory; Czechoslovakia's copping of the football (soccer) crown; and Poland's taking of the equestrian Grand Prix.

PAST, PRESENT AND FUTURE

Is there such a reality as the ultimate human sports performance? The answer is "yes" in some events, a strong "no" in others.

In limited-distance (sprint) running, for instance, coaches and other experts agree that man can accelerate only so much. He may be very near that point today for 100-400m distances. Eventually, human bullets will reach the cracking point where muscles won't take the strain, where physical breakdown will occur. "No one can predict when that limit will come," says leading track coach **Jim Bush** of the University of California at Los Angeles. Sport scientists plot complex equations to arrive at their predictions. They define mean speeds of the past at various distances, figure in increased technical knowlege and training methods, add expected equipment and racetrack improvements and the "bigger and better body" concept for man's evolving physiology. With this input, these scientists can look to the year 2000 and beyond.

A gain of only about .40sec is foreseen in the 100m dash. At 200m, a .86sec gain is seen by the year 2000 and/or the decade following. The most startling expansion of Olympic and world records no doubt will come in the field events and distance runs. It may sound fantastic and even impossible, but either in the Olympic Games or elsewhere:

- a 25′ gain in the **discus** could happen
- **javelin hurling** could improve 31′
- **highjumps** may go up some 10″, **broadjumps** go out by 3′ or more
- **pole vaulting,** nowhere near the ultimate, could bring leaps of over 22′
- **hammer throwing** could show the largest gain of all—more than 70′

Roger Bannister of Great Britain, first man to cover the mile in under 4min (1954), has speculated that some superhuman will run a 3:30 mile by about the year 2010. In Games terms, this would mean the Olympic metric mile (1500m) record would drop from the current 3:34.91 (world record: 3:31.86) to 3:23 or less.

The following chart gives Olympic best marks of 12 years ago, of today, and what the soothsayers think the early 21st century will bring:

Event	1972	1980	2000-2010 (projected)
100 meter	9.95	9.95	9.55
200 meter	19.83	19.83	18.97
400 meter	43.86	43.86	42.49
800 meter	1:44.3	1:43.50	1:38.3
1500 meter	3:34.91	3:34.91	3:22.2
3000-meter steeplechase	8:23.6	8:08.02	7:45.60
5000 meter	13:26.4	13:20.34	12:20.34
10,000 meter	27:38.4	27:38.35	25:44
Marathon	2:12:12	2:09:55	2:00:00
110-meter hurdle	13.24	13.24	12.80
400-meter hurdle	47.82	47.64	47.05
Discus	212′6″ (64.78m)	224′ (68.28m)	249′ (75.9m)
Javelin	296′10″ (90.48m)	310′4″ (94.58m)	341′4″ (104.03m)
Hammer throw	247′8″ (75.5m)	268′4″ (81.8m)	338′4″ (103.11m)
Shot put	69′6″ (21.18m)	70′0½″ (21.35m)	80′ (23.38m)
High jump	7′4¼″ (2.24m)	7′8¾″ (2.36m)	8′6¾″ (2.61m)
Long jump	29′2½″ (8.9m)	29′2½″ (8.9m)	32′2½″ (8.81m)
Triple jump	57′0¾″ (17.39m)	57′0¾″ (17.39m)	59′7½″ (18.18m)
Pole vault	18′0½″ (5.5m)	18′11½″ (5.78m)	22′6″ (6.86m)

CEREMONIAL OPENING

The ritual has changed little in the nearly 90 years since the Olympics was reborn. It's a majestic, beautiful and throat-catching spectacle, especially when the thousands of athletes appear in the ceremonial parade.

At the first Modern Games, begun on Easter Sunday in March, 1896 at Athens, Greece, the opening rites set a standard for the future. An audience of 50,000 sat in solemn silence as the Organizing Chairman spoke a welcome. **King George I** of host nation Greece spoke but 12 tradition-setting words in declaring the Games open. The Olympic Anthem was sung by a 500-voice chorus. Trumpets of silver announced the arrival of the competitors.

For 1984, the multimillions watching on television and crowding Los Angeles Memorial Coliseum will witness drama very much like that of Athens, with some new flourishes added.

1 The ceremony begins with the arrival of the host nation's head of state, in this case **President Ronald Reagan.** He is greeted at the Tribune of Honor by high officials of the International Olympic Committee, the Los Angeles Olympic Organizing Committee, the City of Los Angeles and the State of California. Top hats and tailcoats are *de rigueur* for IOC bigwigs.

2 With a flourish of heraldic trumpets, the national teams parade onto the field. Each team is preceded by a shield bearing its name and by a flag-bearer carrying the country's banner. First comes Greece, as the home of the original Games. Others follow alphabetically. Last of all comes the host (the United States).

3 When the teams form up on the Coliseum floor, the president of the Organizing Committee introduces the president of the IOC, who calls upon the head of state to make the ancient pronouncement. Rigid protocol holds the speech to just 17 words: "I declare open the Olympic Games of Los Angeles, celebrating the XXIII Olympiad of the modern era."

4 An honor guard carries the Olympic flag into the arena and—with a trumpet fanfare—it is raised to the music of the Olympic Anthem. Another special, satin Olympic flag is presented to the IOC president and Los Angeles mayor by officials of the previous host city, Moscow. The mayor of Los Angeles will present the flag to the next host city, Seoul, in 1988. This symbolizes the continuity of the festival.

5 A salute of guns and the release of many doves or pigeons, a peace symbol dating to 1896, follows.

6 The Olympic torch, carried by relays of runners and jet aircraft from the Valley of Olympia in Greece, arrives. The final runner circles the track, climbs the stairs to a brazier and lights a flame which will burn throughout the Games.

7 The Olympic oath is taken by an athlete from the host nation on the behalf of all the participants: "We swear that we will take part in the Olympic Games in loyal competition, respecting the regulations which govern them in the true spirit of sportsmanship for the honor of our team and the glory of sport." A similar oath is taken by one judge for all the judges. The national anthem of the organizing nation is played.

8 The teams march out of the Coliseum and host Los Angeles stages whatever appropriate display or demonstration it wishes.

Opening ceremonies usually extend to about 2 hours; competition begins the following day. The audience is usually asked to remain seated at the conclusion so as to allow the teams to reach their housing quarters free of traffic congestion.

Olympic Flag: Founding father of the Games, **Baron de Coubertin,** discovered the ancient design of interlaced rings at Delphi, near Olympia, in 1913. The 5 linked rings symbolize the 5 continents of the world and include the national colors of virtually all of the Olympic-world countries.

Olympic Torch: The ***Flame of Peace*** was introduced at the 1927 Games of Amsterdam (the Greeks of antiquity held torch races at night as part of the program). In 1936, for the Berlin Games, the ceremony of running the torch from Greece involved 335 runners, who relayed 1.5lb (.7kg) torches for 12 days and over 1864mi (3000km) from Olympia to Berlin. This has continued since.

Olympic Hymn: Several anthems were tried, but always the Olympics went back to slow, solemn **Hymn Olympique** composed in 1896 by **Spyros Samaras** of Greece. Lyrics are by **Costis Palamas,** also Greek. Since 1957, this has been the offical anthem.

Citius, Altius, Fortius (faster, higher, stronger) is the **Olympic Motto.** It was the inspiration of a Dominican monk of Paris, **Father Henri Didon,** who coined it for his college students, and was first displayed at Antwerp in 1920. A second slogan is de Coubertin's: ***The most important thing in the Games is not to win, but to take part, just as the important thing in life is not the triumph, but the struggle. The essential thing is not to have conquered, but to have fought well.***

Flight of Doves: With homing pigeons often substituted, the bird release dates to Athens in 1896 and became a permanent peace symbol in 1920.

Olympic Oath: As the Greeks prayed at the Temple of Zeus to play fair in the Games, so today's oath promises sportsmanship, honor and goodwill. In 1961 the Oath was modified. The term ***honor of our country*** was changed to ***honor of our team*** to lessen nationalistic feeling. Belgian fencer **Victor Boin** was the first to take the Oath, at the 1920 Games.

Parade of Athletes: Until London in 1908, teams straggled in and out. But in Britain they paraded in sport clothes and for the first time carried national flags. These were lowered to **King Edward,** with the exception of the USA banner. Weight-tosser **Martin Sheridan,** the American standard-bearer, said, "This flag dips to no earthly king." For years, the salute to the Royal or Presidential box presented a tough problem. Modern protocol is for marchers to salute the head of state of the host nation by turning their heads toward his or her box. No other demonstration is necessary.

Victory Ceremonial: Until 1932 in Los Angeles, the festival lacked a rousing and climactic crowning ritual. Los Angeles built a 3-step platform, with the gold medalist in an event standing at the top and with silver and bronze winners flanking him on slightly lower steps. Protocol is for the victors to appear in their sport costumes while the IOC president, or his designate, drapes the medals around their necks. The national anthem of the winner's country is played as the group of 3 faces the flagstaffs.

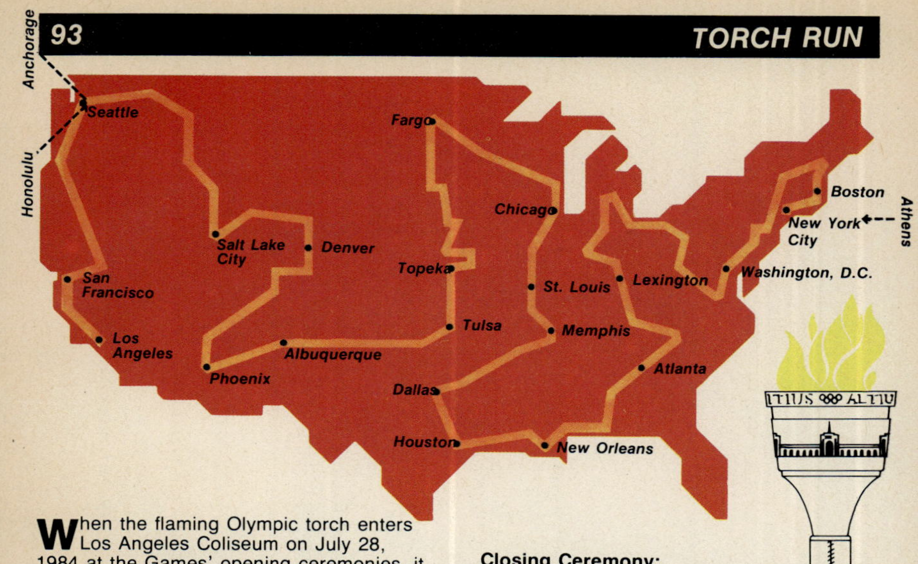

When the flaming Olympic torch enters Los Angeles Coliseum on July 28, 1984 at the Games' opening ceremonies, it will have ended a very special trip across the USA.

During this torch relay, 10,000 legs of the trip are being *sold* for $3000 per kilometer (.62mi), with all of the proceeds to be divided among the YMCA, Boys Clubs and Girls Clubs of America. The expected $30 million total will be the largest donation ever made to youth sports.

It is another example of the Games growing to fit the times, in this case, a strained world economy. The same factor also altered traditional Games sponsorship: Los Angeles' 1984 Games will be the first privately sponsored Olympics.

While this may be one of the most philanthropic of torch runs, it has rivals for sheer spectacle.

For Tokyo's 1964 torch trip, some 101,473 runners covered 7487km (4652.3mi). Four years later, the fiery symbol of international cooperation traced Christopher Columbus' route to the New World before opening the Mexico City Games.

But perhaps Canada gave us a true sign-of-the-times torch relay when an orbiting satellite became one of the *runners.* In 1976, the flames of the Olympic torch were encoded in Athens and beamed by satellite to Ottawa. There the transmission reignited the waiting torch. Human runners completed the trip to Montreal.

The torch, which originates at the Altar of Zeus near the site of the ancient Greek Games, became part of the sportsfest's ceremonies in 1936. In 1984, it will travel from its traditional starting point at Olympia to Athens by runner, by airplane to New York City, then again by runner in the AT&T-sponsored pass through the USA.

On May 8, the first portion of the 50-state, 1500-community run will begin. Carrying the torch will be 2 special USA Olympic guests: **Gina Hemphill**, granddaughter of **Jesse Owens**, and **Bill Thorpe, Jr.**, grandson of **Jim Thorpe.**

For difficult portions of the run—desert and mountain terrain—AT&T will send in a fleet of 150 experienced runners, chosen from among its employees. In addition, the sponsor is providing medical and security personnel, as well as organization for the monumental project.

Exactly 82 days and some 19,000km (nearly 12,000mi) after leaving NYC, and after 10,000 citizens of the USA have had the once-in-a-lifetime experience of carrying the Olympic torch, it will arrive in Los Angeles—and the Games will begin.

Closing Ceremony:
Shorter and less marked by pomp, ceremony and heraldic flourishes than the opening, the concluding rites are often just as emotional as the opening. Fans, carried away, often invade the field, as do spectator athletes, in a spontaneous outpouring of celebration and goodwill. The ceremony:

1 Flag bearers march into the arena, followed by representatives of each nation (a limit of 6 per country) and group themselves.

2 While the IOC president mounts the rostrum, the flags of Greece and the next host nation are hoisted to national anthems.

3 The IOC president makes a short speech of appreciation and calls upon the youth of all nations to assemble again at the Games in 4 years' time.

4 Following a trumpet fanfare, the Olympic flame is extinguished, the Olympic flag is very slowly lowered from its mast and solemnly carried out by an honor guard. A salute of 5 guns is heard in the distance. The bearers and delegates march from the arena. It's over—*finis* another Olympiad.

Some of the most unforgettable Olympic ceremonies:

Rome, 1960—In an impromptu act, thousands of people lit rolled up newspapers in the twilight. The Stadio Olympico seemed to be teeming with fireflies.

Tokyo, 1964—Emotion clutched everyone when 19-year-old **Yoshinori Sakai** ran into Meiji Stadium with the sacred torch. Young Sakai was selected for the honor because he was born August 6, 1945 near Hiroshima, at the time an atomic bomb destroyed the city.

Mexico City, 1968—Perhaps the single most spectacular moment in all of the celebrations was when runners carried the torch to the pinnacle of the great Pyramid of the Sun at Teotihuacan. When the flame was lit, the pyramid erupted like a volcano—spewing rockets, Roman candles and other pyrotechnics across the sky.

Montreal, 1976—At the closing, 500 women in white formed 5 interlocking rings, then removed their robes to reveal the bright colors of the circle symbols. The Indian tribes of Canada marched in native costume. Indians, athletes and spectators danced on the field until long after dark.

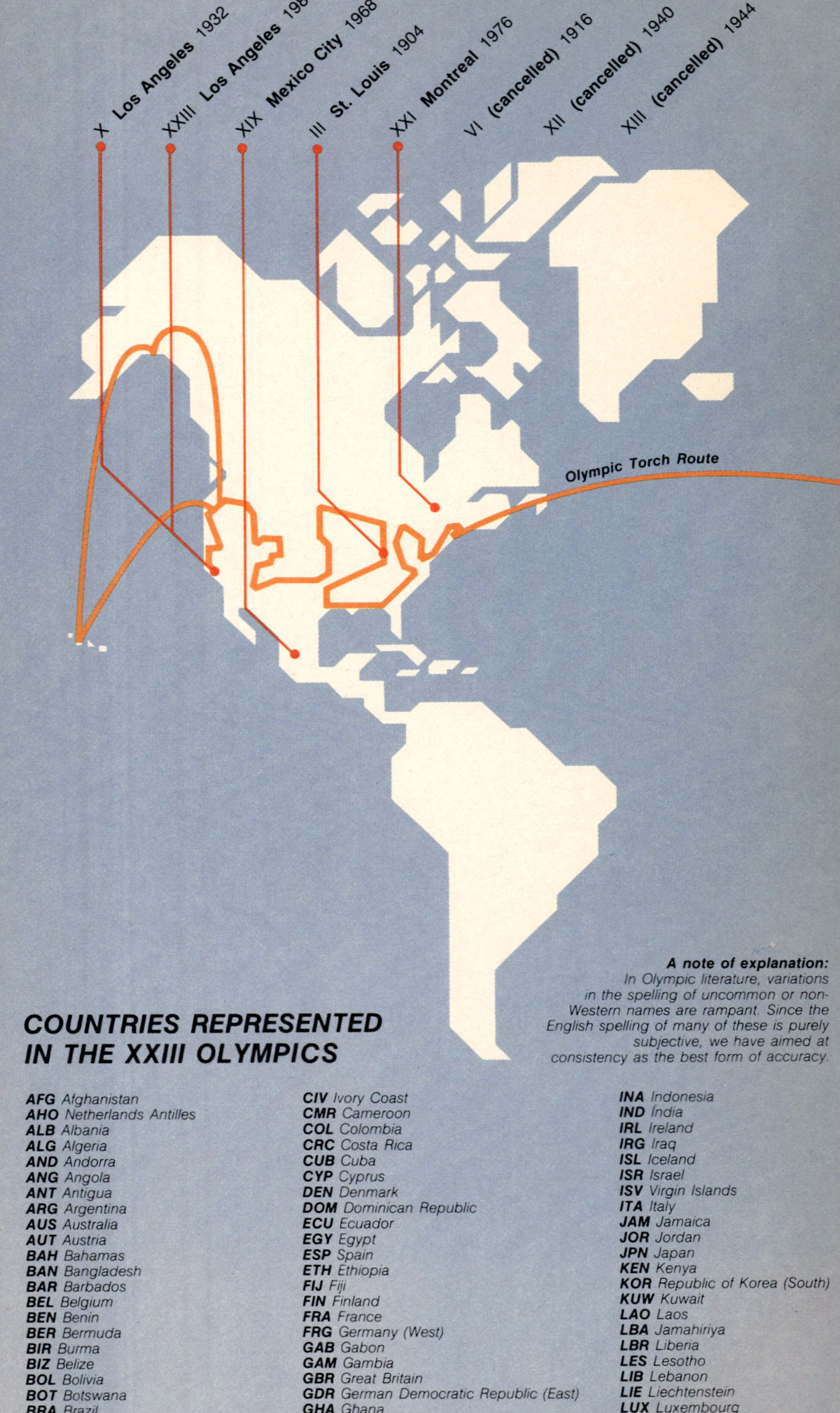

A note of explanation:
In Olympic literature, variations in the spelling of uncommon or non-Western names are rampant. Since the English spelling of many of these is purely subjective, we have aimed at consistency as the best form of accuracy.

COUNTRIES REPRESENTED IN THE XXIII OLYMPICS

AFG *Afghanistan*
AHO *Netherlands Antilles*
ALB *Albania*
ALG *Algeria*
AND *Andorra*
ANG *Angola*
ANT *Antigua*
ARG *Argentina*
AUS *Australia*
AUT *Austria*
BAH *Bahamas*
BAN *Bangladesh*
BAR *Barbados*
BEL *Belgium*
BEN *Benin*
BER *Bermuda*
BIR *Burma*
BIZ *Belize*
BOL *Bolivia*
BOT *Botswana*
BRA *Brazil*
BRN *Bahrain*
BUL *Bulgaria*
CAF *Central Africa*
CAN *Canada*
CAY *Cayman Islands*
CGO *People's Republic of Congo*
CHA *Chad*
CHI *Chile*
CHN *People's Republic of China*
CIV *Ivory Coast*
CMR *Cameroon*
COL *Colombia*
CRC *Costa Rica*
CUB *Cuba*
CYP *Cyprus*
DEN *Denmark*
DOM *Dominican Republic*
ECU *Ecuador*
EGY *Egypt*
ESP *Spain*
ETH *Ethiopia*
FIJ *Fiji*
FIN *Finland*
FRA *France*
FRG *Germany (West)*
GAB *Gabon*
GAM *Gambia*
GBR *Great Britain*
GDR *German Democratic Republic (East)*
GHA *Ghana*
GRE *Greece*
GUA *Guatemala*
GUI *Guinea*
GUY *Guyana*
HAI *Haiti*
HKG *Hong Kong*
HOL *Netherlands*
HON *Honduras*
HUN *Hungary*
INA *Indonesia*
IND *India*
IRL *Ireland*
IRG *Iraq*
ISL *Iceland*
ISR *Israel*
ISV *Virgin Islands*
ITA *Italy*
JAM *Jamaica*
JOR *Jordan*
JPN *Japan*
KEN *Kenya*
KOR *Republic of Korea (South)*
KUW *Kuwait*
LAO *Laos*
LBA *Jamahiriya*
LBR *Liberia*
LES *Lesotho*
LIB *Lebanon*
LIE *Liechtenstein*
LUX *Luxembourg*
MAD *Madagascar*
MAL *Malaysia*
MAR *Morocco*
MAW *Malawi*
MEX *Mexico*
MGL *Mongolia*
MLI *Mali*
MLT *Malta*
MON *Monaco*

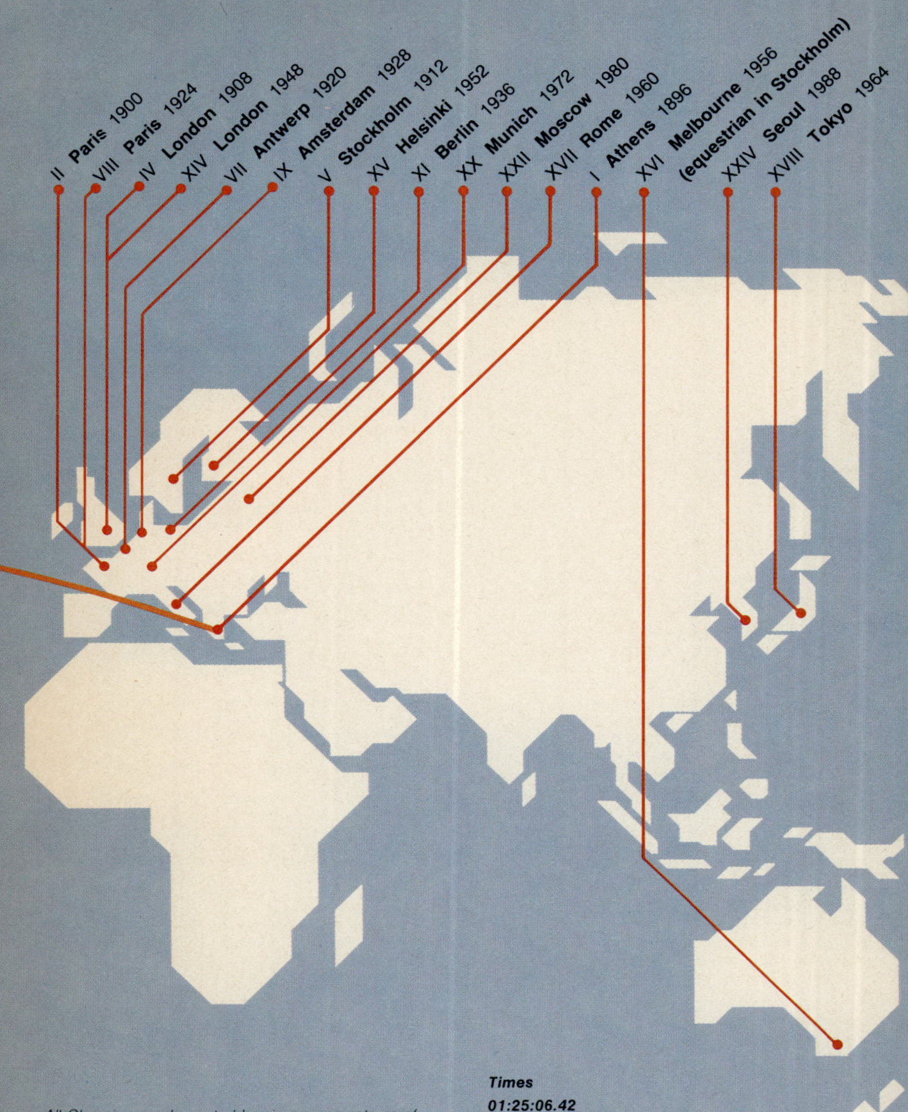

All Olympic records quoted herein are accurate as of the 1980 Moscow Olympics; world records are accurate as of August 15, 1983.

Times

01:25:06.42

hours:minutes:seconds.tenths and hundredths of seconds

MOZ *Mozambique*
MRI *Mauririus*
MTN *Mauritania*
NCA *Nicaragua*
NEP *Nepal*
NGR *Nigeria*
NGU *Papua-New Guinea*
NIG *Niger*
NOR *Norway*
NZL *New Zealand*
PAK *Pakistan*
PAN *Panama*
PAR *Paraguay*
PER *Peru*
PHI *Philippines*
POL *Poland*
POR *Portugal*
PRK *Democratic People's Republic of Korea*
PUR *Puerto Rico*
QAT *Qatar*
ROM *Romania*
SAL *El Salvador*
SAU *Saudi Arabia*
SEN *Senegal*
SEY *Seychelles*
SIN *Singapore*
SLE *Sierra Leone*
SMR *San Marino*
SOM *Somalia*
SRI *Sri Lanka*
SUD *Sudan*
SUI *Switzerland*
SUR *Surinam*
SWE *Sweden*
SWZ *Swaziland*
SYR *Syria*
CTO *Chinese Taipei*
TAN *Tanzania*
TCH *Czechoslovakia*
THA *Thailand*
TOG *Togo*
TRI *Trinidad and Tobago*
TUN *Tunisia*
TUR *Turkey*
UAE *United Arab Emirates*
UGA *Uganda*
USSR *Union of Soviet Socialist Republics*
URU *Uruguay*
USA *United States of America*
VEN *Venezuela*
VIE *Vietnam*
VOL *Upper Volta*
YAR *Yemen Arab Republic*
YMD *Yemen Democratic Republic*
YUG *Yugoslavia*
ZAI *Zaire*
ZAM *Zambia*
ZIM *Zimbabwe*

Metric/English Conversion

1mm = .039″	*1″ = 2.54cm*
1cm = .394″	*1′ = .3048m*
1m = 1.094yd	*1yd = .9144m*
1km = .6214mi	*1mi = 1609.3m*
1mg = .015gr	*1oz = 28.35g*
1g = .0353oz	*1lb = 453.6g*
1kg = 2.205lbs	

Metric conversions used in this book are approximate.

Abbreviations Used

″ = inch ′ = foot
yd = yard
mi = mile
mm = millimeter
cm = centimeter
m = meter
km = kilometer
oz = ounce
lb = pound
mg = milligram
g = gram
gr = grain
kg = kilogram
min = minute
sec = second
pt(s) = point(s)

Richard Saul Wurman

Michael Everitt, *Design Director & Illustrator*
Janet Smith, *Adminstrative Director*

Al Stump, *Writer*
Joy Aiken, *Editor & Writer*

Illustration:
David Candioty
Hugh Enockson
William Fetter
Allison Ann Goodman
Karen Palmerston-Crandall
Mark Park
York R. Parris
Bob Tolone
Art Zendarski

Production:
Wendie Ahrensdorf, *Senior*
Anne Doyle
Suzanne Gibson
Geralyn McGee
Ann McNaughton
Patricia Moritz
George Ochoa
Lisa Selje

Research & Writing:
Freda Wheatley Vizcarra, *Senior*
Morgan Brown
Jan Fenwick
Sara Reeder Ortiz

Typesetting:
Sara Reeder Ortiz
Sue Zepeda, *Associate*

Printing:
Craftsman Press/Seattle, WA 98109
William Dorich

Photocomposition:
Graphic House/Glendora, CA 91740
Frank Kiluk

Richard Saul Wurman, FAIA, is an architect, graphic designer, cartographer and a recipient of Guggenheim, Graham, Chandler, Annenberg and NEA Fellowships. He has authored, co-authored and designed many publications including: *Urban Atlas, Making the City Observable, Cities: Comparison of Form and Scale, Man-Made Philadelphia, Various Dwellings Described in a Comparative Manner, Yellow Pages of Learning Resources, Yellow Pages Career Library, The Nature of Recreation, Notebooks and Drawings of Louis I. Kahn, Whole Pacific Catalog.* Mr. Wurman serves as a member of the policy panel for the National Endowment for the Arts Design Arts Program, Department Chairman at Otis/Parsons Institute and Co-Chairman of **T.E.D.,** The Technology Entertainment Design Communications Conference.

Michael Everitt, whose illustrative passion is represented throughout these pages, is a graduate of the Art Center College of Design and currently serves on the faculties of Otis/Parsons and the California Institute of the Arts.

Al Stump is Chairman of the 1984 Olympic Games World Press Liason Committee for the Greater Los Angeles Press Club. He served as writer for **FOOTBALL**/ACCESS and is a contributing editor with Los Angeles Magazine.

At **ACCESS**PRESS Ltd., our enterprise is fired by a curiosity about *what people do, where they like to go,* and *how they see.* At best, this book will help you see some things you have always seen, but never *seen.*

In production:
HOSPITALACCESS
NEW ORLEANSACCESS
WASHINGTON D.C.ACCESS
BASEBALLACCESS

Co-owners **ACCESS**PRESS Ltd.
Frank Stanton, *President Emeritus, CBS Inc.*
Richard Saul Wurman

ARCO AtlanticRichfield*Company believed that this guide would enhance the comprehension and enjoyment of the XXIII Olympic Games by the largest television viewing audience in history. Their early endorsement and sponsorship have allowed this project to become a reality. Many people from this company gave enormous help and encouragement to this project. These individuals, too many to list here without oversight, were unfailingly interested in quality, accuracy and the spirit of the Olympic movement.*

Sam Adams, Coach
University of California, Santa Barbara
Adidas
AAE *(Aluminum Athletic Equipment Co.)*
Amateur Basketball Association of the USA
Edward S. Steitz, President
American Canoe Association
Billy Bragg, National Coach
Joyce Decot, Executive Secretary
Mary Garland, National Paddling Committee Chairperson
Athletics Congress of the USA
Berny Wagner, Coach Coordinator
Ernest Bland, *author,* Olympic Story
California Judo, Inc., *Hayward Nishioka, President*
Cantabrian Sports Equipment/Lillywhites
Campagnolo USA, Inc.
Federation Internationale Gymnastique
Frank Endo, Judiciary Official
Field Hockey Association of America, Inc.
Susan Charlesworth
Allan S. Woods, General Secretary
Stephanie Grimes, *gymnastics*
Los Angeles Olympic Organizing Committee
Ted Hinshaw, Yachting Commissioner
Arnold Schwartzman, Graphic Design Director
Frank Hotchkiss
Los Angeles Coliseum Commission
Los Angeles Herald-Examiner, *files*
Los Angeles Times/TAC Games Organizers
John MacAllister, *yachting*
Marina Del Rey (CA) Bike & Cycle
Ted Ernst & George Garvey
Darlene May, *Coach,*
California State University at Pomona
Nick McNaughton, *socce.*
Mikasa Volleyballs/Myojyo Rubber Industry Co., Ltd.
Beverly Nairn, *Librarian-researcher, San Marino, CA*
National Archery Association
Alyse L. Glass, Public Relations
National Rifle Association of America
Michael Tipa, Assistant Director
Nike, Inc. *(Beaverton, OR)*
Omega-New York, *Hugh Glenn*
Vanguard Inc. *(Pekaukee, WI), Dan Randeau*
Thane Roberts
Kayak Specialties *(Buchanan, MI), Bill Smoke*
Swiss Timing, *Dennis Oswald, Secretary General*
John Tanzley, *sequence photos, track & field*
Track & Field News
USA Amateur Boxing Federation
Leslie A. King, Director of Communications
Robert Surkein, Board of Directors
US Baseball Federation
Wanda Rutledge, Administrative Director
US Cycling Federation, Inc.
Edmund R. Burke, Technical Director
US Diving, Inc., *Todd Smith, Executive Director*
US Fencing Association
Carla-Mae Richards, Executive Director
US Gymnastics Federation
Roger Council, Past Executive Director
US Modern Pentathlon Association
Daniel Steinman, President
US Olympic Water Polo Team, *Dennis Fosdick, Coach*
US Rowing Association
Eric E. Stoll, Executive Assistant
US Soccer Federation
Richard Rottkov, Director of Media Relations
US Swimming, Inc.
Jeff Diamond, Information Service Director
Shelley D. Valentine, Information Service
US Synchronized Swimming, Inc.
Paula Oyer, Executive Director
US Team Handball Federation
Evelyn Anderson, Administrative Director
Dr. Peter Buehning, President
US Volleyball Association
Albert Monaco, Jr., Executive Director
US Water Polo, Inc., *Dr. Barbara Kalbus, President*
US Weightlifting Federation
Harvey Newton, Executive Director
Patrice Shallow, Adminstrative Assistant
Windsurfer International
Peter Daniels, Director of Olympic Programs
US Wrestling Association
Bob Dillinger, Assistant Executive Director
US Yacht Racing Union
Mimi Dyer, Communications Director
Voit American Division/AMF International
Watchmakers of Switzerland Information Center, NYC
Rudolph Shulthess
John Williams, *Coach, Buena Park, CA*
Vern Wolfe, *Coach, University of Southern California*
York Barbell Company

And to all the federation coaches, directors, friends, advisors and information officers who helped us to compile accurate and comprehensive materials, whose names we missed, our apologies and thanks.